S.H. Chuah is a strategist and former consultant at a top global strategy firm. She has held a regional leadership role at a Fortune 500 company, worked in venture capital, and served as a board observer to portfolio companies. Early in her career, she co-authored a case study for Stanford's Technology Ventures Programme (STVP) and later a white paper for a global management consulting firm.

Her career has taken her across Asia, Europe, and the US, giving her a firsthand view of how different cultures approach leadership, resilience, and strategy. She graduated from Columbia Business School, London Business School, the National University of Singapore (NUS), HKU Business School, and Singapore Management University (SMU). She also attended immersion programmes at Stanford University, Zhejiang University, and in regions spanning Malaysia, Europe, the Middle East, South America, and China. Chuah brings together the wisdom of Eastern and Western philosophy with the pragmatism of global business practice.

The Dao Whispers is both a thank-you to the teachers who came before and an invitation to readers to share the journey.

Praise for The Dao Whispers

"The Dao Whispers curates from a rich tapestry of Chinese classical thought, from philosophers like Confucius, Sun Tzu and Zhuangzi, emperors and empresses and their grand chancellors (zaixiang) to everyday folk sayings, and reinterprets them for today's world. Sue Huey bridges East and West with rare dexterity, offering thought-provoking insights on the applicability of these sage sayings to both daily life and organizational leadership."

Emeritus Professor Wong Poh Kam
National University of Singapore (NUS) Business School, Lee Kuan Yew School of Public Policy

"Sue's writing invites us to pause and reflect: a much-needed practice in today's age of speed and distraction. Her beautifully crafted book offers advice and wisdom to carry into our daily lives."

Dr. Amy Bradley, Affiliate Faculty,
Organisational Behaviour, London Business School

"A sharp and practical resource for meditation, introspection and personal growth."

Mladen Tcherveniakov
General Manager, Strategy – Shell, GE

The DAO Whispers

366 Daily Meditations on Ancient Eastern Wisdom
For a Modern Life Well Lived

S.H.CHUAH

Midnight Jade Press

The Dao Whispers

ISBN: 978-1-9192157-1-6

First edition, 2025
Published by Midnight Jade Press, London
Printed and bound in the United Kingdom

Cover design by the author

To my parents, my brother, and my sister,
for your endless love and support.

To Caylee and Kenji,
the brightest lights in my life.

To the teachers, seen and unseen,
whose guidance and encouragement continue to light my way.

CONTENTS

PREFACE

A Journey Through Seasons

The Blue Moleskine Journal and Meditation for the Monkey Mind

This book began with a blue Moleskine journal, a few handwritten reflections during an executive leadership course at London Business School (LBS).

At first, it was just me attempting to meditate, jotting a few lines, and uploading a screenshot. Then came the group discussions with Sloan, EMBA and MBA classmates, digging into the questions our professor had set and keeping each other accountable. And the self-compassion letters... that took it to another level: "Dear me... be nice."

But over time, it grew. With each classroom insight, late-night conversation, or solo walk home, the reflections grew deeper. What started as scattered thoughts during meditation became a way of making sense of a world that often feels noisy and fragmented.

The lines of writing this book often blurred. I set out to write a book, but in many ways, it also wrote me. In searching for clarity, structuring problems, reflecting on the wisdom we need, and distilling the advice I've received and the stories I've heard, I found myself shaped and moulded in the process.

The journey also began with a nudge: during a leadership course at LBS, a professor invited me to read a page aloud to the class. To my surprise, what I thought was just a "journal" struck a chord with the audience, who encouraged me to finish the book. With readers like them in mind, I've added not only wisdom but also practical tools — small frameworks and references that, I hope, can make a real difference to you, just as they have to me.

The Eastern Sage, the Western Philosopher, and the Messenger

Each entry pairs a classical Chinese proverb with reflections from modern life and Western thought. The Chinese voices include Confucius, Mencius, Sun Tzu, Laozi, Cao Cao, and Emperor Taizong. Western thinkers include Marcus Aurelius, Nietzsche, Seneca, and Einstein. Together, they explore leadership, strategy, power, clarity, boundaries, self-mastery, and human nature.

Notes on the Sages

Confucius (~6th-5th century BCE)

- Teacher of practical wisdom, ethics, and moral leadership, teachings recorded by disciples in the *Analects.*
- Emphasised rén (humaneness), lǐ (ritual propriety) and yì (righteousness); cultivation of the jūnzǐ (noble person).
- Believed order begins with self-cultivation and extends to family, community, and society.
- **Considerations:** Later dynasties used his ideas to justify rigid hierarchies. Some sayings may be later disciples' words, not his own.

Mencius (~4th century BCE)

- Champion of the idea that humans are born good, with seeds of virtue to nurture.
- Advocated benevolent rule and the right to depose tyrants who harm their people.
- Stressed empathy and moral governance as true strength.
- **Considerations:** Often criticised as idealistic about innate goodness. Writings assume a monarchic world order that may not map neatly to modern times.

Laozi (~4th century BCE – traditionally dated earlier, ~6th century BCE)

- Credited author of *Dao De Jing*, teaching harmony with the Dao and effortless action (wúwéi).
- Praised humility, simplicity, and the strength of yielding over force.
- Invites contemplation through paradox and poetic brevity.
- **Considerations:** Authorship disputed; text likely layered over centuries. Wúwéi is frequently misread as passivity rather than skilful flow with life.

Zhuangzi (~4th century BCE)

- Storyteller-philosopher who questioned rigid truths and social conventions.
- Emphasised spontaneity, freedom, and seeing life's paradoxes with humour.
- Famous for the "butterfly dream" and stories that blur illusion and reality.
- **Considerations:** Text has multiple contributors. His scepticism is sometimes mislabelled as nihilism or escapism.

Sun Tzu (~5th century BCE)

- Sun Wu (孫武) is the historical figure traditionally identified as Sun Tzu (孫子), the author and strategist behind The Art of War (孫子兵法), emphasising intelligence, agility, and winning without fighting.
- Advocated preparation, adaptability, and understanding human psychology in conflict.
- Preferred minimal harm over brute force.
- **Considerations:** Historicity debated, often conflated with Sun Bin. Modern business quotes risk turning nuanced strategy into empty clichés.

Cao Cao (~2nd century CE)

- Statesman, warlord, and poet, praised for meritocracy and sharp strategic mind. In ~208 CE, Emperor Xian of Han formally appointed Cao Cao as 丞相 (chéngxiàng) – Chancellor or Grand Chancellor.
- Known for efficiency in governance and bold military campaigns.
- His poetry shows a contemplative side beneath political pragmatism.
- **Considerations:** Ruthless in power struggles, vilified in folklore and *Romance of the Three Kingdoms*. Legacy sparks debate on ends vs. means.

Zhuge Liang (~2nd-3rd century CE)

- Revered as the archetypal Chancellor of Shu Han during the Three Kingdoms era, famed for his brilliance in strategy, governance, and diplomacy.
- Known for the *Longzhong Plan*, laying out Shu's grand vision, and for iconic tactics such as the Empty Fort Strategy and Wooden Ox transport system.
- Remembered for his loyalty to Liu Bei and Liu Shan, serving with diligence and a sense of moral duty, often cited as the embodiment of wisdom and foresight.
- **Considerations**: His cautious strategies sometimes led to missed opportunities, and his northern campaigns against Wei stretched Shu's resources thin. Later generations debated whether his devotion to loyalty and virtue limited his flexibility in pursuit of victory.

Emperor Taizong of Tang (~7th century CE)

- Consolidated Tang rule, valued capable ministers and honest counsel.
- Used history as a mirror for wise leadership and long-term thinking.
- Oversaw reforms and cultural flourishing, setting a standard for emperors after him.
- **Considerations:** Seized the throne after fratricidal conflict. Expansionist policies and frontier wars complicate his image of benevolent rule.

Wu Zetian (~7th–8th century CE)

- First and only female emperor of China, ruled in her own name during the Tang dynasty.
- Expanded the civil service examinations and promoted talent based on merit, including scholars and officials who might otherwise have been overlooked.
- Skilled in consolidating power, using both intelligence and political manoeuvring to secure and maintain authority.
- Patron of culture, literature, and Buddhism, leaving a complex legacy of both flourishing and fear.
- **Considerations:** Her reign challenged gender norms and remains controversial. She is praised as a capable, reformist ruler, yet vilified in Confucian historiography as ruthless and manipulative.

Building Bridges

This collection may also serve as an attempt to build a bridge in response to a gap I kept noticing – a disconnect between cultures, minds, and meanings. People would say, "Eastern classical texts feel inaccessible," or "I wish I understood Eastern thought better." And in some ways, I understood that feeling.

Even for those who grew up with some exposure, the ancient scrolls, as beautiful as they are, can feel distant. Dao De Jing in its original form is as much poetry as it is philosophy: layered, elusive, and deeply ancient.

But the proverbs? They're different. They've survived not through textbooks, but through street slogans, kitchen advice, and everyday conversation. They're fragments from the past that stayed alive. I began to learn simply by asking my parents and friends, "What did you mean when you said that? Why would losing a horse be a good thing? And how could a phoenix be featherless?

This collection isn't a scholarly work. But perhaps it offers one small brick in that unfinished bridge, narrowing the gap just a little. Not only between East and West, but also between people. Between assumption and understanding.

And maybe, in doing so, it reminds us of something deeper...that across borders, languages, and generations, runs a thread of common humanity. The stranger in front of us could be someone's daughter, father, husband, or wife… someone's grandfather or grandmother, and worthy of the same respect, compassion, and dignity we offer to those we love most.

The Tug with the Fog of War

If I'm honest, this book began in discomfort. A tension between what the world seemed to expect and what my own compass told me. As things grew more polarised yet more connected, I kept wondering if there was a way to hold both.

This became my way of trying, searching for whispers from sages and philosophers as I muddled through the fog. A way to honour complexity without needing to pick a side, but also without overthinking it into paralysis and to end up like Thales, the philosopher who was so lost in the stars that he walked straight into a well... Especially when it all feels so much like Robert McNamara's ***The Fog of War.***

The Dance of Yin and Yang

Life is a dance of yin and yang, light and shadow, calm and chaos, truth and illusion, the knowable and the unknowable. This book doesn't aim to judge or tell you what to think. It simply hopes to be a small candle in a dark room, offering just enough light for you to find your own footing. It also invites you to pause, to see both sides, and to choose your response with intention and grace.

The reflections unfold across the year. Some invite quiet introspection, others spark sharper debate, and together they weave a rhythm between reflection and action. Throughout, the book respects your agency. It is not here to speak over you, but to make space for your own voice.

A Note on the Proverbs

Not all the proverbs in this book come from famous sages. Many are folk sayings, everyday wisdom, or anonymous voices passed down through time. They are translated more literally, sometimes left ambiguous on purpose. Some may feel poetic, vague, or even puzzling – and that is part of their charm. At times the meaning lands immediately; at others it reveals itself slowly, in layers. They are not here to wrap everything up neatly, but to offer fragments of old wisdom, leaving space for your own take.

The Mark of an Educated Mind is to be Able to Entertain a Thought Without Accepting It

I once read that reading is like having a conversation with the author, even if it can sometimes feel like a monologue. I hope these pages feel more like a dialogue, not only with the ancient Chinese sages, but with Western thinkers, scientists, leaders, you and I. My hope is that in some of our conversations, we can bring together the voices of East and West, yours, and mine, around the same coffee table where we can question and debate how we each see the world, interpret the proverbs, and add our own points of view. After all, there is always space for the "unknowable," and as Laozi reminds us, any philosophy that can be neatly defined is rarely one that can withstand the test of time.

There is an old Chinese proverb: Three cobblers with their wits combined can outmatch Zhuge Liang, the brilliant strategist of the Three Kingdoms. Well, this book certainly doesn't pretend to be Zhuge Liang. At best, it is the work of cobblers, with fine scraps of leather stitched together from Confucius, Laozi, Zhuangzi, emperors, poets, generals, and a few Western voices thrown in for good measure. The result is not a polished suit of armour, but a patchwork cloak. Perhaps uneven, perhaps imperfect, but if it keeps you warm or makes you smile, then it has done its job.

This book is not here only to offer easy affirmations. At times it will affirm, at others it will provoke. It invites us back into the arena of intellectual debate, where opposing views are not to be feared but tested, like flint striking steel, where the brightest sparks often appear at the collision of strong ideas.

This is also not a book to finish in one sitting. Dip in and out. Read it with your morning tea, on the train, between meetings, or on those quiet days when life feels a little off balance.

More than anything, I hope that something in these pages resonates with you, even if it's just a line or a passing thought. Something timely, comforting, and perhaps, transformative.

S.H. Chuah

QUICK REFERENCE

This book is woven with reflections, but also dotted with a few simple frameworks, reference to external visuals and notes on useful resources. Here, they are gathered in one place, so you can return to them whenever needed.

Select Principles, Frameworks & Tools

Leadership & Self-Awareness

- **Markers of Power:** Subtle signals and behaviours that project – and are perceived as – power and influence. (Jan 8)
- **Communicate with Impact:** Elements for concise communication for clarity, impact, and influence. (April 13)
- **Self-awareness – Johari Window:** Reflection on values, feedback, and recognising blind spots. (April 29)
- **Skill/Will Matrix:** Tailor your leadership style to the ability and motivation of people and teams. (May 11)

Strategy & Focus

- **80/20 Principle (Pareto) & Urgent–Important Matrix –** Most impact comes from a few critical efforts; distinguish signal from noise, focus on the critical few, and separate true priorities from competing distractions. (Jan 5)
- **Strategy Toolkit**
  - **Sun Tzu's Five Pillars of Strategy** (May 12)
  - **From the 36 Stratagems** (Jan 24, Feb 5, Mar 29, Apr 28, May 25, Jun 21, Aug 1, Aug 10, Nov 12)
  - **Strategy Toolkit Laundry List** (May 14)

Reference to External Visuals (Clips)

Readers are encouraged to view the following clips:

- **The Inevitability of Enemies:** Margaret Thatcher recites 'No Enemies' by Charles Mackay to Queen Elizabeth – in the Crown, season four. (Oct 14)
- **What Makes a Good King:** Tywin & Tommen – What makes a good king? (Game of Thrones) (Sep 5)

JANUARY

智

zhì

Meaning of 智 (zhì):

- Wisdom
- Insight
- Discernment
- Good judgement
- Strategic foresight

In Chinese philosophy, zhì (智) is more than being smart. It's knowing how to *use* what you know, with timing, tact, and understanding. It's the kind of wisdom that sees through noise, reads between the lines, and chooses the right move at the right moment. People with 智 don't just know what to do, they know when to speak, what to hold back, and how to move through complexity without being arrogant.

Mastering 智 (zhì) helps us:

- **Stay curious:** Keep learning and listen more than we speak.
- **Be discerning:** Not everything deserves our attention or energy.
- **Speak with intention:** Words have weight, use them well.
- **Know when to pause, when to act:** Timing matters as much as action.
- **Let clarity guide us:** Even in uncertainty, stay anchored in insight.
- **Lead with wisdom:** Let our inner compass guide our actions.

January 1

When Smart Misses the Mark

The trap of thinking fast and knowing little

学而不思则罔，思而不学则殆

xué ér bù sī zé wǎng, sī ér bù xué zé dài

Translation: "Learning without thinking leads to confusion; thinking without learning leads to misjudgement."
— Confucius (孔子), Analects (论语)

Ever nodded along to someone known for being clever, only to realise later they were confidently... wrong? Turns out, a loud voice and certainty are only half the story of intelligence, and not always a sign of wisdom.

Confucius tells us of two traps in learning:

- **The passive sponge:** Soaks up information but never stops to think. They've got facts, but rarely ask what's true, what matters, or why.
- **The overconfident thinker:** Quick with opinions but thin on actual knowledge. Sounds smart and convincing, but the logic often falls apart quickly. Worse, they can mislead others with sheer confidence.

What it teaches us

- **Question what you learn:** Don't just collect information; think about it, challenge it, and connect the dots.
- **Being smart ≠ being right:** Just because someone sounds intelligent doesn't mean they are.
- **Confidence is not competence:** Misinformation often spreads from those who speak with conviction but know too little. Yet confidence is often perceived as competence, deserved or not.

> ***"The greatest enemy of knowledge is not ignorance; it is the illusion of knowledge."***
> — **Daniel Boorstin**

The Dao Whispers: Do I question what I hear, or nod along just because it sounds clever? And if the clever can mislead, can't the intelligent be misled too?

January 2

Why Did You Start?

Sometimes the best way forward is to remember where you began

不忘初心，方得始终

bù wàng chū xīn, fāng dé shǐ zhōng

Translation: "Do not forget your original intention, and you will achieve the aspirations you first set out to accomplish."
— Chinese Saying

It's easy to drift. Years pass, paths twist, and one day we wake up wondering: ***Why did I start this? What was I trying to achieve?***

The proverb urges us to stay true to our ***chū xīn (初心)*** – the heart's original intent. Whether your aim was to serve others, to improve lives, to build something lasting, or to seek recognition, do you still remember that starting point?

What it teaches us

- **Purpose as your compass:** Staying connected to your original "why" keeps daily choices aligned with the kind of life we want to build.
- **Resilience against distractions:** Along your way, there'll be temptations and pressures trying to pull you off-course. Revisiting your purpose helps you refocus, persevere, and keep moving in the right direction.
- **Winning without losing yourself:** Anchoring in your principles prevents ethical drift and lets you succeed without compromising who you are.

> ***"To be yourself in a world that is constantly trying to make you something else is the greatest accomplishment."***
> — **Ralph Waldo Emerson**

The Dao Whispers: What was I hoping to build or become when I began? Have I drifted from that intent? If so, was it through growth, distraction, or fear? Should I return, or is the detour the better path?

January 3

Life's Best Teachers Don't Always Have Titles

Every person we meet carries lessons we have yet to learn

三人行，必有我师焉

sān rén xíng, bì yǒu wǒ shī yān

Translation: "In the company of three strangers walking together, I can always find a teacher."
— Confucius (孔子), Analects (论语)

What if the next person you bump into, someone you'd **normally walk past without thinking twice**, ends up teaching you something that actually changes your life?

Confucius reminds us that wisdom and insight can show up in unexpected places. A child blurting out an unfiltered truth. A stranger quietly doing the right thing when nobody's watching. Even a critic pointing out something we'd rather not hear. Every person we meet, regardless of age, title, or background, has something to teach us if we're open enough to notice.

The people who grow the fastest in life, at work, or in leadership aren't the loudest or the busiest. They're the ones who stay curious, listen well, and keep learning from everyone around them. Treat every interaction as a mini-masterclass and you might walk away smarter, kinder, or at least with a story worth telling later.

> **"The more I learn, the more I realise how much I still don't know."**
> **— Albert Einstein**

> **"Be nice to people on your way up because you'll meet them on your way down."**
> **— Wilson Mizner**

The Dao Whispers

- Everyone we meet knows something we don't, and that makes them worth learning from.
- Am I letting pride or snap judgements get in the way of something I could be learning?

January 4

You Can't Build a House by Just Talking

You have to start putting your ideas into practice

坐而论道，不如起而行之

zuò ér lùn dào, bù rú qǐ ér xíng zhī

Translation: "Better to bring principles to life through practice than to sit around merely discussing them."
— Traditional Chinese proverb

We sip coffee and talk endlessly about goals, values, or plans; but unless we roll up our sleeves and start doing something about them, nothing will change, and nothing will get done.

The proverb calls out that ideas don't matter unless you act on them. It's a call to stop waiting, overthinking, or planning endlessly. Begin. Sometimes, even the most imperfect set of actions can beat perfect intentions.

What it teaches us

- **Don't wait for the perfect moment**: The perfect moment rarely arrives. Done is better than perfect.
- **Ditch self-doubt:** Remove self-limiting beliefs that keep you stuck in place; they are often fears rationalised by logic.
- **Begin anyway:** Start with what you have, where you are. Momentum will follow.

> ***"I always believe that an opportunity comes from opportunity as even the best ideas have flaws...As long as you are willing to take active actions, you will be closer to success...Unfortunately, many people have not remembered this biggest lesson, and as a result, they have resulted to mediocrity."***
> — **John D. Rockefeller,** *Letters to His Son*

The Dao Whispers: What have I been endlessly planning but never starting, what story keeps me stuck, and what is one real step I can take today?

January 5

The 80/20 Rule: What Moves the Needle?

Picking up sesame seeds, but losing the watermelon

捡了芝麻，丢了西瓜

jiǎn le zhī ma, diū le xī guā

Translation: "Picking up sesame seeds but losing a watermelon."
— Traditional Chinese proverb

Have you ever spent hours tweaking a slide font… while ignoring the actual message? Or spent a whole day ***"being productive,"*** only to realise you haven't moved an inch on what really matters?

This old proverb paints a vivid picture: someone so focused on gathering tiny sesame seeds that they drop the big, juicy watermelon they were holding.

It's a perfect metaphor for getting lost in the small stuff and missing the big win.

The 80/20 Rule

- **Consultants call it the Pareto Principle (The 80/20 rule):** the idea that 80% of outcomes often come from 20% of the effort or root causes. In plain English, it means, a small number of things usually create most of the impact.
- **The 20% that moves the needle:** Let's say your team brainstorms 100 ideas to drive growth. In most cases, only 10–20 of those will deliver 80% of the impact. The rest? Nice to have, but they won't move the needle.
- **The 80% sinkhole – high effort, low impact busywork**: Yet even experienced leaders fall into this trap by firefighting low-impact issues, overanalysing the irrelevant, or over-optimising what doesn't matter.

> ***"Things which matter most must never be at the mercy of things which matter least."***
>
> **— Johann Wolfgang von Goethe**

The Dao Whispers: Strategy is a choice. Focus only on what moves the needle.

Urgent vs. Important Matrix: A Secret Sauce for Ruthless Prioritisation

This simple two-by-two (2×2) helps decide where to focus energy – so you can run your life, work, and relationships sustainably, while avoiding chaos and burnout.

	Not Important	Very Important
Very Urgent	**Urgent + Not Important** **Action:** Delegate, set boundaries, deflect	**Urgent + Important** **Action:** Do it Now
Not Urgent	**Not Urgent + Not Important** **Action:** Drop it	**Important + Not Urgent** **Action**: Plan and protect time to address

The idea is simple: Spend time on the 20% of activities that will create 80% of impact. Handle what's important early, so it doesn't creep into the "Urgent + Important" quadrant unknowingly.

What does this mean?

- **Urgent & Important – High Impact:** These crises and deadlines matter, but constant firefighting steals energy from strategic work.
- **Not Urgent & Important – Highest Impact:** Growth, health, and relationships live here. Great leaders defend this space, where lasting results are born.
- **Urgent & Not Important – Low Impact:** This feels pressing but creates little value – the trap of ***"busy but unproductive."*** Impact comes from resisting other people's urgency or chaos.
- **Not Urgent & Not Important – Zero/Negative:** Mindless scrolling, gossip, and no-impact tasks. Every hour here is stolen from impact. Cut ruthlessly.

Urgency tells you what needs attention immediately, while importance tells you where impact really lies.

Using the Matrix for Daily Prioritisation

- **Start each morning:** List your top tasks – ideally top 3 that move the needle.
- Sort them into the four quadrants.
    - **Q1 (Urgent + Important)** – Today's must-dos.
    - **Q2 (Not Urgent + Important)** – Schedule time blocks, don't let them slip through the cracks.
    - **Q3 (Urgent + Not Important)** – Push back or delegate quickly, else you'll be chasing alligators all day.
    - **Q4 (Not Urgent + Not Important)** – Delete.

Rule of thumb: Spend most of your energy in Q2 (high impact, not urgent). Handle Q1 fast, minimise Q3 and Q4.

Over time, you'll intuitively land on three things each day that are urgent and/or important.

- Q1 = Today's must-do's
- Q2 = Block time for them (non-negotiables)
- Q3 = Delegate fast
- Q4 = Delete

Allocate more time to Q2 so important work never becomes an urgent fire.

The Dao Whispers: Apply the **80/20 lens** here – it tells you *which* few activities drive the biggest outcomes.

Wisdom is in acting where urgency, importance, and impact meet – in the life you're building, the day you're living, and the teams and projects you're leading.

January 6

Seize the Moment

Some doors only open once

机不可失，时不再来

jī bù kě shī, shí bù zài lái

Translation: "Do not let the opportunity slip away, as this very chance will not come by again."
— Traditional Chinese proverb

Blink during an online flash sale and suddenly the thing you wanted is gone, sold out to someone faster.

Opportunities in life can be just as unforgiving. It takes the right place, the right people, and the right timing. This proverb reminds us that fortune almost never knocks twice. When we hesitate, it may cost us what preparation alone cannot guarantee – timing.

Opportunity isn't just about being ready; it's about spotting your chance and having the guts to take it before the window closes.

What it teaches us

- **Career moves:** That promotion, connection, or big-deal chat might not come around twice. If you hesitate, someone else will say ***'yes'*** first.
- **Personal growth:** Some opportunities to learn new skills or step out of your comfort zone may not come again, like a chance to speak in public or travel somewhere new. Seizing them may lead to transformative experiences.
- **Relationships:** Some words must be said now, not tomorrow. Moments to mend or strengthen relationships can pass. Say ***'I'm sorry'*** or ***'I love you'*** today. Silence grows heavier the longer you sit on it.

"You miss 100% of the shots you don't take."
— **Wayne Gretzky**

The Dao Whispers: What if I'm not unprepared, but afraid to start?

January 7

It Takes Time for True Colours to Show

Give it long enough, and people will show you who they are

路遥知马力，日久见人心

lù yáo zhī mǎ lì, rì jiǔ jiàn rén xīn

Translation: "Just as a long journey tests a horse's strength, so time reveals a person's heart."
— Traditional Chinese proverb

They say you don't really know someone until you've seen them tired, tested, or stuck in traffic with no coffee. Just like a long journey shows how strong a horse really is, tough times show you who people really are.

What it teaches us

- **Watch who shows up**: See who shows up when it's hard, not when it's easy. That's when you see who stays, who disappears, who hides behind a smile, and who was only around to take.
- **Find out who's behind the mask:** Ask yourself, what does this person want me to notice or feel about them? That's often the first clue to the mask they wear – and what lies beneath it.
- **Give truth time to reveal itself:** Don't rush to decide who someone is. Time, like a long road, will show you more than what first impressions can.

"Time discovers truth."
— **Seneca**

The Dao Whispers: True colours take time to show. Do I give people time to show their true colours, or do I rush to judge?

January 8

Power Has to Be Seen

Influence only matters if others can see and feel it

老虎不发威，当我是病猫？

lǎo hǔ bù fā wēi, dāng wǒ shì bìng māo?

Translation: "Just because (I) the tiger doesn't roar, are you really mistaking me for a cat that's ill?"
— Traditional Chinese proverb

It is still a tiger. Power does not always need to announce itself, but if it stays hidden too long people begin to forget it is there.

The subject of power can make people uncomfortable, but if you want to scale your positive impact and change the world in a good way, power and influence can multiply impact. Let's face it, in life, people often confuse being calm with being weak. If you're quiet, they might think you don't have power, drive, or bite.

Staying composed doesn't mean you're not strong; it means you don't need to prove it all the time. You don't need to show your hand every second, but also, don't let anyone think you've got nothing to play. Unless, of course, you play to a different sort of power – capital – which, as Piketty argued in his seminal work *Capital in the Twenty-First Century*, can outweigh even effort and talent.

> ***"It is not necessary to have all the good qualities, but it is very necessary to appear to have them."***
> — **Niccolò Machiavelli,** The Prince

Core principles of power:

- **Be Seen:** Eye contact, posture, controlled presence.
- **Be Heard**: Louder, steady voice, concise words, silence used with intent.
- **Be Felt:** Energy, emotional congruence, timing, occasional controlled anger.
- **Be Remembered:** Occupy space, frame the narrative, choose moments of revelation.

Tiger's power signals

- **Don't read from notes.** Own your message.

- **Make steady eye contact.** Predators look straight, not down.
- **Keep communication brief.** Concise equals authority.
- **Pause deliberately**. Pauses command attention.
- **Don't apologise unnecessarily.** Apologise only when it's due.
- **Speak with a louder, steady voice**. A clear, anchored voice projects confidence and authority.
- **Use controlled gestures.** Firm, deliberate, not frantic.
- **Stand tall, open posture.** Occupy space without shrinking.
- **Controlled anger.** Sparingly used, signals conviction.
- **Own the stage**. From seating position to body language, claim the space.
- **Guard your availability.** Scarcity signals value.
- **Ask sharp questions**. The tiger is not the one scrambling to answer, but the one setting the frame.

What it teaches us

- **Perception is reality**: Beyond capital or titles, power is often what others believe you have. Research shows taller and more attractive people are more likely to be promoted or paid more. Humans are perceptive creatures who constantly make snap judgements about strength and competence.
- **Assert yourself when you have to:** Restraint is strength, but don't let it be mistaken for weakness. Reserve your power, and when the need arises, use it.
- **Power can feel uncomfortable, but it is necessary:** Talking about power can feel awkward, even distasteful, but without it you cannot scale impact or protect your boundaries. If you want to do good in the world, you need the influence to make it happen.

> ***"If you want power to be for good, more good people need to have power."***
> — **Jeffrey Pfeffer**

The Dao Whispers: Does my presence signal power, or the lack of it?

The Tiger's Laundry List: Markers of Power

While power can be an uncomfortable topic, there is evidence that people who project it – and yes, taller and more attractive people too – are often more successful and paid more. Not all of us stand six foot two, but the signals of power can be learned. Here is a list of markers you can return to whenever you need a reminder.

Voice & Speech

- **Don't read from notes.** Mastery signals confidence.
- **Speak with a louder, steady voice.** Volume conveys confidence, not aggression.
- **Keep communication brief.** Concise equals authority; long-windedness signals insecurity.
- **Pause deliberately.** Silence can command attention better than filling space.
- **Avoid rising intonation at the end of sentences (up-talk).** It sounds uncertain, as if asking for permission.
- **Use declarative statements instead of hedging:** "This is what we'll do" vs. "I think maybe we should…."
- **Notice your pitch, deep voices convey power.** People instinctively link lower pitched voices with strength and stability. A steady and lower pitch signals control under pressure.

Body Language

- **Use solid, steady gestures.** No fidgeting, no flailing. Controlled movements project calm dominance.
- **More gestures (deliberate, not excessive).** Emphasis shows energy and conviction.
- **Maintain eye contact.** Steady eye contact signals presence and dominance.
- **Stand tall, open posture.** Stand with feet apart, shoulders back; not hunched or closed off.
- **Own the space.** Expand slightly (legs uncrossed, arms apart). Don't shrink yourself.
- **Invading personal space.** Use proximity wisely – leaning in or stepping closer can project confidence, but only if done with care.

- **Controlled stillness.** Predators don't twitch. Leaders who can hold still command attention.

Facial Expression & Emotion

- **Anger can sound powerful.** Righteous anger signals conviction (when used sparingly).
- **Neutral or composed expressions.** Don't over-smile; excessive smiling can signal lower status.
- **Micro-expressions of confidence.** Slight nods, subtle frowns, lifted eyebrows at the right time.

Psychological Signals

- **Guard your availability.** Scarcity of words and access signal power. Don't make yourself too available, access given too freely is never valued.
- **Name-drop strategically.** Networks imply power and influence.
- **Be the questioner, not the answerer.** Asking sharp questions frames you as the evaluator, not the subordinate. Set the frame, don't scramble to answer.
- **Own mistakes selectively.** Admit failure with control, not in a self-deprecating way.

Environment & Symbols

- **Dress sharply.** Clothing signals power, or the lack of it. Show up with power – sharp, tailored, no "try-hard" over-accessories.
- **Surround yourself with objects of authority.** Books, documents, or tech can subtly signal knowledge and influence. And yes, some take it further – from Maserati keys dropped on the table to corner offices and private jets. You don't need to play that game yourself, but you should recognise it when others do.
- **Control the stage.** Whether it's a boardroom, Zoom call, or podium, the one who sets the frame sets the tone.

January 9

We Sow What We Reap

If we plant melons, we will harvest melons; plant durians and we'll harvest durians

种瓜得瓜，种豆得豆

zhòng guā dé guā, zhòng dòu dé dòu

Translation: "If we plant melons, we will harvest melons; if we plant beans, we will harvest beans."
— Traditional Chinese proverb

The idiom speaks to the law of cause and effect. Every action plants a seed, and every seed bears fruit in time. In career, relationships, finances, or self-mastery, our choices today affect what we would harvest tomorrow, next year, or a decade later.

And someday, that distant decade will arrive and become the "today" that you'll be living in.

What it teaches us

- **Shaping personal destiny**: Choices in our daily habits, e.g., learning or doing vs. procrastinating, will build up and shape the life outcomes we see later.
- **Long-term impact:** Who you spend time with, what you eat, and how you think will have a long-term impact, in one way or another.
- **Your inner world:** Even thoughts are seeds. Plant bitterness, and bitterness grows; plant curiosity, love, and happiness, and growth and contentment follow.
- **Do what you love**: Spend time doing what you enjoy and build your toolkit around it. Otherwise, you risk spending the first half of your life mastering skills you don't care for, and the second half using them in work you don't like.

"Life is the sum of all your choices."
— **Albert Camus**

The Dao Whispers: What seeds am I planting today, and will they lead me to a future I hope for? How have my past choices, both wise and unwise, shaped my current reality? What can I learn from the seeds I once planted to better choose what I plant next?

January 10

Wisdom Through the Ages

At fifteen, I learn; at thirty, I stabilise; at forty, I gain clarity; at fifty, I recognise my calling

吾十有五而志于学，三十而立，四十而不惑，五十而知天命

wú shí yǒu wǔ ér zhì yú xué, sān shí ér lì,
sì shí ér bù huò, wǔ shí ér zhī tiān mìng

Translation: "At fifteen, I set my heart on learning;
at thirty, I stood firm;
at forty, I had no more doubts;
at fifty, I knew the will of Heaven."
— Confucius (孔子), Analects (论语)

Confucius captured the evolution of human life through the passing decades. Each stage brings more clarity, alignment, and maturity. To remain stagnant is to miss the unfolding wisdom that time offers. Life is meant to be reinterpreted as we grow. If your perspective remains unchanged as you age, you're likely resisting the very experiences that are meant to shape and mature you.

What it teaches us

- **Teens – Set your heart on learning:** This is the age of curiosity, where you build foundations of knowledge and values that guide the rest of life.
- **20s – Test and Learn:** A decade for experimenting, failing, and absorbing lessons from real life. Careers, friendships, love, and values are the arenas where theory gets tested, and mistakes become part of the curriculum. Continuously seeking knowledge, in all its forms, equips you to grow intellectually, emotionally, and relationally.
- **30s – The Foundation Years**: The idea of being "established" at thirty suggests setting clear goals, developing a stable character, establishing your own family unit, being anchored in your career or finances, and finding your place in the world. Signs you are on track include having boundaries that are firm, no longer apologising for your "no," and choosing ***purpose*** over prestige.

- **40s – Things start to click as you seek clarity through reflection:** The gift of this decade is **trusting your gut**. All those years of trial and error finally begin to pay off. You've learned from your wins and your mistakes, you start to trust your own judgment more, and you know who you are and what you stand for. By forty, you either know yourself or know you've been avoiding yourself.
- **50s – You often stop chasing, accept your purpose and start appreciating:** By your fifties, something shifts. You're less interested in proving yourself and more focused on what feels right for your family, your work, your community, and yourself. You begin to honour your story, with all its twists and lessons. Some call it "knowing Heaven's will," while others might just call it clarity. You find your groove and focus on what brings real meaning to your life.
- **60s – You start to progress at your own pace:** By now, you've seen enough to stop rushing. You stop comparing timelines and start trusting your own. The ultimate shift in this is to go from ***achieving*** to ***being.***

Confucius wasn't handing out deadlines. They were more like signposts. Everyone's timeline looks different, and that's okay. Growth doesn't follow a spreadsheet. Maybe at forty you are still searching, maybe at fifty you are only just finding your stride. That doesn't make you behind; it just means life gave you a different curriculum. The real wisdom here isn't in ticking boxes, but in asking: *What is life teaching me right now? And am I willing to learn it?*

> ***"The man who views the world at fifty the same as he did at twenty has wasted thirty years of his life."***
> — **Muhammad Ali**

The Dao Whispers: Ten years ago, you were a different person. Isn't it wild to think how much has shifted?

- **Your questions then vs. now:** Are you still chasing answers, or have your questions become more meaningful?
- **Your heart's verdicts:** Has time made you quicker to judge... or are you now more willing to listen?
- **Your younger self's fears**: Which ones still haunt you? Which did you outgrow without noticing?
- **What you'd fight for now:** The battles that once felt urgent, do they still light a fire, or have your non-negotiables evolved over time?

January 11

The Tale of an Old Man Who Lost His Horse

Who would have known it was a blessing in disguise?

塞翁失马，焉知非福

sài wēng shī mǎ, yān zhī fēi fú

Translation: "When the old man lost his horse, who would have known that it was truly a blessing in disguise?"
— Huainanzi (淮南子)

The Story

Once upon a time, near the northern frontier, there lived a wise old man known for his foresight.

One day, his horse ran away. Everyone came to console him, but he said, "Who knows? This might turn out to be a blessing."

A few months later, the horse returned and brought back a herd of magnificent wild horses. Everyone congratulated him. But he said, "Who knows? This might turn out to be a misfortune."

His family now had many horses. His son loved riding, but one day he fell off a horse while riding and broke his leg. Again, everyone came to express sympathy. But the old man said, "Who knows? This might turn out to be a blessing."

Not long after, nomadic tribes invaded the border region. All able-bodied young men from the village were drafted. Most died in battle, but the old man's son, crippled, was spared. And just like that, his misfortune became a hidden blessing.

> ***"What seems to us as bitter trials are often blessings in disguise."***
> — Often attributed to **Oscar Wilde**

The Dao Whispers: Sometimes, life unfolds in ways we don't understand yet it still serves us. What seems like a loss may carry the seeds of unexpected blessings. Trust that every experience, even the unwelcome or painful, may be guiding us toward our highest good. What past losses in my life might I now see as a hidden blessing?

January 12

When Clever Beats Strong on the Chang Jiang

How one strategist turned fog and straw into 100,000 arrows

草船借箭

cǎo chuán jiè jiàn

Translation: "Borrowing arrows with straw boats."
— A stratagem from Romance of the Three Kingdoms (三国演义)

The Story

The tale of "borrowing arrows with straw boats" is one of the most famous stratagems in Chinese history, a masterclass in deception and resourcefulness.

During a military standoff, strategist **Zhuge Liang** needed 100,000 arrows within ten days to fight **Cao Cao's** forces. Cao Cao was among the era's most brilliant commanders. So, Zhuge Liang devised a plan:

- **Foggy night trick**: On the third day, he sent twenty boats lined with straw-stuffed scarecrows made to resemble soldiers, drifting toward Cao Cao's camp on the Chang Jiang River (Yangtze River).
- **Enemy panic**: Hidden by thick fog, the decoys fooled Cao Cao's archers, who unleashed volleys of arrows, lodging them into the straw figures.
- **Arrow harvest**: Zhuge Liang sailed back with over 100,000 arrows, outsmarting Cao Cao without losing a single soldier.

> ***"It is double pleasure to deceive the deceiver."***
> — **Niccolò Machiavelli**

The Dao Whispers

- Is fighting head-on always the wisest path?
- Are you fully leveraging what you already have, including your insight, timing, goodwill, and network?

January 13

When the Blind Leads the Blind

Why good advice starts with the right advisor

问道于盲

wèn dào yú máng

Translation: "Asking for directions from the blind."
— Traditional Chinese idiom

Imagine you're lost in a city you've never been to. You stop a man on the street and ask for directions. He smiles warmly, speaks with great confidence, and points you toward a winding road. Grateful, you set off, only to discover hours later that you're further from your destination than when you started. Only then do you realise, the man was blind. You're now tired, you can feel the blisters on your feet and your shoulders hurt from the heavy backpack.

Here's the thing... not all advice is good advice. Before you follow someone's lead, ask yourself: ***"Do they actually know the way?"*** Good judgement involves knowing whose judgement to trust. That is why choosing your advisors carefully matters, even if they have the best of intentions.

What it teaches us

- **Choose your guides wisely:** Don't be swayed by charm or credentials; learn from those who have truly succeeded on the path you want, and who share the values you want to live by.
- **Evaluate the advice, not just the advisor:** Even trusted mentors can be wrong. Judge the guidance on its merits, and remember, the final responsibility for your decisions is yours. Don't outsource your judgement, because others may not fully see your context.
- **Empathise with fallibility:** Most who misguide mean no harm. Recognise others' knowledge gaps with compassion and without blame.

> ***"Don't take criticism from someone you wouldn't take advice from."***
> — Anonymous

The Dao Whispers: Am I taking advice that truly fits the life I'm trying to build? When voices conflict, do I have the courage to trust my own?

January 14

Smart Enough to Admit You're Clueless

Because only the smartest know they'll never know it all

知之为知之，不知为不知，是知也

zhī zhī wéi zhī zhī, bù zhī wéi bù zhī, shì zhī yě

Translation: "To know what you know and to admit what you don't know, that is real knowledge."
— Confucius (孔子), Analects (论语)

Ever sat in a meeting, nodding along while secretly hoping no one calls on you to explain what 'macroprudential policy' actually means?

Confucius reminds us it's important to be honest about what we know, and even more honest about what we don't know. Modern psychology calls this the Dunning-Kruger effect:

- People who know little often think they know a lot.
- Those who truly understand a subject often see its depth and complexity and doubt their own mastery.

Admitting we don't know something can be a superpower. The courage to say "I don't know" makes learning possible.

> ***"I am the wisest man alive, for I know one thing – and that is that I know nothing."***
> — **Socrates**

The Dao Whispers

- Can I be honest about what I don't know, even when others are bluffing?
- Am I spending time with people who are honest about their limits, or those who are more focused on looking smart than being clear?

January 15

There is Power in Self-Restraint

A moment of restraint can save a lifetime of regret

忍一时风平浪静，退一步海阔天空

rěn yī shí fēng píng làng jìng, tuì yī bù hǎi kuò tiān kōng

Translation: "Endure for a moment (and watch) the wind calms, the waves settle; take a step back and (see how) the sea broadens, the sky clears."
— Traditional Chinese proverb

You know that sinking feeling, when you hit send too quickly or say something sharp just to make a point, only to make everything worse.

This proverb reminds us that restraint can be a superpower. A pause, a single step back, can change everything.

Especially in moments of anger, pride, or hurt, it pays to stay calm. Choosing to hold back rather than react impulsively can help de-escalate tension and prevent decisions you'll later regret. Rash reactions almost always lead to suboptimal outcomes and often require damage control afterwards.

What it teaches us

- **Patience reveals true character:** When faced with unfairness or hostility, restraint often exposes the real dynamics at play without inflaming the situation.
- **Stepping back can clarify what the system values:** Sometimes, taking a step back shows what truly drives the people or systems around you.
- **Restraint tests integrity of those around you**: When you hold back, do others respond with respect or choose to take advantage of that?

> ***"I cannot trust a man to control others who cannot control himself."***
> — **Robert E. Lee**

The Dao Whispers: Do I master my emotions, or are they my master?

January 16

Words Can Start Wars and Heal Them

A single sentence can shift trust, history, or someone's heart

一言为重百金轻

yī yán wéi zhòng bǎi jīn qīng

Translation: "A single word carries more weight than a hundred pieces of gold."
—Wang Anshi (王安石), Song dynasty

A headline, a tweet, or even a careless office rumour can trigger chaos in minutes. Words may seem small, but they carry enormous weight. They can build trust, win hearts, or light fires that burn for decades. A few sentences can change someone's mind or even the course of history.

Confucius reminds us that the right words, at the right time, can be priceless. Our words stick with people. It's not only about watching what you say, but also about meaning it and saying it with kindness.

What it teaches us

- **Narratives matter**: Narratives can be used to forge alliances and strengthen nations; but they can also be used to spread discord and trigger wars.
- **Talk like it counts:** Every time we open our mouths, we choose: Are we building people up or tearing them down? Do our words build trust, inspire hope, or skew perception?
- **Real leaders watch their words:** One pep talk can shift a whole team's mood – that's the power of words that lift instead of crush.

> ***"A slip of the tongue may haunt you longer than a slip of the foot."***
> — **Benjamin Franklin**

The Dao Whispers: Once something's said, you can't take it back. Do your words leave people feeling safer, smaller, or stronger?

January 17

Don't Say It If You Won't Stand by It

Credibility has only one currency: kept promises

言必信，行必果

yán bì xìn, xíng bì guǒ

Translation: "Keep your word, and follow through on your actions."
— Traditional Chinese proverb

We've all met someone who makes big promises but never follows through. You stop believing their words after the third "next time."

This proverb is a call to close the gap between **what we say** and **what we do**. A promise, once made, becomes part of your public ledger. Pay it in action even when it's inconvenient or uncomfortable. That's how trust, credibility, and self-respect are earned and kept.

What it teaches us

- **Trust is built by showing up:** We've all had that friend who bails last minute or the boss who talks big but never delivers. Credibility is in doing what you said you'd do, even when it's hard.
- **Your reputation is your most valuable currency:** Reliability speaks louder than words – meeting deadlines, honouring commitments, and showing up consistently. People may forget what you said, but they'll always remember what you did.
- **"Yes" needs follow-through:** It's easy to agree in the moment and back out later. Choosing to honour our word not only builds trust but also prevents us from appearing flaky or unreliable.

> ***"Well done is better than well said."***
> — **Benjamin Franklin**

The Dao Whispers: Have I honoured my word by keeping my promises, being careful not to make those I cannot keep, and showing up when I said I would?

January 18

Build Your Mind Like a Fortress

Every book is another stone

立身以立学为先，立学以读书为本

lì shēn yǐ lì xué wéi xiān, lì xué yǐ dú shū wéi běn

Translation: "To establish one's character, one must first learn; to learn, one must read."
— Zhu Xi (朱熹), Song Dynasty Neo-Confucian philosopher

If wisdom came from scrolling, we would all be geniuses. After five hours of doomscrolling, you are left with only two things: tired eyes and questionable life choices. Books feed the mind in a way scrolling never can, as they can build you up page by page, layer by layer.

In this saying, Zhu Xi reminds us that character doesn't appear overnight. It's built over time, layer by layer, through what we learn, reflect on, and practise.

What it teaches us

- **Books are like cheat codes for life:** The more you read across history, philosophy, psychology, and practical skills, the more tools you have to handle whatever life throws at you.
- **Read with intention:** Read across time, disciplines, and cultures so you have enough data points to see patterns and sharpen your judgement.
- **Resilience in the storm:** A mind well-stocked with solid knowledge and wisdom can better draw on its reserves when life's storms hit hardest.

> ***"A reader lives a thousand lives before he dies.***
> ***The man who never reads lives only one."***
> — **George R.R. Martin**

The Dao Whispers: When faced with life's storm, will my mind be a shelter or a house of cards?

January 19

Don't Let Small Storms Sink Big Plans

A single slip can derail a winning strategy

小不忍则乱大谋

xiǎo bù rěn zé luàn dà móu

Translation: "If we do not endure small inconveniences, we may end up disrupting great plans."
— Traditional Chinese proverb

Impatience has a way of turning small bumps into big detours. The email you fired off and instantly regret, the person you snapped at for something small... sometimes, one impatient moment can cost us weeks of peace, progress, or opportunity.

This proverb reminds us that it's rarely the big crises that ruin our plans. It's the little, itchy moments we fail to handle well – the snappy comeback, the irritation that clouds judgement, the pride that refuses a minor setback. What we fail to hold back in a flash can snowball into a chain reaction that derails bigger things.

What it teaches us

- **Guard long-term goals:** Don't let fleeting workplace drama or petty friction derail your broader vision. Pause, breathe, respond... but never, never react impulsively.
- **Lead with composure:** In conflict, calm leaders can better steer teams through conflict and keep them focused on the big picture. If the leader wobbles, the team wobbles.
- **Patience as self-mastery:** We can choose to stay grounded in emotional surges, and not let anger hijack our judgement. With discipline, anger can be transmuted into fuel for constructive action.

"Never lose your temper, except intentionally."
— **Dwight D. Eisenhower**

"A handful of patience is worth more than a bushel of brains."
— Dutch proverb

The Dao Whispers: Do I have the patience to let small storms pass so bigger plans can unfold?

January 20

First, Master the Person in the Mirror

You're the hardest person you'll ever lead, then comes your team

知人者智，自知者明

zhī rén zhě zhì, zì zhī zhě míng

Translation: "To understand others is wisdom; to know oneself is to be enlightened (to be wise, or to have clarity)."
— Dao De Jing (道德经), Laozi

You can be great at reading people. You might even predict what your boss will say before she says it. But turning that spotlight towards the person in the mirror? That's the tricky part.

This saying reminds us that it's one thing to understand others, and quite another to understand yourself. Self-awareness means noticing your patterns, your blind spots, and the stories you tell yourself without realising.

This isn't to say that you need to have a spiritual awakening on a mountaintop. It's the little things every day – catching yourself right before you snap, sulk, or spiral. Very often, that's a lot harder than solving other people's problems.

What it teaches us

- **See yourself clearly:** Notice your emotions before they become reactions.
- **Know your impact:** Understand how you affect others, even when you don't mean to have that effect.
- **Ask for help:** Don't be afraid to ask for help; real strength means knowing when you can't do it all alone.
- **Know your strengths**: Know what you're great at and use it to your advantage.
- **Pay attention to what's not said:** What's left unsaid often speaks the loudest.

"Knowing yourself is the beginning of all wisdom."
— Aristotle

The Dao Whispers: Take five minutes a day to observe, not judge, your emotional responses. Ask: ***"What am I feeling? Why?"***

January 21

The Emperor's Three Truth-Tellers

History, other people, and self-reflections as compasses

以铜为镜，可以正衣冠；以古为镜，可以知兴替；以人为镜，可以明得失

yǐ tóng wéi jìng, kě yǐ zhèng yī guān; yǐ gǔ wéi jìng, kě yǐ zhī xīng tì; yǐ rén wéi jìng, kě yǐ míng dé shī.

Translation: "By using bronze as a mirror, one corrects one's dress; by using history as a mirror, one understands rise and decline; by using people as a mirror, one discerns gains and losses. I keep these three mirrors to guard against my faults."
— Emperor Taizong (唐太宗)

If you've ever been in a fitting room surrounded by three mirrors, you'll know there's nowhere to hide. They show you from every angle, even the one you wish didn't exist. Emperor Taizong's "three mirrors" work the same way. History, other people's perspective, and self-reflection each reveal truths from different angles. Sometimes the view is flattering, other times it's brutally honest. We need both to grow.

Emperor Taizong, one of China's most revered rulers, used this idea as a guide for wise governance during the Tang Dynasty. The "three mirrors" remind us that we need to see our shortcomings clearly in order to correct them and improve.

What it teaches us

- **Study the past:** Learning from historical patterns in personal, corporate, and national history helps us avoid repeating mistakes.
- **Seek feedback for self-improvement:** Listening to honest feedback from friends, mentors, or critics reveals blind spots in how we lead, speak, and behave.
- **Practise self-awareness:** The 'three mirrors' help us see the areas within ourselves that need polishing.

"History doesn't repeat itself, but it does often rhyme."
— Often attributed to **Mark Twain**

The Dao Whispers: Who have I dismissed as a 'hater' when they were telling me a truth I didn't want to face?

January 22

Cheering Someone On Isn't Always Kindness

Good people lift others up, not drag them down

君子成人之美，不成人之恶

jūn zǐ chéng rén zhī měi, bù chéng rén zhī è

Translation: "A person of great virtue helps others to be better, and does not help them to do evil."
— Confucius (孔子), Analects (论语)

Not every 'helping hand' is genuine help. Sometimes, people clap for bad decisions, cheer on poor judgement, or back someone up just because they're friends.

Confucius reminds us that kindness without wisdom isn't kindness at all. Supporting someone means amplifying what's good in them – not feeding their spiral, and certainly not cheering them on as they charge off a cliff. Being a good friend, partner, or leader doesn't mean saying "yes" to everything. It means nudging people toward their better side and stepping back when they're on a path you know leads to hurt, harm, or regret.

What it teaches us

- **Back people up, not their bad habits:** Don't lend energy to grudges, gossip, or recklessness. Back what's right, not what's merely popular or comforting in the short run.
- **Support without enabling**: Encourage others' goals and dreams, but also speak up when you sense self-sabotage or harm; you might have just saved someone from falling flat on their face.
- **Sometimes, love means walking away:** When support turns into enabling someone's impulses or spiral, walking away may be the kindest thing you can do for them.

"Love is not affectionate feeling, but a steady wish for the loved person's ultimate good as far as it can be obtained."
— **C.S. Lewis**

The Dao Whispers: Do I strengthen their better self, or reinforce the patterns holding them back? Do I have the courage to step back when 'support' only fuels the spiral?

January 23

If the Sky is Falling, Use It as a Blanket

Sometimes you've got to let things be

天塌下来当被盖

tiān tā xià lái dāng bèi gài

Translation: "If the sky falls, treat it as a blanket and use it to cover yourself."
— Traditional Chinese folk saying

This playful old proverb reminds us that even catastrophe can be reframed. Resilience, after all, isn't about pretending everything is fine or rushing into problem-solving mode. It's also in knowing when to save your energy, keep your cool, and trust that you will find a way through it all once the dust settles.

When you're in a crisis, your mindset becomes your strongest ally. You can panic, or you can make peace with the absurdity of it all and transform adversity into something oddly comforting, as if to say, "Let it fall. I'll find a way to live with it, or even, sleep under it." The thing is, everything will pass.

What it teaches us

- **Reframe the fall:** If a major plan fails, can you use the rubble to build something new?
- **Turn helplessness into humour:** Playfulness can be a weapon, disarming fear, unlocking creativity, and keeping our spirit intact.
- **Equanimity sharpens problem-solving:** Only by staying calm under pressure can we focus on solutions, rather than be overwhelmed by the scale of the problem.

> ***"Life is ten percent what happens to us and ninety percent how we react to it."***
> — **Charles R. Swindoll**

The Dao Whispers: Can I face this storm with composure and even laughter, and trust that I'll *weather* this one just as I have weathered many before?

January 24

Thirty-Six Stratagems: #36

The strategic wisdom in knowing when to retreat

走为上计

zǒu wéi shàng jì

Translation: "If all else fails, retreat"
— Thirty-Six Stratagems (三十六计, sān shí liù jì)

Once, at a family dinner, we started talking about the legendary Thirty-Six Stratagems of Chinese strategy. My mum leaned in, looking incredibly pleased with herself, and announced, ***"I know number thirty-six."*** I was instantly impressed, thinking I was about to hear some ancient, next-level war tactic. She grinned and said, ***"You run away!!!"***

We laughed, but you know what? She's right. Sometimes, running away is the smartest move you can make. When every path ahead is a mess waiting to happen, the boldest, wisest strategy isn't to push harder – it's to step back, save your energy, and live to fight (or love, or build) another day.

What it teaches us

- **Cut your losses**: As the venture capital world says, *"don't throw good money after bad."* In business, the bravest move can be to pivot or walk away from a bad deal, market, or leadership that drains talent rather than develops it.
- **Exit with dignity:** Some relationships aren't worth the fight. A quiet, graceful exit can be the highest form of self-respect.
- **Step back to reset:** Sometimes clarity only comes once you stop swinging and actually leave the battlefield.

> ***"He who fights and runs away lives to fight another day."***
> — **Menander,** Ancient Greek scriptwriter

The Dao Whispers: Is stepping back now the smartest way to win later? Some playgrounds are designed so the house always wins. In those cases, the wisest move of all may be the 36th stratagem: retreat, regroup, and live to play again. Unless, of course, you can find a way to quietly rewrite the rules.

January 25

A Clear Conscience Helps Us Sleep Well

How not to have a ghost knock at your door at night

平生不做亏心事，半夜敲门心不惊

píng shēng bù zuò kuī xīn shì, bàn yè qiāo mén xīn bù jīng

Translation: "If I do nothing that is against my conscience, I shall not fear when I hear a knock in the middle of the night."
— Traditional Chinese folk saying

In ancient China, a knock in the dead of night could mean trouble. It could mean a guard at the door, a summons to answer for your deeds, or a visit from spirits unsettled by your wrongdoing. Let's be honest, nobody sleeps well if they suspect karma, cops, or ghosts might come calling. Sometimes, it might even be...***that*** ex.

The proverb assures that, when you've done no harm, you don't need to fear the shadows. A clear conscience is the world's best security system – no guilt trips, no cold sweats, no panicked "oh no, is this about *that* thing?"

What it teaches us

- **A clear conscience is the best sleep aid:** Do no harm, tell no lies, and you won't dread that late-night knock or dreaded 'we need to talk' text.
- **Guilt is its own jail**: Anxiety and fear of getting caught weigh heavier than any judge's sentence. That alone can keep you up at night for weeks if not years.
- **Integrity is your invisible armour:** When you have a clear conscience, you don't need anyone else's approval to feel safe and to be at peace.

> ***"Integrity is doing the right thing, even when no one is watching."***
> — Often attributed to C.S. Lewis

The Dao Whispers: *The weight of reckoning haunts.* Is there anything in my life that could bring a midnight knock from ghost or gavel?

January 26

Every Word and Act is Your Signature

Be conscious of what you say and do

慎言慎行

shèn yán shèn xíng

Translation: "Be mindful in what you say and how you act."
— Traditional Chinese proverb

If words and promises were currency, some people would already be bankrupt. This proverb reminds us that everything you say and do leaves a trace, like signing your name on the world. Sometimes it is a masterpiece. Other times it is a messy crayon scribble you'd wish you could erase. The thing is, you often can't erase them.

History is full of examples of people who tanked their careers with one ill-timed joke, an unguarded tweet, a "career limiting move" (CLM) or a "reply all" email they later regretted. The same goes for careless actions that "seemed like a good idea at the time" but ended up damaging trust and goodwill built over years.

What it teaches us

- **Guard your credibility**: Everything you say or do builds your reputation, for better or worse. Before you hit send or speak up, it's good to check, "Would I be okay with this being shared or remembered later?"
- **Strengthen relationships:** What we say to our loved ones and friends either builds them up or tears them down. There's rarely a middle ground, so aim to leave them in a better place than when you found them.
- **Prevent avoidable conflict**: A moment of restraint and measured words now can spare you weeks of conflict, fallout, and strained relationships.

> ***"First learn the meaning of what you say, and then speak."***
> — **Epictetus**

The Dao Whispers: Is my next move one I'll be proud to own, or one I'll wish I could erase?

January 27

Don't Let a Leaf Block the Mountain

When the little overshadows the big picture

一叶障目，不见泰山

yī yè zhàng mù, bù jiàn tài shān

Translation: "A single leaf blocking our view obscures the sight of Mount Tai."
— Traditional Chinese proverb

Picture this: you have a massive, stunning mountain right in front of you, but one oversized autumn leaf gets stuck to your face. Suddenly, no mountain. You would not even notice if Angelina Jolie is waving at you two feet away.

That's what life's little irritations are like. A rude email, a bad commute, a forgotten anniversary text; they feel huge in the moment. But if you take a step back, they are just 'leaves.' The mountain, your bigger goals, your relationships, what actually matters, is still right there.

This proverb is used to describe someone who is short-sighted or narrow minded, focusing on trivial matters (the leaf) while missing the bigger picture or more critical issues (Mount Tai is one of China's most revered mountains).

What it teaches us

- **Do not sweat the small stuff:** A bad mood or snide remark doesn't have to wreck your entire day or week.
- **Keep perspective in relationships:** Don't let small irritations snowball into big fractures; it usually costs more than simply being 'right.'
- **Focus on the mountain:** Learn to tell the difference between what's trivial and what profoundly changes the course of your life.

> ***"The eye sees only what the mind is prepared to comprehend."***
> **— Henri Bergson**

The Dao Whispers: Am I letting today's small irritations distract me from my bigger picture and goals?

January 28

Betrayal Rarely Comes from Strangers

The same hand that pours your wine can pull the rug from under you

知人知面不知心

zhī rén zhī miàn bù zhī xīn

Translation: "You may know a person's face, but not their heart."
— Traditional Chinese Wisdom (民间俗语)

It's rarely the stranger on the street who stabs you in the back. More often, it's the smiling "friend" who knows where you keep the knives. That friend who told you that you could count on them – until the rubber met the road – and then bailed.

This proverb is a reminder that familiarity is not the same as trustworthiness. We can share laughs, dinners, even decades with someone and still be blindsided by their true intentions. Faces are easy to read, but hearts? Probably...*not* so much.

What it teaches us

- **Watch how people manage temptation:** Integrity is shown when someone could take advantage of you but chooses not to.
- **Trust, but with eyes open**: Not everyone who smiles at you has your best interests at heart. A fake friend can hurt you way more than an outright enemy. When someone shows you who they really are, believe them the first time.
- **Listen to your gut:** The little voice in your head, that subtle unease and weird feeling you can't quite explain. It's usually picking up something your brain hasn't put into words yet. Don't ignore the red flags.

> ***"Never open the door to a lesser evil, for other and greater ones invariably slink in after it."***
> — **Baltasar Gracián**

The Dao Whispers: Do I give away trust too quickly? What red flags have I ignored in the past that have cost me?

January 29

The Flying Shoe Problem

Sometimes, the room isn't ready for you

韬光养晦

tāo guāng yǎng huì

Translation: "Hide your brilliance and nurture it in the shadows."
— Traditional Chinese idiom

Talent doesn't just attract lots of cheering, it can also attract daggers or a flying shoe or two. There's an old wisdom that says, before you light up the room, make sure you're not giving insecure people a target to aim at. Across cultures, we see "Tall Poppy Syndrome" where people cut down the one who grows too high, too fast, and too visibly.

This proverb doesn't tell you to dumb down or to dim your brilliance forever. It just says that, perhaps, while waiting for the right moment to act, you can keep a low profile, avoid unnecessary attention, and build your strength in stealth mode.

What it teaches us

- **Don't make enemies unnecessarily**: In ego-sensitive or high-stakes environments, calling things out can backfire. Pick your battles wisely, especially when you're the new player and your presence may disrupt existing hierarchies.
- **Read the power dynamics, understand the game before you play it:** If standing out gets people chopped down, ask, "Is this the right time, or should I stay low and learn the rules first?"
- **Mastery matures best under the radar:** The less noise you make while building, the less pushback you'll attract.

> ***"I am so old that I can remember when other people's achievements were considered to be an inspiration, rather than a grievance."***
> — **Thomas Sowell**

The Dao Whispers: Am I exposing my strengths too soon? Am I visible in a smart way, or attracting a flying shoe?

January 30

You're Not an Exception to Kindness

Love that skips you is not complete

仁者爱人，亦自爱

rén zhě ài rén, yì zì ài

Translation: "The kind-hearted and benevolent people love others, but they also love themselves."
— Traditional Chinese Folk Saying (民间俗语 mín jiān sú yǔ)

仁 (rén) or benevolence, is often thought of as compassion for others. ***But how can you really help anyone in a meaningful way if you're sinking yourself?*** Kindness without self-compassion eventually depletes the tank you draw from.

- The generous give, but they also receive.
- They care for others, but do not abandon themselves.
- They forgive others and extend that same forgiveness to themselves.

What it teaches us

- **Kindness ≠ self-neglect:** Cultures that glorify sacrifice often make people wear exhaustion like a badge of honour. But burnout? That's not a badge of honour. You can't pour from an empty vessel.
- **Self-compassion is a non-negotiable:** It's treating yourself with the same patience, care, and dignity you give others.
- **Recognise your limits with love:** Don't just notice when you are struggling, be kind to yourself when you are.

> ***"Talk to yourself like you would to someone you love."***
> — **Brené Brown**

The Dao Whispers: Do I treat myself with the same kindness I show others? When I stumble, do I offer care or only criticism? Instead of just asking ***"What am I feeling?"***, do I also ask ***"What do I need?"***

Treat yourself with the same patience, care, and dignity you give others. You are not an exception to the kindness you give.

January 31

The Hardest War You'll Ever Fight

Winning against yourself takes more courage

胜人者有力，自胜者强

shèng rén zhě yǒu lì, zì shèng zhě qiáng

Translation: "One who conquers others is strong; one who conquers himself is powerful."
— Laozi (老子), Dao De Jing (道德经)

Sure, you can win arguments, crush competition, even outshout everyone in the room. That's strength. But can you win against yourself? Against the impulse to lash out, the fear that holds you back, the pride that trips you up, or the cheesecake calling your name? That's another league entirely.

Laozi calls this the ultimate power. Not the power to control others, but the power to control your own mind and actions. Truth is, it's easier to bench press 100kg than it is to hold your tongue when you're furious. Okay, maybe not 100kg...2kg.

What it teaches us

- **Train your inner muscle**: It's easy to fight outward battles, but it's a lot harder and far rarer to win the ones within yourself, against pride, fear, anger, and impulse. It takes immense discipline and strength to develop this muscle.
- **Discipline builds real freedom:** Freedom isn't doing whatever you want. It's having the will to choose your response consciously, beyond reflex or impulse.
- **Choose restraint when triggered:** It often takes more courage to pause or walk away than to retaliate or to throw a punch back, verbally, or literally.

> ***"I count him braver who overcomes his desires than him who conquers his enemies; for the hardest victory is over self."***
> — **Aristotle**

The Dao Whispers: What habits or inner battles am I still struggling to overcome? Do I have the discipline to stay disciplined when it counts?

FEBRUARY

道

dào

道 (dào) encompasses the following:

- Natural order
- Authentic alignment
- Effortless flow
- Moral direction
- Integrated living

道 (dào) represents the Way, a principle both cosmic and very personal. It speaks to a life in alignment with natural rhythms, clarity, and purpose. The Way invites us to move with intention, without unnecessary resistance, force, or control. Yet it is not something that can be pinned down as a concept or captured fully in words. It is something that must be lived.

Mastering 道 (dào) helps us:

- **Act with grace:** Life throws curveballs. Instead of forcing things or reacting on impulse, respond with composure, restraint, and flexibility.
- **Trust the flow:** Not every problem needs a bulldozer. Know when to step forward, when to hold back, and when you need to just let things happen on their own.
- **Integrate opposites:** Balance doing with being and recognise that light needs darkness to exist.
- **Live with integrity:** Align actions with inner values, even when you're pressured and it feels a lot easier to just cave.
- **Walk the higher path:** Let your choices be guided not just by ambition, but also by wisdom, harmony, and discernment.

February 1

Know the Game, Know the Players

Half the battle is you, the other half is everyone else

知彼知己，百战不殆

zhī bǐ zhī jǐ, bǎi zhàn bù dài

Translation: "If you know the enemy and know yourself, you can fight a hundred battles and never be defeated."
— Sun Tzu, The Art of War (孙子兵法 Sūnzi Bīngfǎ)

It is powerful to know yourself. But if you stop there, you are only playing half the game.

Sun Tzu's wisdom reminds us that winning is not about pushing harder. It is about seeing the whole chessboard, including ***who is on it, what they want, what they fear, and how they move.*** Too many battles are lost because someone assumed they were the smartest person in the room. ***Most of the time, they were not.***

What it teaches us

- **See people clearly, not how you *want* to see them:** Pride, fear or wishful thinking can distort your judgement. The better you get at reading people – your adversaries, your allies, and the shifting dynamics between them – the more you can improve your judgement over time.
- **Think beyond yourself:** If you only focus on your moves, you'll miss theirs. Knowing others keeps you three steps ahead, helps you anticipate moves, avoid being blindsided, and play the long game.
- **Build alliances with other players:** The best strategists do not just outsmart people, they build trust, forge alliances and sometimes turn rivals into friends.

> ***"To act effectively, one must understand the plurality of human motives."***
> — **Hannah Arendt**

The Dao Whispers: Do I see my own strengths and blind spots clearly? If I understood others' motives and fears, could I have avoided battles or turned them into opportunities?

February 2

Trust Your Journey

Ever noticed how 90% of what we stress about never actually happens?

船到桥头自然直

chuán dào qiáo tóu zì rán zhí

Translation: "When the boat reaches the bridge, its course will naturally straighten."
— Traditional Chinese folk saying

Life loves throwing imaginary curveballs at us. We spend hours, days, sometimes years worrying about ten different versions of problems that haven't even said hello yet. We picture the worst-case scenarios **so vividly it feels like they're already real**; and then, most of them never happen.

This old saying reminds us that not every bump on the path needs to be solved from miles away. Some problems straighten themselves out when you actually get there. The journey, motion, and timing have a way of showing us the next best steps that you simply couldn't plan in advance.

What it teaches us

- **Let go of imagined fears:** Our heads are great at creating monsters. Why borrow worries from the future?
- **Focus on what you can control:** Plan where possible, but don't confuse preparation with prediction.
- **Trust your journey:** Have faith in your resilience. Some answers only reveal themselves when you're on the move.

> ***"My life has been filled with terrible misfortune; most of which never happened."***
> — **Michel de Montaigne**

> ***"Never let the future disturb you. You will meet it, if you have to, with the same weapons of reason which today arm you against the present."***
> — **Marcus Aurelius**

The Dao Whispers: How many hours of peace have I traded for problems that might never come? What's in my control today, and what can I trust will straighten itself out as the journey unfolds?

February 3

When the Real Problem Hides

The root causes no one dares to talk about

引蛇出洞

yǐn shé chū dòng

Translation: "Lure the snake out of its hole."
— Traditional Chinese idiom

The biggest threat in an organisation isn't the problem you can see, it's the one hiding where no one dares to look. When a project is failing, a team is underperforming, or customers are leaving, the first explanation you hear is rarely the truth. People hold back because they fear blame, politics, or simply because no one has asked the right question.

This proverb speaks to using strategic patience to slowly uncover truths, threats, or root causes. In an organisation, that might mean skipping the big confrontation and instead:

- Hold discreet one-on-ones instead of public interrogations.
- Ask open, non-accusatory questions that invite candour.
- Spot patterns in behaviour and results before diagnosing, deciding, or acting.

The goal isn't to trap someone but to create a safe space for people to speak to the real barriers, and to target the solution without wasting time on the wrong problem.

What it teaches us

- **Create a safe space:** Build an environment where people can share their fears, motives, and discomforts without fear of repercussions.
- **Uncover what's unsaid:** Invite others to reveal their cards, rather than escalating tension through direct confrontation.
- **Target the root cause:** Ask targeted questions to surface and solve for deeper issues, not just visible symptoms.

"The truth is rarely pure and never simple."
— **Oscar Wilde**

The Dao Whispers: In difficult situations, do I take the time to uncover what's beneath the surface? Do I create enough trust for people to speak openly?

February 4

Know When to Stop, So You Can See Clearly

If you can't slow down, how can you possibly see where you're going?

知止而后有定，定而后能静，静而后能安，安而后能虑，虑而后能得

zhī zhǐ ér hòu yǒu dìng, dìng ér hòu néng jìng,
jìng ér hòu néng ān, ān ér hòu néng lǜ, lǜ ér hòu néng dé

Translation: "Only by knowing where to stop can you have stability; with stability, you find calm;
with calm, you find peace;
with peace, you can think clearly;
and with clear thought, you can achieve."
— Confucian Classic: The Great Learning (大学)

Life doesn't just push us forward; it shoves us before we're ready. Deadlines, demands, endless decisions; we keep running even when we're not sure if the path makes sense. Confucius tells us that, sometimes, we need to stop for a moment or slow down. Take a breath and let the dust settle. After that, you'll find balance and peace to quieten the mind and think clearly, without panic or pressure. You'll start to see what's important to you, decide where to go next, and how best to get there.

What it teaches us

- **Don't rush:** Rushing often leads to wasted effort and wrong turns - and some paths cost far more to turn back from than they would have to avoid in the first place.
- **Not every option is meant to be chased:** Sometimes knowing what *not* to pursue is more important than knowing what to do next. Not every door is meant to be opened.
- **Lead with calm:** A calm, clear and focused mind is the foundation for sound judgement.

> ***"All of humanity's problems stem from man's inability to sit quietly in a room alone."***
> — **Blaise Pascal**

The Dao Whispers: Have I stopped long enough to see clearly and weigh my options, or am I just rushing blindly forward?

February 5

The Art of Well-Placed Distraction

Create distraction in the East, but strike in the West

声东击西

shēng dōng jī xī

Translation: "Make a sound in the East, then attack in the West."
— The Thirty-Six Stratagems (三十六计)

Life isn't a chessboard where every piece moves honestly. In strategy, sometimes the win does not come from going head-on with resistance, but from **getting people to look the other way**.

This ancient stratagem suggests that we make some noise in one direction, while directing your energy to what counts and staying under the radar. In war, that could mean a surprise flank. In daily life, it could be changing a tricky conversation topic, parking an idea until the moment's right, or distracting your boss with good news before you slide in the bad.

Misdirection isn't always about lies. Used with integrity, it opens minds gently, lowers defences, and creates space for real change. Blunt honesty hurled at a wall usually bounces back, while a discreet message slipped through the side door might just get a foot in.

What it teaches us

- **Begin with common ground**: In communication and persuasion, this can mean starting with shared values before introducing sensitive or disruptive ideas.
- **Don't show all your cards:** Not every move needs to be announced before you make it.
- **Redirect when faced with resistance:** If pushing gets you nowhere, try taking your audience on an alternative route.

> ***"In wartime, truth is so precious that she should always be attended by a bodyguard of lies."***
> **— Winston Churchill**

The Dao Whispers: Sometimes, this tactic is used *against* you. If a message is too loud, too polished, too constant, ask***, What is being hidden? What is not being said? Why now?***

February 6

Pick Your Battles

Sometimes, strategy means saving your energy for a better battlefield

知可以战与不可以战者胜

zhī kě yǐ zhàn yǔ bù kě yǐ zhàn zhě shèng

Translation: "Victory belongs to those who know when to fight and when not to fight."
— Sun Tzu (孙子), The Art of War (孙子兵法)

Sun Tzu teaches that mastery in strategy lies not just in knowing how to fight, but in knowing **when.** It's easy to charge forward on impulse. But a strategic mind knows when to pause to assess the terrain, your own capabilities, the opponent's strengths, and the wider context. The strongest don't fight every battle; they win by choosing the ones worth fighting.

Equally important is the ability to not fight, and to recognise that some battles are unwinnable, untimely, or simply not worth the cost. Sometimes, the best move is to conserve your strength, walk away, and live to fight another day – and on better terms.

What it teaches us

- **Strategic timing**: Acting impulsively often leads to unnecessary losses. Timing can be a source of leverage.
- **Avoiding unnecessary conflict**: Knowing when to walk away protects your energy, focus, and peace.
- **Discipline over ego:** Not every provocation deserves a response.

> ***"You have to pick your battles. Don't pick every fight. Not every hill is worth dying on."***
>
> — **John C. Maxwell**

The Dao Whispers: Can I accept that not every challenge needs my response, and be intentional about where I invest my energy? Looking back, which battles should I have walked away from, and what can I learn to prevent repeating the same mistake?

February 7

Success Can Make You Forget Who You Are

The Monk who wandered from the mountain and lost his path

出山的和尚忘了路

chū shān de hé shàng wàng le lù

Translation: "The monk who left the mountain forgot his way back."
— Traditional Chinese proverb

The Story

This proverb tells of a monk who leaves his mountain temple, coming from a place of discipline, humility, and clarity, and goes off to explore the world. He gains success, wealth, and prestige. But along the way, he forgets the path home, not only the physical road but also the spiritual one. His sense of self, once rooted in simplicity, is now clouded by worldly distractions.

This story serves as a reminder that the higher we climb, the easier it is to forget where we started. We chase goals, build careers, and keep moving forward… but somewhere along the way, do we forget why we started? Or who we were before success took over?

Even monks, it seems, can lose their way once they trade mountain air for emails, deadlines, and the busyness of modern life.

> ***"You have wandered all over and finally realised you never found what you were after: to live rationally."***
> — **Marcus Aurelius**

The Dao Whispers: Have I gone so far that I've lost touch with why I started? Am I only chasing goals, or also paying attention to the kind of person I'm becoming? As I grow, do I stay grounded, or am I becoming what I once hoped to rise above?

February 8

Leaders Look in the Mirror First

Accountability starts with "What's mine to own here?"

君子求诸己，小人求诸人

jūn zǐ qiú zhū jǐ, xiǎo rén qiú zhū rén

Translation: "A person with good character first looks within to reflect on whether they're at fault; whereas the petty (small-minded, self-interested) is quick to blame others."
— Confucius (孔子), Analects (论语)

Confucius said there are two kinds of people in a crisis: the junzi (君子), principled and self-aware, and the xiaoren (小人), small-minded, insecure, and quick to shift blame.

The *junzi* asks, "What could I have done better?"
The *xiaoren* asks, "Who else can I blame?"

What it teaches us

- **Accountability is self-leadership:** The real test of character is how we correct ourselves, not how we criticise others. Accountability is holding ourselves to a standard even when no one's watching.
- **Leadership is not just a title, but a test:** The first test of leadership isn't in directing others, but in correcting ourselves. A team mirrors what it sees. If its leaders dodge blame, so will everyone else.
- **Protect the culture, or it will change you:** If you're the leader, you have the chance to shape and protect a healthy culture. If you're not, and the culture rewards perception over substance, it's not just broken, it's a slippery slope. ***If you stay, are you sure it won't quietly change you too?***

> ***"A man may fall many times, but he won't be a failure until he says someone pushed him."***
> **— William J. Brown**

The Dao Whispers: Am I consistent in owning my part, even when it's uncomfortable? Do my role models hold themselves to the same standard?

February 9

The Gift of Showing Up

Why time with our parents is the most irreplaceable currency

父母在，不远游

fù mǔ zài, bù yuǎn yóu

Translation: "When parents are alive, do not travel far."
— Confucius (孔子), Analects (论语)

Honouring our roots is a source of strength. Often, our family becomes a source of peace we may not realise until much later.

Confucius reminds us that staying near our parents in distance, spirit, or intention, can strengthen and lift the spirits of both our elders and ourselves. In ancient times, staying close to one's parents was tied to survival. Today, it can still offer emotional grounding. While modern life celebrates ambition and independence, The Analects gently remind us that amidst all our striving, staying rooted can offer meaning, perspective, and strength.

Even across time zones or continents, presence can still be felt: a message, a shared memory, a moment of listening.

What it teaches us

- **Presence** is an act of love.
- **Care** is a form of gratitude.
- **Time spent** with our parents is irreplaceable and finite.

> ***"You never know the value of a moment until it becomes a memory."***
> — **Dr. Seuss**

The Dao Whispers: How do I stay true to where I came from while still growing into who I'm meant to be? What small ways can I show love to the people who raised me before it's too late?

February 10

The Classiest Exits Don't Need a Mic Drop

The mark of real class is to walk away gracefully without badmouthing anyone

君子绝交，不出恶声

jūn zǐ jué jiāo, bù chū è shēng

Translation: "When a gentleman severs a friendship, he does not speak ill of the other."
— Confucius (孔子), Analects (论语)

Some people exit with grace. Others turn it into a three-act drama, complete with a mic drop and a group chat blow-up. The real test is what you say after you've closed the door behind you.

Confucius teaches us that a *junzi* (君子) – a person of moral strength – parts ways with respect and dignity. He doesn't slander or seek revenge.

Why does this matter? Because the way you exit says as much about your character as the way you showed up. Your integrity should not be conditional on how others behave.

What it teaches us

- **Character shows in how you leave:** Ending things without drama or trash talk says a lot about your character.
- **Emotional maturity matters:** Letting go of anger instead of lashing out shows real strength, maturity, and self-control.
- **Respect for others:** Choosing not to speak badly of someone honours both their dignity, as well as your own.

"Speak ill of no man."
— Benjamin Franklin

The Dao Whispers: The way we leave is as important as the way we love. Talking badly about someone usually says more about us than it does about them. Can I leave with grace, even if things didn't end well?

February 11

Fortune Favours the Bold

You don't get the tiger cub by tiptoeing outside the den. You've got to enter it

不入虎穴，焉得虎子

bù rù hǔ xué, yān dé hǔ zǐ

Translation: "If you do not enter the tiger's den, how can you capture the tiger cub?"
— Traditional Chinese proverb

This proverb says it plainly – if you want something valuable, you have to take a risk. No one ever caught a tiger cub by standing safely at the edge of the forest hoping it wanders out. But it is not a call to reckless leaps. Courage works best when paired with a plan sharp enough to keep you alive while you go for what matters. That said, I'm not sure I'd volunteer for the tiger's den…the proverb doesn't come with a rescue plan.

What it teaches us

- **Boldness matters:** Meaningful goals rarely come without fear or discomfort. We may have to step into challenging situations in spite of our fear, adversity, or uncertainty.
- **Know the risk and stack the odds:** Walking into the tiger's den without foresight or skill is how you become lunch.
- **Courage looks the same everywhere:** It can be quitting a dead-end job, having that awkward conversation, or betting on yourself...it all starts with telling yourself fear doesn't get the final say.

> ***"If you're not worried, you haven't thought enough about the risks. If you're too worried, you've thought too much."***
> — **Ray Dalio**

The Dao Whispers

- What tiger's den am I circling instead of entering?
- If I stepped in with courage and preparation, what prize might finally be within reach?

February 12

You Can Be Polite but Unyielding

Even the softest cotton can hide a sharp needle

绵里藏针

mián lǐ cáng zhēn

Translation: "A needle hidden in cotton."
— Traditional Chinese idiom

The idiom paints a picture of someone who's soft on the outside, but hard as steel on the inside. Think of it as the human equivalent of a fluffy pillow with a sewing needle tucked inside. It's the art of staying polite, gracious, and calm, all while holding a line that cannot be crossed. You disarm people with warmth, but there's no mistaking that sharp core if they push too far.

We probably know someone who's mastered this art in diplomacy, leadership, or daily life, while never compromising on what matters. Being soft-spoken doesn't mean being a pushover. You've simply figured out how to wrap your strength in civility.

What it teaches us

- **Negotiate with velvet and steel:** Be gracious, but don't give away what matters, especially to those who win by pushing others over.
- **Kind, but not a doormat:** Aggressive people push harder when they sense softness. Push back when needed, even if it feels uncomfortable or out of character. Protecting yourself is your moral duty.
- **Lead with poise under bias:** Women often face double standards, where assertiveness is admired in men but criticised as "hierarchical" or "aggressive" in women. This strategy empowers women to lead with poise while defending what matters.

> ***"One must govern men with a hand of iron covered with a glove of velvet."***
> **— Napoleon Bonaparte**

The Dao Whispers: Where in my life do I need to be velvet outside, steel inside? Do I mistake kindness for weakness in others, and have others mistaken mine?

February 13

What Makes a Real Teacher

Old lessons have a funny way of turning up in new clothes, and only the wise can connect those dots

温故而知新，可以为师矣

wēn gù ér zhī xīn, kě yǐ wéi shī yǐ

Translation: "Revisiting old knowledge while grasping new insights empowers one to become an exceptional teacher."
— Confucius (孔子), The Analects (论语)

Think about the best teacher you've ever had. They didn't just hand you information. They helped you *see*. They could pull lessons from the past, link them to what's happening today, and make sense of things in a way that felt alive and real.

That's what Confucius meant here. A good teacher doesn't just store knowledge or interpret information "as-is." They revisit it, rethink it, and use it to light the path for others in the present moment.

***f*(Wisdom Worth Following) = Knowledge of History + Present Clarity + Applied Wisdom**

What it teaches us

- **Revisit old lessons:** When we revisit old lessons with fresh eyes, hidden layers of meaning reveal themselves; often ones we were too inexperienced to grasp before.
- **Understand lingering legacies:** The past often casts long shadows. Its systems, traumas, and power structures often outlive those who created them. To read the present clearly – and anticipate the future – we must trace its roots.
- **You bring new eyes every time:** The past doesn't change, we do. Each time we revisit familiar ground, we bring new perspective. Those who reflect deeply become not just learners, but teachers.

"The past is never dead. It's not even past."
— **William Faulkner**

The Dao Whispers: Do I see today's patterns through the lens of history? Which old lessons deserve a wiser re-read?

February 14

Love Takes a Lifetime of Nurturing

Love isn't found. It's nurtured, one day, one choice at a time

百年修得同船渡，千年修得共枕眠

bǎi nián xiū dé tóng chuán dù, qiān nián xiū dé gòng zhěn mián

Translation: "It takes a hundred years of nurture to share the same boat; and a thousand to share the same pillow."
— Traditional Chinese proverb

This proverb suggests that meaningful relationships, especially love or deep companionship, are not accidents. They are the fruit of spiritual effort, karmic grace, and emotional labour across lifetimes. Sharing a boat symbolises a fleeting encounter, while sharing a pillow, lasting intimacy. Both are rare, sacred, and worthy of reverence.

Lifelong love is a shared practice across:

- **Self-growth:** Choosing to become a better version of yourself each day.
- **Mutual support:** Encouraging each other's growth, goals, and wholeness.
- **Conscious forgiving:** Accepting imperfection with grace and choosing compassion, even when it's hard.
- **Gratitude:** Recognising the daily quiet miracle of being truly seen and still chosen.

> ***"When you meet someone who makes your heart feel at home, it is as if the universe conspired to bring you together."***
> — **John O'Donohue** (Anam Cara)

The Dao Whispers: Do I treat my relationship as a path of shared cultivation? Am I nurturing love with presence, patience, and kindness?

Love survives not by fate, but by the grace you extend to each other... one ordinary day after another ordinary day.

February 15

Only Exceptional People Break Limits

Extraordinary missions demand extraordinary people

盖有非常之功，必待非常之人

gài yǒu fēi cháng zhī gōng, bì dài fēi cháng zhī rén

Translation: "To achieve extraordinary accomplishments, you must rely on extraordinary people."
— Emperor Wu of Han (汉武帝)

Emperor Wu's words highlight the belief that exceptional results require individuals – those with rare talent, vision, and moral courage. To build exceptionalism in any field, we must seek, recognise, and empower those whose capabilities rise above the ordinary – exercising discernment to spot the truly extraordinary.

What it teaches us

- **Game-changing missions need game-changing people:** To pull off a ***mission impossible,*** you need **extraordinary hires**, those with not only technical skill but also resilience, judgement, and grit – those who maintain grace under fire and find a way forward even when the odds look impossible.
- **A team of rockstars beats a solo superstar every time:** Leverage ***each person's unique genius*** so the whole crew outperforms what any one person could do alone.
- **You're the average of the five people you surround yourself with:** Exceptional mentors and peers don't just teach you, they ***pull you up*** to their level.

> ***"The best executive is the one who has sense enough to pick good men to do what he wants done, and self-restraint enough to keep from meddling with them while they do it."***
> — **Theodore Roosevelt**

The Dao Whispers: Am I surrounding myself with people who raise the bar, and do I dare to hire the best, including those better than me, to get the job done?

February 16

The Talent Snowball Effect

You don't just hire a person, you hire their network

为官择人，不可造次。用一君子，
则君子皆至；用一小人，则小人竞进。

wéi guān zé rén, bù kě zào cì. yòng yī jūn zǐ,

zé jūn zǐ jiē zhì; yòng yī xiǎo rén, zé xiǎo rén jìng jìn

Translation: "Do not be rash when you appoint people to office. Employ one good person, and good people will join in; employ a weak character, and the rest with similar character will rush in."
— Emperor Taizong of Tang (唐太宗)

Emperor Taizong reminds us that **talent replicates itself**. Whom you empower shapes the culture. Empower someone, and their influence ripples. The principled attract the principled; the mediocre attract more mediocrity. Over time, any system rises – or collapses – by the character it elevates.

What it teaches us

- **A-players hire A-players. B-players hire C-players:** Hire the best and the principled, and they'll attract their kind. But keep mediocrity, and excellence quietly quits. ***Eventually, you won't need to build a circus, it builds itself.***
- **Smart people build smart systems:** Great people use the right tools, make sound decisions, and build intelligent systems. The results are simply the compounded effect of consistent good judgement.
- **One hire sets the tone for another:** Character is contagious. Bring in someone with integrity and competence, and birds of a feather will follow; hire poorly, and mediocrity multiplies.

> ***"If you do not include your best people in government, you will be led by the mediocre."***
> — **Lee Kuan Yew**

The Dao Whispers: Have I been intentional in choosing the people I trust, hire, or follow?

February 17

The Ruthlessness to Rule

Is self-preservation necessarily bad? What good comes when selflessness becomes your downfall?

人不为己，天诛地灭

rén bù wèi jǐ, tiān zhū dì miè

Translation: "If a person doesn't act for themselves, heaven and earth will come to an end."
— Ancient Chinese proverb

This saying makes a blunt but fair point: **people naturally look out for themselves first**. Ignoring this fundamental piece of human nature often ends with avoidable loss. Far from promoting selfishness, the saying calls for strategic awareness. To protect one's values, one must first survive.

Machiavelli echoed this in ***The Prince***, warning that the man who is good all the time will be destroyed by those who are not. Both Eastern and Western strategic thinkers recognise this: ***harmlessness isn't the same as being good.*** A man must be capable of being ruthless and consciously choose not to, if his goodness is to mean anything at all.

What it teaches us

- **Be kind, but don't be a pushover:** Be kind, but never at the cost of your dignity, safety, or by letting others take advantage of you. Unprotected kindness is easy prey.
- **Being good means having strength, and keeping it under control:** You've got to be ***able*** to fight back, but ***choose*** not to.
- **Seek respect, not just "niceness":** In a world of wolves, being respected is essential while being liked is a bonus. Leaders who are merely liked can be overrun when tough decisions upset people.

> ***"A harmless man is not a good man. A good man is a very dangerous man who has that under voluntary control."***
> **— Jordan Peterson**

The Dao Whispers: Kindness means having the power to hurt someone and choosing not to.

February 18

The Fog of Truths

Some things are better felt than spoken

道可道，非常道；名可名，非常名

dào kě dào, fēi cháng dào; míng kě míng, fēi cháng míng

Translation: "The Way that can be spoken is not the enduring Way; the name that can be named is not the lasting name."
— Laozi, Dao De Jing (道德经)
Note: A famously cryptic, multi-layered line; this rendering preserves the intent

This proverb is famous yet cryptic, from the opening lines of Laozi's Dao De Jing. It says the deepest truths about life and the universe can't really be boxed into words or neat labels. The moment you try to pin them down...they slip through your fingers.

Some things transcend human expression and definition.

It's a reminder to stay humble, curious, and open to mystery. Not everything can be "figured out," and maybe that's not the point.

What it teaches us

- **Hold on to truths lightly**: Let fresh data, seasons, and growth refine your conclusions.
- **Be careful of false certainty:** What's most neatly labelled are not always what they seem; they could be artificial constructs.
- **Welcome mystery:** Not every question needs a quick answer. Grey areas give us space for questions while black-and-white thinking tends to limit them.

> ***"What can be said at all can be said clearly; and what we cannot talk about we must pass over in silence."***
>
> — **Ludwig Wittgenstein,** *Tractatus Logico-Philosophicus* (closing line, emphasising the limits of language)

The Dao Whispers: Can I stop rushing to "figure it out" and simply sit with today's uncertainty, even if I cannot yet define it or name it?

February 19

How to Get Mauled in Three Easy Steps

Asking for what threatens someone's survival

与虎谋皮

yǔ hǔ móu pí

Translation: "To ask a tiger for its skin."
— Traditional Chinese idiom

The Story

Long ago, a man longed for the finest coat in the land. Nothing else would do. It had to be tiger skin.

So, in a moment of either bravery or sheer foolishness, he marched into the mountains and found a great tiger basking in the sun. Bowing politely, he said, "Great Tiger, your fur is magnificent. Would you be so kind as to donate your skin to me? I promise to put it to good use."

The tiger stared at him, blinked once… and then pounced. His fatal mistake was simple: he asked for something that would kill the giver to give.

What it teaches us

- **Don't ask for the impossible:** You can't expect others to surrender what is core to their survival, identity, or power, like asking the tiger to hand over its own skin. It's just not going to happen.
- **Think before you push:** Is what you're asking for even realistic? If it goes against someone's basic nature or survival, you're probably wasting your time or worse, you'd be making an enemy out of a friend.
- **Pick your battle wisely:** Provoking a "tiger," a powerful or dangerous adversary, usually backfires. Sometimes, it's better to walk away and find a path where no tiger stands in your way.

> ***"Pick battles big enough to matter, small enough to win."***
> **— Jonathan Kozol**

The Dao Whispers: How often do I waste energy trying to change the unchangeable?

February 20

Think Thrice Before Acting

Slowing down is sometimes the fastest way forward

三思而后行

sān sī ér hòu xíng

Translation: "Think three times, then act."
— Confucius (孔子), Analects (论语)

There's an old story about Ji Wenzi (季文子), a minister in the state of Lu who was famous for never rushing decisions. He was said to "think three times" before acting, not because he was slow, but because he knew mistakes made in haste cost more time and pain later.

This proverb is a reminder that quick action isn't always smart action. Slowing down to think things through often gets you further, faster, and with fewer regrets.

What it teaches us

- **Thinking things through pays in the long run**: Quick decisions can feel efficient in the moment, but taking the time to really weigh your options means fewer regrets down the line.
- **You'll have fewer fires to put out:** Taking a moment to think before you respond can save you from misunderstandings, conflict, or having to backtrack later.
- **Slow down to speed up:** Tight timelines often lead to poorly framed problems, weak hypotheses, and wasted effort on solutions that miss the mark. Investing time to define the problem, to structure your thinking, and to challenge your initial set of solutions to uncover the most robust answer can prevent wasted effort.

"Haste makes waste."
— Benjamin Franklin

The Dao Whispers: Before my next big move, could I take a moment to breathe, think twice, maybe even thrice? How many mistakes could I have avoided if I had simply taken a step back?

February 21

Look Before You Leap, But Don't Wait Forever

Thinking twice is good enough

季文子三思而后行。
子闻之，曰：“再，斯可矣。”

jì wén zǐ sān sī ér hòu xíng. zǐ wén zhī, yuē: zài, sī kě yǐ

Translation: "Ji Wenzi always thought three times before acting. Hearing this, Confucius said, 'Twice is enough.'"
— Confucius (孔子), Analects (论语)

When Confucius heard about how Ji Wenzi had to 'think thrice before acting' (三思而后行, sān sī ér hòu xíng), he replied, **"Twice, is enough."** According to Confucius, prudence is smart. But too much of it becomes hesitation. There's a fine line between being careful and being stuck in an endless spin cycle of *"Should I? Shouldn't I?"* At some point, **meaningful impact requires timely action, not endless calculation**.

What it teaches us

- **Balanced decision-making:** A pause to think is good. A full-on analysis marathon is not, you might end up with analysis paralysis and stall completely.
- **Confidence to act**: Thinking twice builds enough certainty to act with conviction.
- **Don't let perfect ruin good:** Sometimes you just need to jump, preferably after looking where you're landing.

> *"The perfect is the enemy of good."*
> — **Voltaire**

The Dao Whispers: Where in my life am I triple-checking what only needs two checks? What would change if I trusted my judgement and acted a little sooner?

February 22

Smoke, Mirrors and Mastery

In warfare, you need to be unreadable

兵者，诡道也

bīng zhě, guǐ dào yě

Translation: "Warfare involves deploying 'The Art of Deception.' Strategy requires misdirection."
— Sun Tzu (孙子), The Art of War (孙子兵法)

In the Art of War, Sun Tzu was not at all being subtle when he said that **all warfare is based on deception**. It made a lot of sense, though it had more than just a pinch of cunning to it. I mean... if you tell your opponent exactly what you're about to do, when and how, of course you shouldn't then be surprised if they're waiting with popcorn and a counterattack ready.

The proverb alludes to how strategy can use some finesse – acting weaker than you are, concealing your true intent, and making your moves while everyone is looking elsewhere.

What it teaches us

- **Being too readable is a disadvantage:** Wherever strategy is at play, those who always act in straight lines are easily read and countered quickly. They are almost telling the counterparties what moves they need to make for a swift kill.
- **Strategic ambiguity is a form of defence:** Sometimes, appearing weak when strong, or uncertain when prepared, isn't deception, it's just playing your hand wisely.
- **Read the players and watch for the illusions:** Who's using smoke and mirrors on you, and are you able to see beyond what they want you to see?

"All warfare is based on deception."
— **Sun Tzu**

The Dao Whispers: Am I as intentional in what I withhold as in what I share? Where could I bring more subtlety without losing integrity?

February 23

Big Fish in a Small Pond, or…?

Better be the beak of a chicken than the rear of a cow

宁为鸡口，无宁为牛后

níng wéi jī kǒu, wú nìng wéi niú hòu

Translation: "Better to be the beak of a chicken than the rear of a cow."
— Traditional Chinese proverb

Is it better to run the show in something small, or just be the tail end of someone else's big parade? This old proverb leans toward the first. The chicken may be modest, but its beak leads the way; while the ox may be mighty, its tail just follows.

Sometimes, being the "chicken's beak" gives you more say, more impact, and more dignity than being a silent cog in a massive machine. You might have fewer resources, but you're not stuck waiting for permission to act.

Still, it's not always so simple. The best choice depends on your goals, your stage of life, and how much freedom or support you need right now.

When this could be a good strategy

- **Autonomy and influence:** Being a "chicken's beak" means you get to call the shots. You're shaping direction, culture, and deliverables, not just following them. If you've built up experience, have a clear vision, and know how to get things done, that kind of independence can be incredibly rewarding.
- On the flip side, being the "cow's rear" can feel stifling, especially when you're stuck in a system that doesn't value your voice or give you room to lead.

- **Self-respect and dignity:** Even small leadership roles can bring meaning and pride. But in a big, impersonal system, especially one that feels cold or transactional, you can end up feeling like just another cog in the machine, overlooked and worn down.

- **Growth and visibility:** In smaller settings, you're more likely to have opportunities to step up, take initiative, and actually be noticed. You won't be buried in layers of hierarchy or stuck in office politics, which matters even more in cultures where merit isn't always rewarded.

- **Flexibility and adaptability:** Smaller teams can move fast. You can pivot, experiment, and make things happen. Big organisations love their red tape and ten approval layers. Blink and you would have lost three weeks.

When it might not be a good strategy

- **Limited resources:** Smaller entities may lack funding, reach, or influence, making it harder to innovate, scale, or access key infrastructure.
- **More pressure on you:** Being the "chicken's beak" means you're in charge. That also means you carry the stress such as hitting targets, solving problems, and dealing with crises. The "cow's rear" may be slower, but it's usually lower stress.
- **Less structured learning:** Big organisations often have formal training, mentors, and clear systems. That's useful if you're still early in your career and want to build a solid foundation.
- **Scale of impact:** If your goal is system-level influence, small-scale leadership may not get you there. That said, technology increasingly enables small players to scale rapidly and break traditional limitations.

The Dao Whispers

- Do you want autonomy and the chance to lead, or stability and the power of something bigger?
- Choose the "chicken's beak" if you value autonomy, dignity, and the chance to lead, even if it means less prestige or fewer resources.
- Choose the "cow's tail" if you want structure, stability, or the ability to leverage something larger.
- There's no universal right answer. It depends on what matters to you right now, and where you want to grow next.

February 24

There Comes a Time When a Lion Must Roar

Don't wait to be discovered, make yourself heard

狮子不开口，谁知它会吼

shī zi bù kāi kǒu, shuí zhī tā huì hǒu

Translation: "If the lion doesn't open its mouth, who knows it can roar?"
— Traditional Chinese proverb

We're taught not to be boastful, to avoid arrogance, to stay modest. All true. But there's a danger: stay quiet too long, and people assume you're small, weak, or irrelevant. A lion that never roars risks being mistaken for a house cat. Humility has its place, but leadership also demands presence. Playing small may keep you safe but it won't change the world. Occasionally, playing small can also mean that you'd be gobbled up by the lion next to you.

The proverb reminds us: even the lion must roar, not out of vanity, but to make its presence and strength known.

What it teaches us

- **Silence can be complicity:** If you never step up, don't be surprised if others step over you.
- **Visibility matters:** You can't lead from the shadows forever. Step up, speak to your work, and take credit when it's due, especially if others overlook it. That's how the world works. Like it or not, if no one sees your work, it's as if it never happened, and worse, someone else will claim it.
- **You must have your own back:** People follow voices they can hear. Authority needs to be exercised, not hidden. The roar signals that strength, courage, and vision are present. It signals that you've got your own back, because if you don't, who will?

"Find your voice. Use your voice. Own your voice."
— The Dao Whispers

The Dao Whispers: Leadership doesn't *ask* you to 'assert yourself' – ***it demands it***. Don't be afraid to be seen – ***stand up, speak up, and be a leader.***

February 25

Concise Communication: The Gravity of Brevity

The fewer the words, the stronger the message

长话短说，短话精说

cháng huà duǎn shuō, duǎn huà jīng shuō

Translation: "Shorten lengthy speeches and refine short speeches to convey the core message."
— Traditional Chinese proverb

There's a scene in *Interstellar* where the team approaches the black hole Gargantua. The closer they get, the heavier time bends under gravity. Every second counts. Imagine trying to explain Einstein's gravitational time dilation in that moment with a ten-minute lecture… you'd lose your audience, or worse, lose the mission. Your colleague still orbiting the planet would have been seventy years older by the time you finished. A single sharp sentence would've saved everyone time.

This proverb says just that. Clear thinking doesn't need endless words. Eloquence is not verbosity. It is the skill of stripping away fluff, sharpening the point, and landing it where it matters. Many confuse long-winded talk with intelligence.

What it teaches us

- **The best minds explain complexity simply:** If you can't make it plain, you don't fully get it. The brightest minds make the complex accessible. The confused often do this: ***"If you can't convince them, confuse them."***
- **Respect others' time:** Every extra word costs time. Being precise honours both the speaker and the listener.
- **Land the message:** Keep it short, sharp, and sticky. Make your point in a way that they'll remember after you've left the room.

> ***"I didn't have time to write you a short letter, so I wrote you a long one instead."***
> — **Mark Twain**

The Dao Whispers: Where am I using ten words where five would do? Am I adding weight to my message, or am I diluting my core message with a list of other points that just don't matter?

February 26

The Right Partner Changes Everything

Love doesn't stop life's storms, but it makes the umbrella bigger

家有贤妻，夫不遭殃

jiā yǒu xián qī, fū bù zāo yāng

Translation: "A man with a wise wife avoids suffering."
— Traditional Chinese proverb

This proverb reminds us that a wise and supportive partner isn't just a "nice-to-have," they can be a lifeline when life gets messy.

A strong relationship isn't one that is perfect. It's two people having each other's backs, even on the bad days. It's not a fairy tale of roses and butterflies, it's consciously choosing each other through 2 a.m. arguments, unwashed dishes, and life's curveballs… and somehow still laughing together after. When you find someone like that, life doesn't suddenly get easier and the tough bits disappear, they just feel a little less heavy and a lot less scary when you're not facing them alone.

What it teaches us

- **A solid partner may not fix your life but can change the game:** They can help you see more clearly, act more wisely and stay calm in times when you'd otherwise spiral.
- **Good ones save you from yourself:** A good partner might save you from bad decisions, not by nagging, but by saying, "Uh… maybe don't do that," when you need to hear it.
- **The keepers:** Anyone who's got your back, has patience, a clear head, and a sense of humour is a real win already.

> ***"By all means, marry. If you get a good wife, you'll become happy; if you get a bad one, you'll become a philosopher."***
> — **Socrates**

The Dao Whispers: What kind of partnership brings out the best in me, makes me wiser, calmer, and maybe even funnier? Am I choosing love with a clear head… or just because I'm tired of bad first dates or don't want to keep eating bad takeaway dinners solo?

February 27

Chicken and Duck Talk

Know when to speak and when to walk away

鸡同鸭讲

jī tóng yā jiǎng

Translation: "A chicken talking to a duck."
— Traditional Chinese idiom

This proverb illustrates the frustration of miscommunication, where two people speak, but nothing lands. They almost look like a chicken and duck clucking and quacking without mutual comprehension.

It's often used for moments when people have different mindsets, goals, or frames of reference, making it less a dialogue and more two different radio stations broadcasting on full volume.

What it teaches us

- **Talk *with* people, not *at* people:** Most conversations are just two monologues crashing into each other. Slow down, make sure they're following, and you'll actually get your point across. Sometimes, having a shared context is what lets you bring people with you on the journey.
- **Barriers to understanding:** Differing perspectives, experiences and knowledge bases can prevent meaningful dialogue. Clarifying assumptions and framing our message with empathy often helps bridge the gap.
- **Know when to walk away:** Not every conversation is worth salvaging. Sometimes, being wise means knowing when someone simply isn't ready or willing to understand.

> ***"The single biggest problem in communication is the illusion that it has taken place."***
> — **George Bernard Shaw**

The Dao Whispers: When our worlds differ – in culture, experience, and belief – do I make the effort to see through another's eyes, or do I insist on my own?

February 28

If the Leader Panics, Everyone Sinks

A leader who remains composed builds teams that are unshakable

将不愠，则军不溃

jiāng bù yùn, zé jūn bù kuì

Translation: "If the general holds steady, the army will be unbreakable."
— Traditional Chinese military philosophy

When things get tough, a leader's mood sets the tone for the whole team. Stress, panic or anger at the top spreads quickly and morale sinks with it. Composure does not mean pretending everything is fine. It means holding steady even when things feel chaotic and the rug is yanked from under everyone's feet, including yours. Your message to the team is clear: ***We've got this.***

A leader who shows up daily, stays steady and inspires strength will have teams that also stand firm.

What it teaches us

- **Emotional resilience matters:** Your composure when things go wrong sends a very powerful message to your teams without you saying it, *"We are going to make it."*
- **Don't offload downward:** Offloading your stress onto the team doesn't "share the burden," it multiplies it. A leader's job is to stabilise, not destabilise. And yes, we know it can be a lonely place to be.
- **Stand taller in storms:** It is exactly in times of crisis that a leader needs to be even more solidly grounded to help the team rise together.

> ***"Your job as a leader is to inspire and to galvanise, not to share your distraught thoughts. You make your people dispirited."***
> **— Lee Kuan Yew**

The Dao Whispers: When the storm hits, am I the anchor or the wave that knocks everyone off balance?

February 29

Power with a Steady Hand

Ruling a great nation is like frying small fish,
gentle handling, but with an iron pan

治大国若烹小鲜，但需铁腕手段

zhì dà guó ruò pēng xiǎo xiān, dàn xū tiě wàn shǒu duàn

Translation: "Ruling a large country is like frying a small fish, you need an iron frying pan."
— First half of proverb by Laozi (老子), Dao De Jing (道德经)
Note: The first half of the proverb is by Laozi, the second half was an adaptation in modern political discourse to represent a pragmatic interpretation. Added here to give additional flavour to the ancient proverb.

This metaphor explains that leading a vast, complex system requires delicacy, not brute force. Like frying a small fish, too much interference breaks it apart. Wise leaders act with restraint, trusting order to emerge without heavy-handed meddling. But when disorder threatens the whole, ***the pan must be iron.***

But Laozi wasn't naïve. Finesse alone doesn't always keep things standing. At times, stability, justice, or even survival demand a firm, decisive hand.

> ***"And let there be no mistake about this...whoever governs Singapore, must have that iron in him, or give it up. This is not a game of cards – this is about your life and mine. I spent a lifetime building this – and as long as I am in charge, nobody is going to knock it down."***
> — **Lee Kuan Yew**

> ***"Speak softly and carry a big stick; you will go far."***
> — **Theodore Roosevelt**
> (a reminder that diplomacy works best when backed by real authority)

The Dao Whispers: Leadership is contextual. There is no one-size-fits-all style. The art lies in knowing when to let the fish simmer – and when the iron pan must hold it together.

MARCH

忍

rěn

Meaning of 忍 (rěn):

- Patience
- Endurance
- Emotional discipline
- Strategic restraint
- Tolerance, inner strength

忍 (rěn) is generally used daily to mean patience, and tolerance.

忍 (rěn) does not mean that we should simply passively submit to the external pressures or injustice, but rather, an active mastery of the self. It's the ability to deliberately choose patience over impulse, wisdom over knee-jerk reaction, and clarity over chaos.

Mastering 忍 **(rěn)** allows us to:

- **Endure:** Handle struggles or delays without losing focus or determination.
- **Restrain:** Keep anger, ego, or retaliation in check when it serves no purpose.
- **Observe:** Give yourself space to fully assess the situation before choosing your next move.
- **Protect:** Save your time and energy for what moves you forward and avoid conflicts that derail you.
- **Act when it counts:** Wait for the right time, then act decisively and with control.

March 1

Timing Can Change Fates

When the timing is right, the universe will roll out the red carpet

时来天地皆同力，运去英雄不自由

shí lái tiān dì jiē tóng lì, yùn qù yīng xióng bù zì yóu

Translation: "When the time is right, even the heavens and earth will lend you their strength; but when fortune fades, even heroes aren't free to do as they wish."
— Traditional Chinese folk wisdom

Some days, life feels like magic. The right people show up, opportunities fall into your lap, and everything clicks. Other times, you sweat buckets, knock on doors, and the universe pretends it's not home.

This old saying reminds us that effort matters, yes, but so does timing. You can't force fate to say "yes" before it's ready. Some external conditions are simply beyond our control, yet they can affect outcomes significantly. Sometimes it's as mundane as market shifts, policy changes, or pure dumb luck.

What it teaches us

- **Timing is leverage:** Do something at the wrong moment and you're pushing a boulder uphill. When the time is right, you can put in the same effort and get ten times the results.
- **Control is an illusion:** When things go sideways, don't beat yourself up. Even heroes trip when luck takes a coffee break.
- **Be kind to those who are waiting for their season:** There's a pinch of luck in every win. Don't puff your chest out too much when you win, and don't mock those who miss.

> ***"For there is no creature whose inward being is so strong that it is not greatly determined by what lies outside it."***
> — **George Eliot**

The Dao Whispers: Have you noticed how some days the world just opens doors, and on others, nothing moves no matter what you do? Before doubling down, take a step back and ask: ***"Is this the right time?"***

March 2

You Can Disagree Without Burning Bridges

You can assert yourself respectfully, then walk away without leaving wreckage behind

君子之争，行礼而退

jūn zǐ zhī zhēng, xíng lǐ ér tuì

Translation: "When a cultivated person disputes, he remains courteous and then withdraws."
— Xunzi (荀子)

If you must clash, do it with class. Nothing says ***"I've got this"*** like a well-timed, classy exit.

This old saying is a reminder that you can stand your ground without raising your voice, and sometimes the smartest move isn't to "win" the argument at all. You can disagree while staying composed, keep your dignity, and step away before things get messy.

What it teaches us

- **Be civil – fight fair or don't fight at all:** Disagreements are inevitable, but they don't have to turn hostile. Speak firmly but never forget your manners.
- **Doesn't hurt to have some self-control:** Sometimes, walking away takes more courage than staying in the fight.
- **Take the high road:** Grace beats pride. Not every battle needs a winner, and fewer still need casualties. Some battles are best fought with a classy exit.

> ***"Never wrestle with pigs. You both get dirty and the pig likes it."***
> **— George Bernard Shaw**

The Dao Whispers: How can I best put my point across respectfully, and leave the bridge standing?

March 3

Interim Solutions Have Their Purpose

Ride the donkey while looking out for the stallion

骑驴找马

qí lǘ zhǎo mǎ

Translation: "Ride a donkey while looking for a stallion."
— Traditional Chinese proverb

Not every ride is glamorous. Sometimes, you're on a donkey and not a racehorse, but the donkey gets you moving. This proverb is a reminder to use what you've got now, even if it's far from perfect, while keeping your eyes open for a better ride ahead.

Standing still gets you nowhere, but jumping straight on the first shiny stallion you see isn't smart either. The donkey is your temporary ride, not your destiny.

What it teaches us

- **Work with what you have**: Be practical. This isn't forever, it's just "for the time being."
- **Play the hand you have, stack the deck for the next round:** Win now and set up your next win.
- **Don't be complacent**: Don't get too cosy on the donkey – it's a seat, not a throne.

> ***"Do what you can, with what you have, where you are."***
>
> **— Theodore Roosevelt**

The Dao Whispers

- What "donkey" keeps me moving now, and what clear trigger tells me it's time to dismount?
- While I ride, how am I upgrading my saddle – skills, proof points, and network – to attract the stallion?
- What guardrail stops me from settling: a review date, hard metrics, or a hard stop

March 4

Turn the Impossible into the Inevitable

With persistent grinding, even an iron bar can be turned into a needle

只要功夫深，铁杵磨成针

zhǐ yào gōng fū shēn, tiě chǔ mó chéng zhēn

Translation: "Grinding an iron pestle into a needle."
— Traditional Chinese proverb

The Story

When Li Bai was a young boy, he was talented but lazy and disliked studying. One day, while playing outside, he saw an elderly woman kneeling by a stream, who seemed to be scraping a thick iron rod (铁杵) on a rock; a rather odd sight indeed.

Curious, Li Bai asked, "What are you doing?"

The old woman replied, "I'm grinding this iron rod into a needle."

Shocked, Li Bai laughed and said, "That's impossible! Such a thick rod can never become a needle!"

The woman smiled and answered, ***"As long as I work hard and don't give up, even an iron rod can be ground into a fine needle."***

Hearing this, Li Bai was deeply inspired. He realised that greatness and success aren't achieved through talent alone. It takes patience, persistence, and effort over time. From then on, he studied diligently, eventually becoming one of China's greatest poets.

> ***"Nothing in this world can take the place of persistence. Talent will not; nothing is more common than unsuccessful men with talent."***
> **— Calvin Coolidge**

The Dao Whispers: Do I expect to see results quickly and give up when progress feels slow?

March 5

Sometimes You Must Retreat to Advance

Like a slingshot, you pull back to launch farther

以退为进

yǐ tuì wéi jìn

Translation: "In order to advance, first retreat."
— Traditional Chinese wisdom, commonly associated with philosophical thought and influenced by Sun Tzu and Daoist strategy

The proverb reminds us that sometimes, the fastest way forward is not in bulldozing our way through something, but in pulling back gracefully and deliberately, with the long game in mind.

Occasionally, the best move is a well-timed sidestep, a little pause, or even a tactical "*nope*, not today."

Stepping back doesn't mean you've lost, it means you're saving energy, sizing things up, and planning a comeback that actually works.

What it teaches us

- **Step back to see the full picture:** Stepping back gives you space to reassess and recalibrate.
- **Not every fight is worth it:** A timely retreat can cool tempers, de-escalate tensions, protect relationships, and conserve energy.
- **Give ground to gain ground:** Sometimes losing a battle wins you the war and saves you a few grey hairs in the process.

> ***"Patience is not passive; on the contrary, it is concentrated strength."***
> — **Bruce Lee**

The Dao Whispers: Not all progress is forward, sometimes, not moving is the move, other times, taking a step backward is the right move. Where in your life would a small pause or even a temporary retreat, set you up for a bigger win later?

March 6

The True Measure of Character

Do not unto others what you do not wish for yourself

己所不欲，勿施于人

jǐ suǒ bù yù, wù shī yú rén

Translation: "That which you do not wish for yourself, do not impose on others."
— Confucius (孔子), Analects (论语)

Confucius didn't invent the golden rule, but he gave it teeth. He didn't mean you have to be polite or "nice," but that you stay fair when you hold the upper hand. The test is also not about how kind you are to friends or equals. It shows up:

- **in how we speak** to people who can't push back.
- **in how we lead** when no one's watching.
- **in how we treat others** when we're the ones with the power, or when we're sure we're right.

It's easy to justify our behaviour when we're in control. It's even easier to brush off criticism or act cold toward someone quieter or less confident. But that's often where our true character shows.

Before you act, ask yourself one question: ***Would this still feel fair if the roles were reversed?***

The Dao Whispers

- Power reveals character. How do you act when you're the one with the power to decide?
- The golden rule is not about being nice, it's about being fair. Do you apply it only when it suits you, or every time?
- If the roles were reversed, would your behaviour still feel fair and right?

DIGNITY - 尊严 (zūn yán)

March 7

I'll Respect Myself, Even If You Don't

When the line is crossed, redraw it

人不敬我，我必自敬；
人辱我，我必报之

rén bù jìng wǒ, wǒ bì zì jìng; rén rǔ wǒ, wǒ bì bào zhī

Translation: "If others do not respect me, I will respect myself. If they insult me, I will respond accordingly."
— Modern Chinese martial saying, echoing the spirit of Sun Tzu's strategy

This saying is a reminder that **self-respect isn't up for debate**. If someone won't give you basic respect, you keep yours intact. If they cross the line, you don't roll over – you respond. Not with rage or drama, but with a clear stance that says *"enough."*

What it teaches us

- **Set boundaries with class:** Staying graceful doesn't mean letting people walk all over you. You don't need to raise your voice to be strong. But you must be clear: disrespect has no place. To respect others does not mean tolerating humiliation. There is a line between grace and self-erasure. When someone crosses a line deliberately, you must respond.
- **Your worth isn't up for debate:** Self-respect is non-negotiable. Even if others ignore it, you don't get to.
- **Fight fire with water, not gasoline:** "Respond accordingly" is a call to ***proportionality***. A wise response need not mirror the insult.

> ***"Never be bullied into silence. Never allow yourself to be made a victim. Accept no one's definition of your life, define yourself."***
> — **Harvey Fierstein**

The Dao Whispers

- Am I respecting myself, even when others don't?
- Have I tolerated something that violates my values?
- Is it time to set a boundary or to enforce one?

March 8

Leading in a World That Expects You to Fail

The hidden rules women in power must break

女人不狠，地位不稳

nǚ rén bù hěn, dì wèi bù wěn

Translation: "A woman who isn't ruthless won't secure her position."
— Empress Wu Zetian (武则天)
Empress Wu Zetian remains a controversial figure. Revered for her leadership, condemned for her ruthlessness. Some argue that history judged her more harshly for being a woman in power than for her actions.

In imperial China, survival at the top was brutal – especially for a woman. Empress Wu Zetian knew it, lived it, and ruled anyway.

I may venture to say that, in this proverb, "ruthless" (狠) is not about cruelty. It points instead to ***determination, assertiveness, or strategic boldness*** – qualities needed to counter challenges like ***discrimination, competition, or instability,*** particularly in environments where women are not expected to lead. The proverb reflects a cultural reality and a commentary on gender dynamics, advocating agency rather than aggression.

History shows us that perceptions of power are slow to evolve. People still instinctively equate height with strength, attractiveness with competence and trustworthiness, confidence with authority. These are all primal biases, powerful yet often detached from reality. And gender bias carries the same stubborn weight. Despite progress, women's authority remains judged more harshly, their confidence misread, their ambition seen as unsettling, their firm voices condemned.

What it teaches us

- **Double standards:** Assertive women are often labelled 'difficult' or 'intimidating,' while men are praised as 'strong' or 'decisive.' The first step is to call it out.
- **Primal instincts:** These biases aren't just cultural, they're primal. Like peacocks or wolves, many still respond to power and gender through instinct, not intellect. Primal instincts

may explain bias, but they don't excuse us from overcoming it. So, the real test of humanity is whether we rise above it.

- **Strategic agency:** Setting boundaries, negotiating firmly, or speaking up, especially with support, enables women to counter bias, gain respect, and unlock their potential.
- **Impostor syndrome:** Many women, even in positions of power, wrestle with the inner voice that says, "I don't belong here." Recognising this for what it is – a reflection of systemic bias, not personal inadequacy – is crucial. Agency starts by silencing that false voice and standing fully in earned authority.

> ***"When a man gives his opinion, he's a man.***
> ***When a woman gives hers, she's aggressive."***
> — **Bette Davis**

Naming this as bias, not truth, is key to standing in authority. The answer isn't to play by unfair rules but to reframe "ruthless" as clarity, build allies, and use resolve as strategy, not cruelty.

The Dao Whispers: Have I judged someone for the very traits I admire in a man?

March 9

Don't Roll in the Mud Just Because They're Dirty

When people throw dirt, you don't have to join in

以德报怨

yǐ dé bào yuàn

Translation: "Repay hatred with kindness."
— Confucius (孔子), Analects (论语)

Confucius wasn't telling us to be doormats or to just take it. He was saying, ***"Revenge rarely makes life cleaner. It drags you into the mud."*** When hostility comes your way, you don't have to match it. Sometimes the best response is no response, self-restraint, or simply walking away. It's the kind of choice that keeps your hands and your conscience clean.

What it teaches us

- **Choose kindness:** When the harm is small, unintentional, or born from ignorance – like a rude stranger, a friend's bad day, or an oversight by an elderly person – choose kindness over bitterness. And don't let it live rent-free in your head.
- **Flip the script with empathy:** In misunderstandings, forgiveness or an honest conversation can better restore mutual respect and heal rifts.
- **Refuse to play dirty:** If a colleague undermines you, don't go down to their level. Respond with professionalism, not petty retaliation. You reset the game when you refuse to play dirty.

> ***"Darkness cannot drive out darkness; only light can do it. Hate cannot drive out hate; only love can do that."***
> — **Martin Luther King Jr.**

The Dao Whispers

- Next time someone annoys you, ask: "Will matching their energy improve anything or drag me down to their level?"
- Can I set boundaries without hostility?

Mud doesn't stick if you don't roll in it.

March 10

You Can't Force Growth

Pulling the sprouts does not help them grow faster, it kills them

拔苗助长

bá miáo zhù zhǎng

Translation: "Pulling up the sprouts to help them grow."
— Traditional Chinese idiom

The Story

Long ago, in the state of Song, a farmer grew anxious that his rice seedlings were not growing fast enough.

One afternoon, unable to bear it any longer, he went into the field and gently tugged each sprout upward, convinced it would help them grow taller.

Exhausted but proud, he returned home that evening and said, ***"Today I helped the sprouts grow."***

Curious, his son ran to the field and found every seedling wilted and dying.

The man's well-meant help had destroyed what only time and nature could nurture. In his rush to see progress, he killed it.

The Dao Whispers

Some things can't be rushed. Pulling forward what isn't ready often breaks the roots you cannot see, and you may end up with a dead plant and dirty hands.

March 11

The Art of Playing to People's Strengths

A wise leader places people where they thrive

用人如器，各取所长

yòng rén rú qì, gè qǔ suǒ cháng

Translation: "Deploy the gifts of people as you would tools, by leveraging their strengths."
— Emperor Taizong of Tang (唐太宗)

Ever seen the office spreadsheet handed to the one person allergic to Excel? That's how teams fall apart.

This principle is exactly that. It implies that no one is inherently useless, only misapplied. Like tools in a kit, each person has unique strengths. A wise leader doesn't force everyone into the same mould but matches the task to the talent, using strengths as leverage rather than setting people up for failure.

What it teaches us

- **Sharpen strengths, don't obsess over weaknesses:** When we invest in strengths in ourselves or others, we accelerate mastery and achieve outcomes that far exceed the average.
- **Design teams smartly:** Assign roles where people can shine, not where you hope they'll survive.
- **Get more done with less:** When you put strengths in the right places, everything works faster and better, especially when resources are lean.

> ***"Focus on strengths, not weaknesses. A person's greatest room for growth is in their areas of strength."***
> ***— Donald O. Clifton***

The Dao Whispers

- What strengths do I have, and where will they make the biggest difference?
- Do I focus on what people do best, or where they fall short?
- How different would things be if I built my day, team, or life around strengths?

March 12

Control What You Can, Then Let Go

You can steer the ship, but sometimes, the weather still calls the shots

人算不如天算

rén suàn bù rú tiān suàn

Translation: "Man's plans cannot match Heaven's plans."
— Traditional Chinese proverb

We've all been there – the perfect plan, the flawless spreadsheet, the "this can't go wrong" moment – and then life shows up with its own ideas.

This old saying isn't telling us to give up planning; it's just reminding us that **no matter how hard we try to script things, there's a bigger script running that we don't control.** It speaks to the unpredictable workings of ***tian*** (天, Heaven), which means fate, nature, or some larger order. Whether we believe in it or not… well, that's a discussion for another day.

What it teaches us

- **The trap of endless planning:** Overthinking every move doesn't guarantee success. Sometimes you need to stop refining the plan and just get moving
- **We are not in charge of everything:** Life rarely follows our blueprint, but that doesn't mean you give up. Focus on what's in your hands and stop sweating the stuff that isn't. Some doors won't open no matter how hard you push.
- **Embrace adaptability in uncertainty:** When plans fail, life may be redirecting us to something better. Many good things come from unexpected twists, like meeting the love of your life because you missed a flight. (that hasn't happened to me yet, but still...)

> ***"Let me not pray to be sheltered from dangers, but to be fearless in facing them."***
> **— Rabindranath Tagore**

The Dao Whispers: Life has its own script and rarely checks with our plans first. Am I willing to let go and move with it?

March 13

The Conundrum of Strength

Why strength demands both kindness and ruthlessness

量小非君子，无毒不丈夫

liàng xiǎo fēi jūn zǐ, wú dú bù zhàng fū

Translation: "A petty man is no gentleman; a man without ruthlessness is no true man."
— Attributed to Wu Zetian, China's only female emperor

History is rarely gentle to those who rise against the odds. Wu Zetian, the Tang dynasty concubine who became China's only female emperor, understood this better than anyone. She knew that to rule, you needed the heart of a sage but the steel of a warrior.

This proverb captures a paradox most leaders wrestle with: tolerance makes you a gentleman, but without the capacity for ruthlessness, you may never hold power long enough to practise that gentleness. Put differently: compassion without strength is weakness, and strength without compassion is tyranny. The art lies in holding both – power and mercy.

What it teaches us

- **Balanced leadership**: A good leader doesn't sweat small stuff or meaningless slights. But when the situation calls for tough decisions, they do not hesitate.
- **Real-world pragmatism:** A CEO who never fires, a general who never disciplines, or a parent who never sets boundaries will soon lose control. Mercy has its place, but so does steel.
- **Personal takeaway:** Being underestimated as "too soft" can be a mask of power, but only if you have the backbone to act when it matters.

"You should be a monster. An absolute monster. And then you should learn how to control it."
— **Jordan Peterson**

The Dao Whispers: Strength without mercy is tyranny. Mercy without strength is fragility. Where do you stand?

March 14

When Life Gets Rough, Watch Who Stays

Hard times show you who's worth keeping

疾风知劲草，板荡识诚臣

jí fēng zhī jìng cǎo, bǎn dàng shí chéng chén

Translation: "Strong winds reveal tough grass, turbulent times reveal loyal ministers."
— Cited by Emperor Taizong of Tang

Everyone appears supportive when skies are clear and sunny. But when the storm comes, that's when you see who stands beside you.

Adversity is a filter. It separates fair-weather friends from those who are loyal. Some disappear at the first sign of difficulty, while others stay by your side, even when there's nothing left to gain.

Hard times don't just test people, they show you who's really in your corner.

What it teaches us

- **The gift of hardship:** Do not fear difficult seasons. They reveal the sincere and the self-serving among those around you.
- **Pay attention to presence:** Notice who stays when things fall apart, those are the ones worth keeping close. Turbulent times reveal a person's true character and intentions.
- **Let go wisely:** When someone walks away in your lowest hour, don't chase them. Their absence is its own answer, and often, a gift.

"Et tu, Brute?" ("You too, Brutus?")
— **William Shakespeare**
(A lament from Julius Caesar as he is being assassinated by a group of Roman senators. He expressed his shock seeing his close friend Marcus Junius Brutus, among his assassins.)

The Dao Whispers

- Who stayed with me when things were hard?
- Who came around only when they had something to gain?

March 15

Be So Good They Can't Ignore You

Do not seek to be known, but to be worth knowing

苟全性命于乱世，不求闻达于诸侯

gǒu quán xìng mìng yú luàn shì, bù qiú wén dá yú zhū hóu

Translation: "I sought only to preserve my life in chaotic times, not gain recognition among the lords."
— Zhuge Liang (诸葛亮)

Zhuge Liang's words reflect the humility of a brilliant mind during a turbulent era. A famed strategist and statesman, he had the talent to command armies and shape nations, yet he did not seek power or fame. Instead, he chose to step back, refine his thinking, and act only when the time was right.

Today, visibility is currency. Everyone's curating their "personal brand," posting hot takes, and angling for attention. But visibility only opens doors, it's substance that keeps them open.

The real question is not ***"How do I get noticed?"*** but ***"When the right time comes, will what I've built be worth noticing? And am I worth knowing?"***

What it teaches us

- **Balancing ambition with discipline:** Chase the right opportunities, not every opportunity. Be intentional about where you build and where you show up.
- **Be ready, not restless:** Preparation beats scrambling for attention. Big wins go to those who've done the work, not those jostling for the spotlight.
- **Anchor yourself in mastery:** Build so much depth into your craft that it speaks for you – especially when you're not there to explain it.

> ***"Pursue what is meaningful, not what is expedient."***
> **— Jordan Peterson**

The Dao Whispers: Am I building something so valuable it speaks for me when I'm not in the room?

March 16

Patch the Boat Before It Sinks

It's too late to rein in the horse at the cliff's edge

临崖收缰晚，船到江心补漏迟

lín yá shōu jiāng wǎn, chuán dào jiāng xīn bǔ lòu chí

Translation: "It's too late to rein in the horse at the cliff's edge; patching the boat midstream comes too late."
— Traditional Chinese proverb

Patience is usually a virtue. But there's patience, and then there's waiting so long that you're practically waving at the cliff edge thinking, "Maybe the brakes will fix themselves." Foresight is not useful without timely action. It's not just about seeing what's coming, but actually moving before the cost of delay compounds.

This proverb speaks exactly to that. When we delay decisions or ignore early warnings, we may find ourselves reacting when it's already too late. It uses the vivid metaphors of "reining in at the cliff's edge," or "trying to patch a boat in the middle of the river, when the water's already rushing in," to remind us that early action often saves more than late correction.

What it teaches us

- **Don't be paralysed by fear:** Don't delay decisions because you're afraid. Stay focused, find out where the problem is and define the problem clearly.
- **Fix problems early:** Red flags are easier to manage when they first appear. They are less visible, cheaper, and simpler to deal with at the start.
- **Delay has a price:** Don't pay more than the fair price for your delay. Don't suffer more than you need to.

> ***"An army of sheep led by a lion would defeat an army of lions led by a sheep – but only if the lion trains the sheep beforehand."***
> — **Alexander the Great** (attributed)

The Dao Whispers: What am I ignoring now that will cost me tenfold if I delay?

March 17

The Fish Doesn't Know It's Wet

It's hard to see the mountain when you're standing in it

不识庐山真面目，只缘身在此山中

bù shí lú shān zhēn miàn mù, zhǐ yuán shēn zài cǐ shān zhōng

Translation: "We fail to see the true face of Mount Lu, simply because we are in the mountain."
— Su Shi (苏轼), Song Dynasty

This verse from Su Shi speaks to perspective and how easily we lose it. The fish doesn't know it's wet because water is all it's ever known. Similarly, when we're immersed in our own story, emotions and assumptions can blind us to the bigger picture.

What it teaches us

- **Distance brings clarity:** When you step back emotionally, mentally, or physically, put on a pair of fresh eyes, you'll often see what was hidden before.
- **Being too close to the mess clouds your judgement:** When you're too close to a situation, it's hard to think straight. Emotions can blur your judgement and make small problems look bigger or hide obvious truths.
- **Change your lens:** When stuck, try to see things from a different angle. Even a slight shift in vantage point can unlock new answers or direction.

> ***"You cannot solve a problem from the same level of consciousness that created it."***
> **— Albert Einstein**

The Dao Whispers: Sometimes the best decision comes after a walk, a night's sleep, or a shift in vantage point. What am I too close to, to see clearly right now?

March 18

Rumours Have No Off Switch

It's harder to guard against sharp tongues than a raging river

防人之口，甚于防川

fáng rén zhī kǒu, shèn yú fáng chuān

Translation: "Guarding against people's mouths is harder than guarding a river."
— From the Discourses of States – Zhou Discourses (国语·周语)

You can build a dam to stop a river, but you can't build one big enough to stop a loose tongue. One sentence, said with malice, can travel further than a flood and leave a mess that's harder to clean up.

This ancient proverb teaches that the spoken word, in the form of slander, gossip, or false flattery, can be more insidious than visible threats. It started as a warning to rulers who feared words more than armies. But it also applies to our daily lives. One careless line can destroy reputations, break relationships, or leave a mark that's hard to wash off.

What it teaches us

- **Don't wrestle every rumour:** Don't waste energy trying to silence every critic. Actions over time can speak louder than you can.
- **Build your reputation, let rumours starve of oxygen:** If you spend all day correcting lies, you'll never have time to live your life. The best response to gossip? Live your life well.
- **Remember where gossip comes from:** Most rumours are born from envy, projection, or sheer boredom. Don't give it more weight than it deserves.

> ***"Reputation is what men and women think of us; character is what God and angels know of us."***
> — **Thomas Paine**

The Dao Whispers: Do I verify what I share, or do I become a link in someone else's rumour chain? When I hear something second-hand, do I ask: ***"Who benefits from this?"***

March 19

Not Everyone in Your Circle is in Your Corner

Keep the small-minded at arm's length

远小人，近君子

yuǎn xiǎo rén, jìn jūn zǐ

Translation: "Keep petty people away; and noble ones near."
— Traditional Chinese saying

This proverb reminds us to be discerning about who we allow into our lives. In ancient Chinese thought, the 君子 (jūn zǐ) represents a person with virtue, depth, and integrity. The 小人 (xiǎo rén) is small-minded, petty, and self-serving. They are often driven by envy or hidden agendas, tend to nurse grudges, spread gossip, and seek revenge. Knowing the difference matters because not everyone around you wishes you well.

The small-minded drain your energy, test your boundaries, rarely show their true face, and smile while they scheme. Whereas the principled can disagree with you without being unkind. They make you feel safe, even when they see things differently.

"Be careful who you share your bad news with, but be even more careful who you share your good news with."
— **Jordan Peterson**

Not everyone clapping is happy for you. Some celebrate your success on the surface, while quietly hoping for you to stumble.

"Unsafe people blame others instead of taking responsibility... Unsafe people only apologise instead of changing their behaviour... But you'll also find yourself guilt-ridden, compliant, and unable to make mistakes without tremendous anxiety."
— **Henry Cloud** (Safe People)

The Dao Whispers: Pay attention to how you feel after spending time with someone: uplifted, drained, or like they're an energy vampire? Do they celebrate your growth or feel threatened by it?

This week's exercise: Take five minutes to Google *"traits of safe and unsafe people by Henry Cloud & John Townsend."* Compare what you read with the people in your own circle.

March 20

People Never Let Things Go

Better to offend a kind soul than a mean-spirited one

宁可得罪君子，不可得罪小人

nìng kě dé zuì jūn zǐ, bù kě dé zuì xiǎo rén

Translation: "It is better to offend a gentleman than to offend a petty person."
— Traditional Chinese proverb

The proverb speaks to the quality of a person's response when they feel slighted.

- **The 小人 (xiǎo rén)** is small-minded, petty, self-serving, and often driven by envy or hidden agendas, tends to nurse grudges, spread gossip, and seek revenge.
- **The 君子 (jūn zǐ)** is noble in character, with integrity and depth, is more likely to respond with grace, understanding, or quiet disengagement.

This is not an invitation to provoke, but a reminder to be discerning. Petty minds often weaponise offense, while the noble are more inclined to absorb and move on.

What it teaches us

- **Not all offence is equal:** The kind-hearted may forgive or forget, but the small-minded can hold on to grudges for life.
- **Don't overshare your journey:** Don't overshare or explain your path to those who might not truly wish you well, even if they seem close.
- **Choose your proximity wisely**: Stay clear of those who turn small bumps into big vendettas.

> ***"Never wrestle with a pig. You both get dirty, and the pig likes it."***
> **— George Bernard Shaw**

The Dao Whispers: Who around me can handle honest disagreement? Where do I need to step lighter or step away?

March 21

Say It Before the Moment Slips

I fear our next meeting can only be in a dream

只恐相逢是梦中

zhǐ kǒng xiāng féng shì mèng zhōng

Translation: "I fear our next meeting may only be in a dream."
— Tang Dynasty, Bai Juyi (白居易, in 长恨歌)

This haunting line captures the fragility of love and time – the aching fear that a cherished encounter may never come again or may have existed only in dreams. It speaks to the *heartbreak of missed chances, unspoken words, and lives lived too cautiously.*

Too often, we wait for better timing, the right words, or a sign. But life is not patient. What if the moment passes and all we are left with is silence and memory?

What it teaches us

- **Say it while you can:** Sometimes the hardest part isn't feeling love, it's saying it. Fear, pride, and poor timing hold us back. It takes courage to say it before it's too late.
- **Cherish what's real**: In our race for success, don't overlook those sitting quietly beside us, offering the most precious things... *their presence and love.*
- **Choose depth**: Seek genuine relationships and connections that matter. Life is too short for bad wine, meaningless connections, or cold company.

> ***"Think yourself as dead. You have lived your life. Now take what's left and live it properly."***
> — **Marcus Aurelius**

The Dao Whispers

- Who do you love, but haven't told?
- Are you present with those who matter to me, or those that are conveniently nearby?
- If today were your last meeting with them, would it be enough?

March 22

The Battle is Often Won Before It's Fought

Winners secure triumph before they move;
losers fight first, then scramble to win

胜兵先胜而后求战，败兵先战而后求胜

shèng bīng xiān shèng ér hòu qiú zhàn, bài bīng xiān zhàn ér hòu qiú shèng

Translation: "The winning warriors win first and then go to war; the losing troops go to war first and then seek to win."
— Sun Tzu (孙子), The Art of War (孙子兵法)

According to Sun Tzu, outcomes are often shaped long before the battles begin.

The ***'winning troops'*** (胜兵, shèng bīng) prepare relentlessly by studying terrain, stacking the odds, securing alliances, and creating conditions that favour success. They don't go into a battle unless they know that the odds are in their favour.

By contrast, **the *'defeated troops'*** (败兵, bài bīng) tend to rush in hoping to figure it out as they go. They skip the groundwork, reacting as they go along and very often end up paying a hefty price.

What it teaches us

- **Win before you play the hand:** Preparation stacks the odds in your favour – whether it's a presentation, job interview, market entry, negotiation, or major life decision.
- **Plan, but be ready to adapt:** Plan your moves, secure what you can, and be ready to adapt to what you can't control. But move decisively.
- **Don't confuse motion with strategy:** Activity ≠ progress. Are my motions generating lots of movement but little impact?

> ***"Give me six hours to chop down a tree, and I will spend the first four sharpening the axe."***
> **— Abraham Lincoln**

The Dao Whispers: Before I act, am I truly setting myself up for success or just moving to avoid waiting? Am I shaping the game, or playing by someone else's rules?

March 23

Play the Hand You're Dealt

Change your game plan to fit what's happening, not the other way round

因敌制胜

yīn dí zhì shèng

Translation: "Understand and adapt to the enemy to win."
— Sun Tzu (孙子), The Art of War (孙子兵法)

As military strategist Helmuth von Moltke once said, "No battle plan survives first contact with the battlefield." Life does not always deal you the cards you wanted, and people rarely follow your script. This proverb from Sun Tzu reminds us that winning is not about clinging to a fixed plan. It is about reading what is happening in front of you and shifting your play.

In a tense meeting, a messy negotiation, or when life throws curveballs, survival and success often hinge on adaptability, not stubbornness.

What it teaches us

- **Learn to read the room:** In meetings, relationships, or negotiations, pay attention to what is really going on, not just what you hoped would happen.
- **Workplace challenges:** With difficult colleagues, first understand their mindset, motives, and style, then adjust your approach accordingly.
- **Study competitors' strategy:** Understand how rival companies operate, then adjust your game plan to outmanoeuvre and capture market share.

> ***"There is a strange but never-failing relation between the honest madman and skilful knaves; and whenever one meets with collected numbers of the former, one may be very sure that they are secretly directed by the latter."***
>
> — **Earl of Chesterfield** (Letters to His Son)

The Dao Whispers: Am I playing their game, or lost in my own?

March 24

The Strongest Strategy? Unpredictability

Strike where they are not looking

故善攻者，敌不知其所守；善守者，敌不知其所攻；虚则实之，实则虚之

gù shàn gōng zhě, dí bù zhī qí suǒ shǒu; shàn shǒu zhě, dí bù zhī qí suǒ gōng; xū zé shí zhī, shí zé xū zhī

Translation: "The master of attack makes the enemy unsure of where to defend; the master of defence makes the enemy unsure of where to strike. When strong, appear weak; when prepared, appear unprepared."
— Sun Tzu (孙子), The Art of War (孙子兵法)

This proverb speaks to the power of unpredictability in outmanoeuvring opponents. It also alludes to the art of misdirection – not deception for malice, but the wisdom of not broadcasting your hand.

When you show too much strength, you may be marked as a threat or even as an enemy. But when you are underestimated, you have room to move. Strategy isn't just about your plans, but how others perceive them.

What it teaches us

- **Information is leverage**: Don't overshare your intentions. Power needs privacy.
- **Make opacity your strategy**: If they don't know what to expect, they can't predict your next move.
- **Control the narrative**: What people believe about you shapes what they do next.

> ***"Have a real reserve with almost everybody; and have a seeming reserve with almost nobody; for it is very disagreeable to seem reserved, and dangerous not to be so...many are ridiculously mysterious and reserved upon trifles; and many imprudently communicative of all they know."***
> — **Earl of Chesterfield** (Letters to His Son)

The Dao Whispers: Let them see only what you want them to see, not the math behind the move.

March 25

The Wisdom of Crowds

Three ordinary cobblers can sometimes outmatch the brilliant strategist Zhuge Liang

三个臭皮匠，顶个诸葛亮

sān gè chòu pí jiàng, dǐng gè zhū gě liàng

Translation: "Three ordinary cobblers can beat Zhuge Liang."
— Traditional Chinese proverb

Zhuge Liang, often considered the 'Einstein of ancient China,' symbolises peak intelligence and strategic brilliance. This proverb may sound humourous, but its meaning is profound: the **collective wisdom can rival – or even exceed – the individual genius.**

This saying doesn't reduce Zhuge Liang's brilliance; instead, it underscores that even the greatest minds don't always operate alone or have all the answers. When individuals share knowledge, challenge blind spots, and pool perspectives, they may produce extraordinary results, even from the most unlikely collaborators.

What it teaches us

- **Not everyone is Zhuge Liang, Einstein, or Musk, and that's fine:** Genius is rare, and most breakthroughs don't come from lone geniuses. They happen when ordinary people share ideas, challenge each other, and build on what works.
- **Further together:** Team-based ideation often outperforms individual brilliance, especially in strategy, innovation, and systems design.
- **Crowdsourcing intelligence:** In fields like AI, climate science, or policy, no one person knows it all. Collective minds can fill in the gaps.

> ***"The wise man learns more from fools than fools learn from the wise."***
> — **Cato the Elder**

The Dao Whispers: Do I have both the intelligence and humility to know that teamwork can help us achieve more?

March 26

The Face Behind the Poker Face

Beneath the smile hides a knife

笑里藏刀

xiào lǐ cáng dāo

Translation: "A knife hidden behind a smile."
— From the Old Book of Tang (旧唐书·李义府传) – Biography of Li Yifu

Li Yifu, the Tang Dynasty official this phrase was written about, was known for his outward gentleness and inner cruelty. He often smiled while plotting others' downfall.

This ancient saying warns us that charm can be a mask, and flattery may hide malicious intent. We should be careful to not confuse politeness for sincerity, or charisma for character. A smile can conceal a blade.

Malice wrapped in silk is still a blade, and not all smiles are kind.

What it teaches us

- **Guard your trust**: Be careful of excessive charm from new acquaintances. Watch their actions, not just their words.
- **Office politics**: Don't be disarmed by flattery. Ask yourself: *Why now? What's at stake?*
- **Negotiating**: A handshake and smile may hide sharp terms. Read both contracts and intentions with equal care.

> ***"Men are so simple and so subject to present necessities that he who seeks to deceive will always find someone who will allow himself to be deceived."***
>
> **— Niccolò Machiavelli**

The Dao Whispers

- Am I quick to assume that kindness is always genuine?
- Are there masks that I am ignoring just because they are smiling?
- When was the last time someone's words didn't match their actions?

March 27

What Your Posture Says About You

Master your presence, your body sets the stage before you even speak

立如松，坐如钟，行如风

lì rú sōng, zuò rú zhōng, xíng rú fēng

Translation: "Stand like the pine tree, sit like a bell, move like the wind."
— Traditional Chinese military and Confucian body training disciplines

In ancient China, students were taught not only to think but also to carry themselves with dignity. This proverb captures the ideal posture and conduct – poise, groundedness, and agility – reflecting Confucian values.

- ***Stand tall like the pine tree*** – rooted, dignified.
- ***Sit like a bell*** – still, grounded, composed (and present).
- ***Move like the wind*** – swift, graceful, intentional.

Thousands of years later, psychologist **Jordan Peterson** echoed this idea through the humble **lobster,** one of Earth's oldest creatures. Lobsters establish dominance through posture. A lobster that's standing tall produces more serotonin, gains status, and improves its chance of survival. But if it slouches, its brain registers defeat.

What it teaches us

- **55% of our communication is body language:** According to research, posture speaks louder than words. The remaining 38% is the tone of voice, and 7% lies in the words we speak.
- **Presence reflects mastery:** How we carry ourselves shows confidence. But it's the mastery beneath that confidence that drives and commands presence.
- **Composure is strategic:** Stand firm under pressure, stay centred amid criticism, adapt in fast-changing moments.

> ***"A leader is a dealer in hope. His presence alone must steady the men."***
> — **Napoleon Bonaparte**

The Dao Whispers: Does my posture speak to strength, composure, and agility, or does it signal defeat or weakness?

March 28

Reframing Scarcity

It's not how much there is but how it's shared that shapes a society

不患寡而患不均

bù huàn guǎ ér huàn bù jūn

Translation: "Do not worry about scarcity, but do worry about inequality."
— Confucius, Analects (论语)

Confucius once shared that what unsettles a society isn't scarcity itself, but a sense of unfairness. Poverty alone rarely fuels unrest. It's the belief, whether real or perceived, that wealth, power, or opportunity are unevenly distributed. Social harmony depends not just on abundance but on fairness, dignity, and trust in those who lead.

What it teaches us

- **Meritocracy in action**: A culture of meritocracy doesn't just attract talent. It attracts principled talent driven by purpose, not entitlement.
- **Moral leadership matters:** Leaders are responsible for ensuring fairness in resource allocation, championing fairness and shared dignity over the interests of a select few.
- **Rethinking freedom:** According to modern economists, freedom isn't just about speech or choice. It also means being free from the traps of poverty, systemic bias, or economic exclusion.

Nobel Prize winner **Joseph Stiglitz**, in *The Road to Freedom*, said,

> ***"Freedom is meaningless when people are chained by poverty, inequality, or lack of opportunity."***

The Dao Whispers: Am I building freedom ***with others*** or ***at their expense***?

March 29

Stratagem #31: The Beauty Trap

Use charm and emotions to disarm the enemy

美人计

měi rén jì

Translation: "The beauty tactic: use charm, seduction, or emotional entanglement to manipulate or destabilize an opponent."
— 31st Stratagem of the Thirty-Six Stratagems (三十六计)

The Story

In Chinese folklore, **Daji,** the stunning concubine of the Shang dynasty's last king, helped bring down an empire. Often portrayed as a fox spirit or ***femme fatale,*** she personifies 美人计 (*měi rén jì*): desire as a weapon, softness as subversion.

This stratagem says to use charm, attraction, or emotional pull to:

- Distract leaders from clarity.
- Stir jealousy or rivalry among allies.
- Undermine unity and morale.

A well-set trap does not announce itself and does not chase you. It lets you walk right in.

What it teaches us

- **Read the fine print**: Deals cloaked in *seductive* terms often hide traps in the details. Be wary of flattery or "too-good-to-be true" offers.
- **Strategic persuasion**: Charm and diplomacy can be used as tools to advance ambitious goals, especially in politics, negotiation, or influence.
- **Grace as strategy**: A calm, empathetic response may dissolve conflict faster than confrontation.

> ***"When dealing with people, let us remember***
> ***we are not dealing with creatures of logic,***
> ***but creatures of emotion."***
> — **Dale Carnegie**

The Dao Whispers: Do I notice when persuasion is dressed as charm, affection, or flirtation?

March 30

Keep Battles Short and Wins Clean

A swift win beats a long-drawn fight

故兵贵胜，不贵久

gù bīng guì shèng, bù guì jiǔ

Translation: "In war, winning is what matters, not prolonged engagement."
— Sun Tzu (孙子), The Art of War (孙子兵法)

We admire grit but forget that some of the wisest generals prefer to win before lunchtime. Sometimes, there is no correlation between grinding in the trenches for a year to win, vs. the same win that can be done in an hour. The latter probably makes more sense.

Sun Tzu explains that drawn-out battles drain resources, morale, and momentum. The longer the fight, the more unpredictable the ground. A good win isn't about how long you stay in the fight, but how cleanly and effectively you strike.

The best strategies often win fast, cost little, and leave no mess. The most compassionate move is often the most decisive.

Win well, then move on.

What it teaches us

- **Indecision drains more than mistakes ever will:** Waiting too long often does more damage than simply choosing and adjusting.
- **Dragging things out doesn't fix things:** It just builds tension, fuels resentment, and drains your time, money, and energy.
- **Overcommitting is a slow leak:** Overcommitting time, energy, or money isn't strategy, it's often just poor judgement.

> ***"The greatest results come from the rapid execution of well-laid plans."***
> — **John Stuart Mill**

The Dao Whispers: Do I confuse grit with wisdom, by staying in battles that drain more than they serve me?

March 31

The Scales Will Balance

Good is rewarded with good, and evil with evil – usually in its own time

善有善报，恶有恶报
不是不报，时候未到

shàn yǒu shàn bào, è yǒu è bào
bú shì bù bào, shí hòu wèi dào

Translation: "The good is rewarded with good, the evil with evil. It's not that there is no retribution – only that the time has not yet come."
— Traditional Chinese saying

I reckon karma feels like a call centre on a Monday morning. It's probably sitting there with a hundred thousand tickets saying, "Yes, yes, bad deeds logged, we'll process them sometime this century."

This proverb speaks to the same spirit. It reflects a belief in moral causality, often tied to karmic principles, where actions – good or bad – inevitably lead to corresponding consequences, though the timing may be delayed.

What it teaches us

- **Patience with the journey:** Doing things the right way often takes more time, but it pays off better in the end.
- **Shortcuts have strings attached:** Cutting corners with gossip, tricks, or manipulation usually catches up eventually.
- **Build credibility:** Integrity may not bring quick wins, but it earns trust and respect over time.

"Every action has its pleasures and its price."
— Immanuel Kant

The Dao Whispers: Do I stand by my core beliefs and values – trusting that the scales will balance in their own time – even when the world rewards cunning over character?

APRIL

思

sī

思 (sī) encompasses the following:

- Reflection
- Discernment
- Critical thinking
- Mindful learning
- Deep contemplation

思 (sī) means "to think." More broadly, it is the discipline of clear thinking, reflection, discernment, structured reasoning, mindful learning, and deep contemplation. It anchors us when decisions are complex, problems are tangled, and distractions pull us in every direction.

Mastering 思 (sī) allows us to:

- **Reality:** See people, situations, and reality for what they truly are.
- **Problems:** Define the problems accurately and distinguish between problems that are – "**important and urgent**," "**urgent only**," or "**important only**." This will better help us prioritise.
- **Root causes:** Identify and solve for root causes rather than chasing one symptom after another.
- **Structured problem-solving:** Apply structured thinking to problem solving to design high-impact solutions that are also practical.
- **Impact:** Prioritise and focus our energy on where it will make the biggest difference.

April 1

Time: Priceless and Non-Refundable

You can trade it, waste it, or invest it, but not reclaim it

一寸光阴一寸金，寸金难买寸光阴

yī cùn guāng yīn yī cùn jīn, cùn jīn nán mǎi cùn guāngyīn

Translation: "An inch of time is worth an inch of gold, but even gold cannot buy back an inch of time."
— Traditional Chinese proverb

The Story

A young man once idled away his days in the marketplace, leaning against stalls and watching the hours drift by. An old goldsmith, polishing a piece of jewellery in his tiny shop, watched him waste hour after hour. Finally, he stepped outside and placed a small piece of gold in the young man's hand. The young man looked puzzled. "You treat time as worthless," the elder said, "but even gold can't buy back a moment once it's gone."

What it teaches us

- **Guard against time leaks:** Time slips away easily in doom-scrolling, compulsive multitasking, or meaningless distractions... there's no buyback option for lost time.
- **Live your life, not someone else's:** Years can disappear chasing someone else's dreams, stuck in the wrong rooms, or buried in spreadsheets nobody reads.
- **Respect other people's time – time theft is real:** When we make someone wait, cancel last minute, drag meetings, or make "urgent" requests that don't matter tomorrow, force others to trade their nights for work no one remembers; that's stealing hours they'll never get back.

> ***"Your time is limited, so don't waste it living someone else's life. Don't be trapped by dogma – which is living the results of other people's thinking... And most important, have the courage to follow your heart and intuition. They somehow already know what you truly want to become."***
> **— Steve Jobs**

The Dao Whispers: Is this worthy of my time?

April 2

On Staying Away from Crossfires

When power clashes, the innocent pay

城门失火，殃及池鱼

chéng mén shī huǒ, yāng jí chí yú

Translation: "When the city gate catches fire, the fish in the moat suffer."
— Chinese proverb from the Three Kingdom period (三国时期)

When the powerful clash, it's rarely their own homes that burn. This ancient proverb reminds us that collateral damage often skips those responsible and falls instead on the innocent. Whether it's emperors at war, political factions colliding, or corporate titans feuding, it's usually those with no voice, no choice... yet they bear the cost.

As **Tyrion Lannister** said in *Game of Thrones:*

> ***"The powerful have always preyed on the powerless. That's how they became powerful in the first place."***

A **Malay proverb** echoes:

> ***"Gajah sama gajah berjuang, pelanduk mati di tengah-tengah."***
> *("When elephants fight, the mousedeer dies in the middle.")*

That said, **Plato** gave a perspective on the alternative:

> ***"One of the penalties of refusing to participate in politics is that you end up being governed by your inferiors."***

Tyrion and the Malay proverb remind us how easily the powerless become collateral damage when the powerful lock horns. Plato takes it one step further, warning how unchecked power or apathy can pave the way for demagogy – the rise of loud, unworthy rulers. There's rarely a perfect playbook in such moments. Sometimes you speak up, sometimes you step aside. The choice is yours, but ignoring it isn't always safe either.

The Dao Whispers:

- Who is caught in the crossfire?
- Do I step in, or step aside?

April 3

Look Beyond the Obvious

Complexity reveals itself in layers.
Read between the lines and look for patterns

玄之又玄

xuán zhī yòu xuán

Translation: "There is mystery upon mystery."
— Laozi (老子), Dao De Jing (道德经)

Life's mysteries are like onions. Peel one layer and you'll probably cry before you get to the core. Anyone selling you a three-step formula to truth is probably also selling magic beans.

The Daoist phrase, literally "mystery within mystery" reminds us that the world isn't always what it looks like. Truth is layered, tangled, and full of twists... rarely the clean story we're first told.

The word ***xuán*** (玄) means 'mystery' or 'mysterious,' and evokes something deep, elusive, and beyond comprehension. It's a reminder that real understanding is rarely found on the surface.

What it teaches us

- **Truth unfolds in layers**: What looks clear at first often conceals deeper motives, meaning, or complexity. If something feels too loud, too polished, or too easily explained, it may be crafted to mask, to sway, or to mislead.
- **Stay curious, stay humble:** None of us see the full picture. Our own habits, filters, and blind spots twist reality more than we realise.
- **Embrace the unknown:** Life rarely gives tidy answers. Uncertainty feels uncomfortable, but it's often where we grow fastest and see things we'd otherwise miss.

Kant echoed this by pointing to the ***ultimately unknowable thing-in-itself (das Ding an sich),*** which alludes to the reality *unfiltered* by our senses or cognitive frameworks. We can never fully know reality as it really is. We only experience ***filtered versions of it*** through our senses and minds, and those senses are far from perfect.

The Dao Whispers: Do I stop to question anything that feels too certain?

April 4

The Smart Fight Is the Fight You Never Have

Plan so well that conflict becomes unnecessary

夫未战而庙算胜者，得算多也

fū wèi zhàn ér miào suàn shèng zhě, dé suàn duō yě

Translation: "Those who win battles without fighting have done many calculations at the temple."
— Sun Tzu (孙子), The Art of War (孙子兵法)

Battles are not won with muscles or loud threats, Sun Tzu would say, they are won with the thinking you do before the fight even starts. Wise generals don't charge into a battlefield hoping that their enemies are somehow incompetent or weak. They win the war on paper first, weighing every move before a single sword is drawn.

The term **"庙算" (miào suàn)** refers to 'sacred calculations' made in ancestral temples, a metaphor for disciplined thought, measured foresight, and deliberate strategy.

What it teaches us

- **Beyond warfare:** In business, data-driven insight, scenario planning, and strategic positioning are today's form of *庙算 (miào suàn)*. Smart leaders don't just act, they simulate, prepare, and position to win the long game.
- **Invisible groundwork prevents reactive scrambling**: In life, those who move confidently have usually done the unseen groundwork by thinking ahead, aligning, and anticipating outcomes.
- **Anticipation over reaction:** Reacting well matters but anticipating matters more. Thinking ahead gives you the time and space to craft a thoughtful response, or mitigation plan.

"Plans are worthless, but planning is everything."
— Dwight David Eisenhower

The Dao Whispers: Do I take time to think clearly before I act, or do I react before I think?

April 5

Talking Too Much Reveals What You Don't Know

The wise say more with less

知者不言，言者不知

zhī zhě bù yán, yán zhě bù zhī

Translation: "He who knows does not speak; he who speaks does not know."
— Laozi, Dao De Jing (道德经)

We've all met that person who can talk for twenty minutes without saying anything… and the one who drops a single line that makes the whole room stop. It feels like they've already figured it all out.

Laozi's take? The ones who know the most rarely feel the need to prove it. Silence doesn't mean they've got nothing to add. They just don't see the need to join the chatter.

Conversely, those who speak excessively, eager to explain or quick to argue, often reveal the gaps in their understanding. Their need to dominate conversations often comes from a place of pride, insecurity, or the need to be noticed.

What it teaches us

- **Be contextually aware:** In Eastern culture, silence may mean strength and reflection. Elsewhere, it may be mistaken for passivity or uncertainty. There's no universal rule, really, just read the room and choose what serves you best.
- **Speak less, but with more weight:** Talking too much often comes from the need to prove or impress and may signal insecurity or inexperience. A few well-chosen words coupled with sharp insights often carry more weight than long explanations.
- **Don't fall for volume**: Loud narratives often drown out reason. But loud doesn't mean right.

"The more you know, the less you need to say."
— Jim Rohn

The Dao Whispers: When was the last time you spoke to feel seen, not to add value? If I said half as much, would my words land twice as well?

April 6

Does the Fish Rot from the Head?

Plato once said, unjust cities cannot raise just people

上梁不正下梁歪

shàng liáng bù zhèng, xià liáng wāi

Translation: "If the top beam is not straight, the lower beams will be crooked."
— Traditional Chinese folk proverb, rooted in Confucian thought

The tone of a team, a company, even a country often mirrors those steering it. When leaders cut corners, the effect trickles down; just as if the main beam is bent, it's difficult to expect the house to stand straight.

This proverb reminds us that moral uprightness starts at the top. When those in power lack integrity, it distorts everything underneath them, shaping behaviours, values, and expectations in ways that are hard to undo. Plato echoed this in ***The Republic,*** warning that the justice of a city reflects the character of those who rule it. If leaders are unjust, expecting fairness from the system they've built is wishful thinking.

What it teaches us

- **Leaders shape reality:** In any setting, from boardrooms to living rooms, people take cues from those above. You become the moral compass for those you lead, whatever its direction.
- **The system leaves a mark:** If you're in an unhealthy or exploitative environment, spot the pattern early and don't let it rewrite your values.
- **Fairness isn't automatic:** Some structures are rigged by design. Step back, assess, and choose where you stand before you sink with them.

> ***"Justice in the city is the same as justice in the individual."***
> — **Plato**

The Dao Whispers: What example am I setting for others, whether I mean to or not? And in this house, are the beams straight?

April 7

History Is Our Inevitable Teacher

By using history as a mirror, we can understand the rise and fall of nations

以史为镜，可以知兴替

yǐ shǐ wéi jìng, kě yǐ zhī xīng tì

Translation: "By using history as a mirror, we can understand the rise and fall of nations."
— Emperor Taizong of Tang (唐太宗)

Every time someone says, ***"this time it's different,"*** history cheekily rolls its eyes. Civilisations rise and fall not at random, but through familiar patterns. If we don't learn from them, we may unknowingly repeat the very mistakes we hoped to avoid. History isn't just a record of the past, it's a mirror for the present and a map for the future.

Emperor Taizong's insight echoes across cultures:

- **George Santayana: *"Those who cannot remember the past are condemned to repeat it."***
- **Cicero: *"To be ignorant of what happened before you were born is to remain always a child."***

Maturity means looking back not only to our own lives, but to the systems, struggles, and choices that shaped the world we live in. To understand the forces at play today, we must study the decisions that brought us here. Avoiding the discomfort of history doesn't absolve us, it blinds us. Reflection, then, is a responsibility.

What it teaches us

- **History is a blueprint:** Wise leaders study history ***not to romanticise it,*** but to avoid repeating its mistakes.
- **Old thinking writes the same stories:** Patterns repeat until we trace their roots and address them.
- **Historical honesty polishes our rough edges:** Healthy societies depend on historical honesty.

The Dao Whispers: Do I make time to understand the history of my culture, my country, my world? Do I take a moment to ask: *What happened before, and what might be affecting this story today?*

April 8

When You Hit an Impasse, Shift Gears

Change turns dead ends into new beginnings

穷则变，变则通，通则久

qióng zé biàn, biàn zé tōng, tōng zé jiǔ

Translation: "When things reach an impasse, they must change; when they change, they flow; when they flow, they last."
— I Ching (易经)

This phrase comes from **I Ching** (Book of Changes), one of China's most ancient and profound philosophical texts. It teaches that when we hit a wall, we must shift, because change isn't just a way out, it's a way for us to move past the block.
Let's break it down:

- **穷则变** (qióng zé biàn): When one is stuck, change becomes necessary.
- **变则通** (biàn zé tōng): Change creates movement and opens the way for solutions; and this leads to breakthroughs.
- **通则久** (tōng zé jiǔ): Breakthroughs then lead to sustainable success.

What it teaches us

- **Embrace change in crisis:** When you hit rock bottom, it can be life's cue to pivot.
- **Obstacles become openings:** Challenges can force us to get out of our comfort zone. A health scare, for instance, might trigger us to change our lifestyle for the better.
- **Refresh your network: "When you feel stuck, don't go deeper into the same circle. Refresh your network to refresh your perspective."** (Synthesized from Grant, Hoffman & Ibarra)

> ***"It is not the strongest or most intelligent who survive, but those most responsive to change."***
> — **Charles Darwin** (paraphrased)

The Dao Whispers: Feeling stuck is life's invitation to transform. If that happens, would you accept that invitation, or refuse it?

April 9

Give & Take: Why Reciprocity Is the Heartbeat of Connection

Why give-and-take decides who stays in your life

礼尚往来，有来不往非礼也

lǐ shàng wǎng lái, yǒu lái bù wǎng fēi lǐ yě

Translation: "Courtesy demands reciprocity. If one gives and the other does not return, it's not in line with propriety."
— The Book of Rites (礼记 · 曲礼上)

In Confucian thought, 礼 (lǐ) – propriety or ritual – governs human interactions, built on respect and mutual obligation. It suggests that relationships thrive on mutual exchange. When someone extends kindness, a gift, or time, it is only proper to respond in kind. Otherwise, it's like crashing a party and never bringing a bottle, then wondering why the invitations stop coming.

What it means

- **Keep the balance:** When giving is one-sided, the relationship can become draining. Relationships thrive when we stay mindful of give-and-take, respect, and balance.
- **Watch out for takers:** Even the kindest people have limits. If someone keeps taking without giving back, their goodwill will eventually run dry.
- **Know when to step away:** If you're always the one making the effort, it's okay to pause or move on. Healthy connections feel mutual, not like a solo workout.

"Unreturned kindness becomes unseen labour."
— Author unknown

The Dao Whispers

- When was the last time someone was kind to you and how did you respond?
- Are there areas in your life where you tend to take more than you give?
- Or are you giving more than you're getting back?

April 10

Fighting Poison with Poison

Beware confronting darkness with darkness,
it may leave its mark on you

以毒攻毒，必受其害

yǐ dú gōng dú, bì shòu qí hài

Translation: "He who fights poison with poison will surely be harmed by it."
— Traditional Chinese proverb

At times, when faced with cruelty, injustice, or corruption, we want to fight fire with fire. But remember, you might just end up with a nasty burn yourself.

This old saying reminds us that, ***if you fight poison with poison, you don't walk away untouched.***

Nietzsche put it well in ***Beyond Good and Evil:***

> ***"He who fights with monsters should look to it that he himself does not become a monster."***

Don't let what you resist define what you become.

The Dao Whispers

- Have I absorbed the very darkness I once stood against?
- In confronting betrayal, cruelty, or deceit, have I started to mirror it?

April 11

Dancing with Wolves

Sometimes, you've got to learn to deal with the devil to be an angel

与狼共舞

yǔ láng gòng wǔ

Translation: "To dance with wolves."
— Traditional Chinese proverb

This proverb reminds us that life doesn't always let us choose our company. Sometimes, we find ourselves across the table from liars, manipulators, and even predators. Yet, for strategy, survival, or a cause greater than ourselves, we must still dance.

Niccolò Machiavelli once said,

> ***"A prince must learn how not to be good... and use this knowledge when necessary."***

A respected senior corporate leader once said,

> ***"Sometimes, you've got to learn to deal with the devil... that's the reality of the corporate world."***

The world is rarely pure, but your purpose can be. Just make sure that you don't lose yourself in the dance.

The Dao Whispers

- **Discern:** When facing wolves, am I clear with them and with myself about where I'll bend, and where I won't?
- **Boundaries:** If I must engage, can I do it on my own terms?
- **Integrity:** Can I move through darkness without letting it cling to me?

Sometimes, we must engage dangerous forces – not to befriend them, but to protect what is important to us.

April 12

The Price of Saying Yes Too Often

Generosity without boundaries invites exploitation

得寸进尺

dé cùn jìn chǐ

Translation: "Give an inch, they'll take a foot"
— Traditional Chinese proverb

You offer to help a colleague "just this once" with their report. Next thing you know, every week they're forwarding their workload to you, calling it "team collaboration." Generosity turns into unpaid overtime fast.

The proverb describes someone who, after receiving a small favour or concession, immediately pushes for more, often in a greedy or opportunistic way.

- A favour becomes an expectation.
- A compromise becomes a weakness.
- Gratitude turns into entitlement.

Adam Grant, in ***Give and Take***, offers a useful lens on human exchange:

- **Givers** offer time, energy, and help freely.
- **Takers** extract value without reciprocity.
- **Matchers** trade based on fairness.

If you're a Giver, recognising when someone pushes beyond reasonable limits helps protect your boundaries and energy. Being generous is great, but without boundaries, it can open the door to being taken advantage of.

> ***"Appeasement is feeding the crocodile, hoping it will eat you last."***
> — **Winston Churchill**

The Dao Whispers:

- When you meet new people, can you tell if they're Givers, Takers, or Matchers?
- Do you give from choice, or from guilt?
- When someone crosses a line, do you call it out or let it slide?

April 13

Communicate with Impact

Lead with the point, speak clearly and keep it short

言简意赅

yán jiǎn yì gāi

Translation: "Keep your speech short, but its meaning whole."
— Texts from Han Feizi (韩非子)

Ever started telling a story and halfway through even you forgot the point? Now imagine that in front of your boss or a room of tired executives. This idiom reminds us that clarity isn't about saying more but about saying what matters, fully yet concisely. Leaders have little time, and shorter attention spans. When you're talking to a senior stakeholder, presenting to a crowd, or answering an interview question, if you ramble, you'll lose them in 30 seconds (or less).

What it teaches us

- **Headline first**: Lead with the key point. Don't bury it or make your audience guess.
- **Start with the answer:** Then explain your reasoning.
- **Provide context:** Only you know what you're talking about, the audience usually don't.
- **Always include the so-what:** What are the implications? Why are you saying this? Why should they care?
- **Use the power of "Why":** When the "why" is clear, the "what" and the "how" land more effectively.
- **Explain simply:** If a child can't understand it, neither will your audience.
- **Use the power of three:** People remember three points, not seven.
- **Use the two-minute rule:** Most things – intros, answers, explanation – can (and should) be said in under two minutes.

> ***"If you can't explain it simply, you don't understand it well enough."***
> ***— Albert Einstein***

The Dao Whispers: Be concise, be simple; but never simplistic. The most powerful stories are often told with the simplest words.

April 14

The Beauty of Impermanence

The most beautiful seasons are sometimes brief

花无百日红

huā wú bǎi rì hóng

Translation: "No flower stays red for a hundred days."
— Traditional Chinese proverb

Life moves in cycles, ups and downs, highs and lows, bumpy paths, and smooth-sailing ones. When things are going well, celebrate them, but stay humble. When things fall apart, remember: ***this too shall pass.***

The proverb reminds us that beauty, success, and prosperity are fleeting. Just as a flower's bloom eventually fades, so too do our moments of fame, fortune, and vitality.

What it teaches us

- **Let go lightly:** Clinging to status, beauty, or recognition makes change feel like a loss. Be grateful for life's bright chapters and let them go with grace.
- **Savour what's here**: Recognise that joyful seasons, career highs, and love's early blossoms won't last forever – and that's what makes them so precious.
- **Grow through change:** When momentum slows or certainty slips away, don't let it define you. Downturns are part of the cycle. What matters is moving through them with equanimity, finding balance even as seasons shift.

> ***"The wheel of fortune turns, and those at the top will soon be at the bottom."***
> **— Boethius**

The Dao Whispers: In clinging to what is slipping away, have I neglected my health? My family? My peace of mind? Myself?

April 15

Good, Not Gullible

Harbour no ill-will towards others, but don't stand unshielded

害人之心不可有，防人之心不可无

hài rén zhī xīn bù kě yǒu, fáng rén zhī xīn bù kě wú

Translation: "Do not harbour malice but never go unprotected."
— Traditional Chinese proverb

It's great to be kind. But kind and clueless? That's just asking for trouble. Life has plenty of people with good intentions, but a few who'll happily take advantage if you let them. This proverb is a reminder that you don't need to grow claws, but you should probably have a fence.

- Being good doesn't mean being gullible.
- Forgiving doesn't mean forgetting the lesson.
- Being compassionate doesn't mean ditching your common sense.

What it teaches us

- **Don't ignore the red flags:** Forgive, sure, but don't overlook repeated deceit or harmful behaviour.
- **Be wise in trust:** In life or business, trust must be earned, not assumed. Do your due diligence before delegating or investing your time and resources.
- **Stay open, not exposed:** You can be open-hearted without leaving yourself completely exposed and defenceless. Not everyone has good intentions.

> ***"The only fence against the world is a thorough knowledge of it."***
> **— John Locke**

The Dao Whispers:

- Do I trust too easily?
- Do I know how to stay kind without being naïve?
- Do I set boundaries, or let people keep testing them?

April 16

When Life Disappoints, Have Some Fun

Loosen your grip, untie your hair, and escape to Santorini or Bali

人生在世不称意，明朝散发弄扁舟

rén shēng zài shì bù chèn yì, míng zhāo sàn fà nòng piān zhōu

Translation: "When life in this world goes against your will, let down your hair and sail away in a boat by morning."
— Li Bai (李白), a famous poet

Li Bai knew what he was talking about. Some days, no matter how hard you plan or push, life simply refuses to cooperate. Plans stall, people let you down, doors slam shut. In those times, doubling down isn't grit, it's banging your head on a locked door.

What it teaches us

- **Choose grace:** Letting go is not giving up, it's choosing sanity over meaningless struggle.
- **Stop fighting the current**: When life pushes back, pushing harder may not be the answer. Sometimes, drifting downstream with the current is wiser than forcing your way upstream.
- **Reset with nature**: A walk in the woods, a day by the sea, or even an impulsive road trip won't fix everything, but it might give you clearer eyes and a lighter heart.

> ***"Sometimes we must let go of the life we have planned, so as to accept the one that is waiting for us."***
> **— Joseph Campbell**

The Dao Whispers

- What am I clinging to that clearly isn't working?
- If I gave myself permission to let go for a while, would life feel different?

April 17

When Power Rewrites Reality

When someone calls a deer a horse, think twice before you nod

指鹿为马

zhǐ lù wéi mǎ

Translation: "Calling a deer a horse."
— Shiji, historical records by Sima Qian

The ancient story

During the Qin Dynasty, the powerful minister Zhao Gao staged a loyalty test among the court officials. He brought a deer before the Emperor Qin Er Shi and called it a horse. When the emperor questioned him, Zhao insisted it ***was*** a horse. Officials who dared speak the truth were either punished or executed.

Zhao Gao wasn't confused, and he wasn't joking. He was displaying power and control. By forcing others to accept an obvious lie and punishing dissent, he exposed disloyalty and strengthened his grip on power.

What it teaches us

- **Spot manipulation:** When you sense that reality is being twisted, stay alert. Question the narratives that contradict observable evidence.
- **Think for yourself:** If everyone is agreeing on something that feels off, pause and ask if it really makes sense.
- **Know when to walk**: If you're in a place where speaking honestly is punished and blind conformity is rewarded, ask yourself if it's where you want to stay.

> ***"Those who can make you believe absurdities can make you commit atrocities."***
> — **Voltaire**

The Dao Whispers:

- Who is asking me to call a deer a horse?
- Am I doing it to others?
- Do I need to call a deer a horse to thrive where I am?

April 18

The Unread Chapters in Every Person

Even the people you trust keep parts of themselves hidden

人心隔肚皮

rén xīn gé dù pí

Translation: "The heart is hidden behind the ribs (belly) – meaning you'll never truly know what others think."
— Traditional Chinese proverb

People can surprise you, and not always in good ways. This old saying reminds us that no matter how close you are to someone, you'll never fully know what's in their heart. Thoughts, intentions, emotions... much of it stays hidden, out of reach.

What it teaches us

- **Accept human complexity:** Recognise that everyone has private thoughts and motives. Avoid rushing to judge what you cannot fully see or understand. A silent colleague may be grieving a loss or quietly dealing with difficult news.
- **Protect your own intentions:** Be strategic about revealing your thoughts, particularly in competitive environments. Sharing too much about your plans might make you vulnerable to others' unspoken agendas.
- **Develop emotional intelligence:** Learn to read subtle cues, like body language or small contradictions. A friend who speaks warmly but acts otherwise may be showing you their truth without saying it.

"Human nature doesn't change."
— **Robert McNamara** (The Fog of War)

The Dao Whispers:

- Am I too quick to assume that every smile reflects goodwill?
- Even those closest to us carry shadows we may never see. Do I leave myself exposed to harm by those I trust most?

April 19

The Persistence of Memory

The harder you try to forget, the more it sticks

抽刀断水水更流，举杯消愁愁更愁

chōu dāo duàn shuǐ shuǐ gèng liú, jǔ bēi xiāo chóu chóu gèng chóu

Translation: "Drawing a sword to cut the water will only make it flow on, and raising a glass to drown sorrow will only make it deepen."
— Li Bai (李白), a famous poet

Some pain cannot be hacked away or drowned out. Li Bai reminds us that we need not fight our struggles head-on. Trying to force grief away, or drink heartbreak into numbness, often makes it sting more. It's like being told not to think about a purple giraffe and suddenly it's all you can see. Memories don't just disappear with a drink, or simply because we tell them to. The harder we try to forget a memory, the more it lodges itself in our minds.

- Be kind to yourself. You don't have to "move on" overnight.
- Don't fight your feelings too hard, let them be.
- Let memories sit with you. They will fade with time anyway, at their own pace.
- Life moves forward, even when you feel stuck. Little shifts, like going to a new place, having a chat with a stranger, or tasting a pleasantly unexpected ice cream flavour, can gently ease you along.
- Stop forcing healing. The more space you give to it, the more likely it will find you.

> ***"Nothing fixes a thing so intensely in the memory as the wish to forget it."***
> — **Michel de Montaigne**

The Dao Whispers

- Am I trying too hard to forget something that needs time to fade?
- What happens if I stop fighting the memory and just let it be?
- What if healing is about living with the past, not erasing it?

April 20

Suffer No More Than What Gives It Meaning

Emotions are part of life, but they shouldn't run your life

哀而不伤，乐而不淫

āi ér bù shāng, lè ér bù yín

Translation: "Mourn, but without being overwhelmed by grief; rejoice, without being excessive."

— Confucius (孔子), Analects (论语)

Confucius reminds us that emotions aren't enemies, they're part of living. Grief is human, but we don't need to suffer more than life already demands. Joy is precious, but it shouldn't sweep us so far away that we lose our footing.

Confucius wasn't saying "don't feel." He was saying "don't drown." Balance is not about numbing how we feel; it's about staying steady enough to keep living on your terms.

What it teaches us

- **Do not suffer more than needed**: Grieve what you've lost, feel your emotions, but don't let them take over your life. Suffer no more than what life demands, and no less than what gives it meaning.
- **Build emotional resilience:** Whether it's a bad day at work, a family fight, or a breakup, let yourself feel upset. It's okay to feel upset. But don't let it break your focus, confidence or derail you.
- **Love without losing yourself:** Care deeply but leave room for both you and them to breathe.

> ***"Virtue is a golden mean between two vices, the one of excess and the one of deficiency."***
> **— Aristotle**

The Dao Whispers

- Am I carrying more pain than this moment truly demands?
- Do I hold on to highs and lows so tightly that they throw me off balance?

April 21

When They Misread You, Let Them

You don't have to explain yourself to everyone

知我者谓我心忧，不知我者谓我何求

zhī wǒ zhě wèi wǒ xīn yōu, bù zhī wǒ zhě wèi wǒ hé qiú

Translation: "Those who know me say my heart grieves; those who don't, will misunderstand me and assume I'm chasing something else."
— Qu Yuan, Li Sao, Warring States Period

Qu Yuan, poet and patriot, and exile, wrote this line after being cast out by the court he had loyally served. To those who knew him, he was a man of principle, saddened by what was happening to his country. To outsiders, he appeared ambitious, self-serving, and calculating. That pained him.

It's a kind of pain that many of us may know. Your grief when it is mistaken for weakness, your silence read as arrogance, and your values misconstrued and twisted into some kind of selfish motives.

Qu Yuan's line suggests that ***being understood by a few is worth far more than being liked or accepted by everyone.***

What can we learn from Qu Yuan?

- **Stop over-explaining:** People determined to misunderstand you won't be convinced by more words. You don't owe everyone an explanation.
- **Speak where you're safe:** Share your heart with those who've earned the right to hear it.
- **Protect your inner compass**: When the world misunderstands you, stay close to the people who don't and more importantly, to the version of yourself that you know to be true.

> ***"Don't explain. Your friends don't need it, and your enemies won't believe it."***
> **— Elbert Hubbard**

The Dao Whispers: Who in my life really gets what I'm going through? Am I wasting energy to explain myself to those who just don't want to understand?

April 22

Crucibles Are Forged in Fire

Tough times don't just test you, they reveal who you are and help you become who you can be

艰难困苦，玉汝于成

jiān nán kùn kǔ, yù rǔ yú chéng

Translation: "Through hardship and suffering, one is turned into jade."
— Traditional Chinese proverb

A professor at London Business School asked, ***"Do we all know what crucibles mean?"*** A few nodded, a few looked blank, and some gave that perfectly unreadable consultant-banker stare.

She explained it simply: **the strongest steel is forged in the hottest fire.** This proverb alludes to the same idea, that raw jade only becomes precious after it's cut and polished.

Life works like that too. Storms don't just test us; they carve and shape us into who we can become. **How we stand in the storm moulds the version of us that walks out when the skies finally clear.**

What it teaches us

- **Growth hides in hardship:** Even when you feel you're barely holding on, life is subtly forging your resilience, clarity, and depth of character. Today's "just surviving" often becomes your unshakeable strength tomorrow.
- **Pressure builds character:** Struggles lay bare who we are. Each time we push through when it'd be easier to quit, you're not just surviving, you're becoming stronger.
- **Kindness matters:** Struggles bring out different sides of us, not all are pretty, but all are real. Instead of judging yourself, offer the same compassion you'd give a friend.

> ***"Circumstances don't make the man, they only reveal him to himself."***
> — **Epictetus**

The Dao Whispers: Do I show myself compassion when life gets hard? When times are tough, what would I say to a good friend? Can I be that friend to myself?

April 23

The Conundrum of Justice

Would it still feel just if the tables were turned?

不偏不倚，公正无私

bù piān bù yǐ, gōng zhèng wú sī

Translation: "Be neither biased nor partial; and be just without prioritising self-interest."
— Traditional Chinese saying

Confucian scholars once trained for years to live up to this ideal, judging without leaning toward friends, fear, or self-interest. It all sounds noble until you're in the middle of it yourself. Emotions, loyalties, and consequences tug at you, and before you realise it, the straight line of justice has already bent.

The real dilemmas

- **The mediator's dilemma:** Two friends are at odds. Speaking truth may hurt one and staying silent may feel like betraying both. What feels fair then?
- **The leader's paradox:** Can you allocate resources purely on merit when team dynamics – ***and your own survival*** – pull you toward favouring loyal allies? Where do you draw the line?
- **Two concepts of liberty: *One man's freedom is another man's unfreedom.*** When values clash, who gets to define what's fair?

> ***"There are no facts, only interpretations."***
> — **Friedrich Nietzsche**

The Dao Whispers

- Did I call this 'fair' just because it worked out for me?
- Would I still think this was fair if I were on the losing side?
- Am I defending a principle, or just my position?

April 24

The Illusion of Consent

Consent means little without freedom to refuse

强买强卖，非礼也

qiáng mǎi qiáng mài, fēi lǐ yě

Translation: "Forced buying or selling is contrary to propriety."
— Contemporary Chinese saying reflecting Confucian moral values

Not every "yes" is real. Sometimes, contracts subtly strip away basic rights, turning choice into an illusion. On paper, a deal can look fair. Two parties sign, a contract is sealed, and everyone calls it consent. But without the freedom to refuse, a signed deal is just a polite form of pressure.

This proverb explains that when one party holds overwhelming power, consent becomes questionable. Agreements made under pressure may be legal, but are they ethical?

- qiáng mǎi qiáng mài (强买强卖) literally means forcing someone into a transaction against their will.
- (fēi lǐ yě) 非礼也 says it **violates lǐ** (礼) – which means dignity and proper conduct.

Joseph Stiglitz, in ***The Price of Inequality,*** said something similar about contracts:

> ***"When contracts are formed under significant inequality or asymmetrical information, their fairness and ethical standing come into question."***

So, what these thinkers remind us is that justice isn't only about what the law permits. It's about whether both sides really had the freedom, not simply the formality, to say no.

The Dao Whispers

- When I evaluate a deal or decision, do I ask who really had the freedom to choose?
- Does agreement mean fairness, or just the absence of resistance?
- Am I mistaking formality for legitimacy?

April 25

Strong Smiles Often Hide the Deepest Scars

Behind every smile, there may be someone fighting a battle

笑中有泪

xiào zhōng yǒu lèi

Translation: "There are tears behind the smile."
— Traditional Chinese Saying

The kindest hearts have known the deepest pain, weathered the darkest storms, and emerged with souls of steel. What makes them extraordinary is that, in spite of it all, they still choose to be kind.

Some smiles are brave disguises, worn by people carrying battles they'll never show you. They hold others up even while fighting to stay on their feet. They reach out because they know what it feels like to suffer, and they don't want you to feel alone.

It speaks to **invisible courage**:

- The mother who stays strong for her children.
- The friend who jokes through heartbreak.
- A colleague who shows up for the team even when they're unwell.
- A caregiver who supports others while barely coping inside.
- A soul whose grief and grace live in the same face.
- Someone who helps you rise while barely holding themselves up.
- Someone who smiles through injustice, not because it doesn't hurt, but because they've made peace with the imperfections of human nature.

Behind many smiles we pass on the street are struggles we'll never see.

> ***"Life is a tragedy when seen in close-up, but a comedy in long-shot."***
> — **Charlie Chaplin**

The Dao Whispers: Who around me looks okay, but might be fighting their own storm? Do I take for granted how much strength it takes to stay kind when life isn't kind in return?

April 26

When in Rome... Or Any Other Village

When we go to a village, let's honour their history and people by following their local customs

入乡随俗

rù xiāng suí sú

Translation: "When one goes to a village, follow its customs"
— Traditional Chinese proverb

We've all seen travellers on social media stomping through a new place, stirring discomfort as if their way is the only way. By demanding things to "feel like home" or "be like how we do it at home," they miss the gift of what's right in front of them.

This idiom nudges us to respect the traditions and soul of a place, to pause, observe, and honour the community we're entering. Cultural humility doesn't mean losing our own roots. It's about understanding what's different, appreciating it for what it is, and joining in the local customs without stomping on them.

What it teaches us

- **Adapt to local norms:** A few small gestures go a long way. For example, pouring drinks for others in Korea, lowering your voice on the London tube, or skipping eye contact where it feels intrusive.
- **Respect different worldviews:** It's easy to judge what we don't understand, but respect means allowing others the dignity to live by their own values.
- **Blend into new environments:** In unfamiliar teams or companies, observe the tone, pace, and dynamics. Aligning with local culture often helps with collaboration and earns trust.

> ***"To hold another culture is to hold a mirror to your own."***
> — **Margaret Mead**

The Dao Whispers: Do I enter others' space with respect, or impose my preferences without regard for local norms? Do I ask, observe, and adapt, or rush to judge what's different?

April 27

People Who Really Care Show Up for You

Because "I'll be there for you" means nothing if you never show up

口惠而实不至

kǒu huì ér shí bù zhì

Translation: "Promising help but without actually delivering it."
— Traditional Chinese proverb

Ever met one of those "don't worry, I've got you" types, who disappear faster than the last cookie in the office pantry when it's time to actually show up? Generous promises, fancy words, and zero follow-through. It calls out the flaky ones... big promises, no delivery.

Hard times are funny like that. You barely remember what people said, but you'll ***never forget who turned up at the door.*** And when someone keeps promising and disappearing, it's not bad luck or timing, it's who they are.

There's wisdom in believing what actions show, not just what words promise.

> ***"You are what you do, not what you say you'll do."***
> — **Carl Jung**

The Dao Whispers

- Who showed up when I had nothing to give back?
- Do I keep my own promises, or just hand out words for free?
- When someone's absence speaks louder than their vows, do I listen?

April 28

Offer a Brick, Gain a Jade

Why putting your "initial hypothesis" or "rough draft" on the table is a smart strategy

抛砖引玉

pāo zhuān yǐn yù

Translation: "Throw a brick to attract jade."
— Thirty-Six Stratagems (三十六计, sān shí liù jì)

In classical Chinese thought, jade symbolises wisdom and refinement. A brick, on the other hand, is… well, a brick is rough, ordinary, and rather unremarkable, most would say.

This proverb speaks to making a small, imperfect offer to unlock something far more valuable from others. You don't hoard your ideas until they're perfect. You toss out a rough sketch, a flawed first draft, to inspire a better, richer response. Sometimes you need to offer a brick to get someone to throw you a gem.

In the context of the Thirty-Six Stratagems, used well, this isn't manipulation but thoughtful, even calculated leverage. You take a small risk to open doors, invite genius, or draw out what's hidden. It's the art of going first, even if it's clumsy, knowing it could lead to something priceless.

What it teaches us

- **Share your hypotheses to kickstart discussions:** Offer a partial idea to invite deeper contributions.
- **Trade small for big:** Making a modest concession or gesture can earn trust or bigger opportunities in return.
- **Offer building blocks to refine:** In mentorship, sharing basic advice can prompt mentees to explore and develop their own, often more refined approaches.

"A candle loses nothing by lighting another candle."
— James Keller

The Dao Whispers: Am I holding back my "brick" because I'm afraid it looks dumb? Am I willing to go first, even if imperfect, to create space for others to shine and to get a better collective result?

April 29

Please Show Me My True Colours

To see myself clearly, I must see how others see me

以铜为镜，可以正衣冠
以人为镜，可以明得失

yǐ tóng wéi jìng, kě yǐ zhèng yī guān, yǐ rén wéi jìng, kě yǐ míng dé shī

Translation: "The bronze mirror reflects how well we're dressed, while people as mirrors reflect our strengths and flaws." — Emperor Taizong of Tang

Have you ever wondered why certain people disappear from your life without warning?

Emperor Taizong said these lines after the death of the famous advisor Wei Zheng (魏征), a man known for his honesty and critical counsel. In mourning, the emperor said he had lost his most precious mirror – not the bronze mirror, but the mirror that tells the truth.

Here, the emperor alludes to how self-awareness cannot be found through introspection alone. It is found in insights from how others experience us. The hard truths, kind corrections, and subtle exits. All of them are reflections of how others experience us, pleasant or otherwise.

> ***"Criticism may not be agreeable, but it is necessary. It fulfils the same function as pain in the human body."***
> — **Winston Churchill**

The Dao Whispers

The people around us tell us a lot about our own true colours.

- If you are kind, kindness often echoes back.
- If you are selfish or biased, the fair will quietly leave.
- If you act with malice, goodness will fade from your circle.
- If you are superficial, you attract people who disappear when life gets hard.
- If you are overly agreeable, you may be surrounded by those who use you, not those who value you.
- If you are cruel or combative, the wise simply go silent.

When someone holds up a mirror to your blind spots, thank them. They just gave you a gift.

Johari Window: The Hidden Gem for Self-Awareness
Awareness is a gift. The Johari Window, created by Joseph Luft and Harrington Ingham in 1955, is sometimes dismissed as an old training tool. At its heart, the model is about two things modern leaders still struggle with: sharing openly and inviting feedback.

	What I know	**What I don't know**
What you know	**Open:** What I know and what you know about me	**Blind Spot:** What you know about me that I don't **Action**: Ask for feedback – what I should start, stop, or keep
What you don't know	**Hidden:** What I know about me that you don't **Action:** Choose when and what to reveal to build trust, while keeping healthy boundaries and good judgement	**Unknown:** What neither of us knows yet **Action**: Learn & experiment – books, videos, lectures, coaching, experiences

The idea is simple: Growth comes from widening the "open area." We do this in two ways: by sharing more of ourselves (reducing the hidden area), and by inviting feedback (shrinking our blind spots). The more we reveal and the more we learn, the greater our self-awareness.

The framework has four key quadrants:

- **Open Area:** What is known to self and others.
- **Blind Spot:** What others see in you but you don't see in yourself.
- **Hidden Area:** What you know but choose not to reveal.
- **Unknown:** What neither of us knows yet.

The Dao Whispers: Self-awareness lives in our willingness to face the person in the mirror – and to accept the mirror held up by those around us.

April 30

The Door to Life's Big Mysteries

Some truths can't be Googled. Laozi said so himself, right in chapter one of the Dao De Jing

众妙之门

zhòng miào zhī mén

Translation: "The gateway to all mysteries."
— Laozi (老子), Dao De Jing (道德经)

This phrase comes from the **opening chapter of Dao De Jing**, where Laozi describes ***the Dao***, or ***the "Way,"*** as something that can't be pinned down with words or logic. It's the source of everything, yet you can't see it, touch it, or hold it. It's mysterious, subtle, and only revealed when you stop trying to force understanding.

The "gate" is that threshold between what we think we know and the vastness we don't. Laozi hints that the door only opens when we quiet the noise, let go of our obsessions with control, and allow space for life to show us its hidden wisdom.

What it teaches us

- **Simplicity helps clear the fog:** A calm, uncluttered mind often sees what busyness hides. Meditating, or a simple walk in nature, can declutter our thoughts.
- **Gut feelings matter:** Logic helps, but when you make a logical decision and you feel that deep tugging in the gut; pay attention to it and re-assess the situation again.
- **Stay open to mystery:** Uncertainty can be an opportunity for transformation if you stay curious instead of clinging rigidly to fixed answers or outcomes.

> ***"The more I learn, the more I realise how much I don't know."***
> — **Albert Einstein**

The Dao Whispers: Not everything needs to be solved today. Sometimes, when you stop pushing for an answer, it finds you.

MAY

行

xíng

Meaning of 行 (xíng):

- Action
- Practice
- Conduct
- Execution
- Walking the path

行 (xíng) means "action", or "to do." 行 (xíng) is where ideas meet the real world, where insight turns into change, vision into momentum, and knowledge into results.

行 (xíng) is not just doing something for the sake of doing. It is thoughtful movement that is decisive yet deliberate, courageous yet considered.

Mastering 行 (xíng) means we can:

- **Follow through:** Take real action to deliver on our plans and aspirations, not just make them.
- **Walk the talk:** Let our daily choices reflect who we want to be and do what we say we will do.
- **Stay disciplined:** Show up even when we don't feel like it.
- **Live with integrity:** Align our actions with our values.
- **Be flexible:** Adjust when things change without losing the big picture.

May 1

Sun Tzu's Rule on Striking Fast

A 'good enough' move now beats 'perfect' tomorrow

兵贵神速

bīng guì shén sù

Translation: "In war, speed is of the essence"
— Sun Tzu, The Art of War (孙子兵法)

Picture two armies:

- One hesitates, waiting for perfect conditions. The troops grow restless, their plans leak, and they lose momentum.
- The other strikes like lightning at dawn. Before the other side can even grab their armour, it's over.

Sun Tzu wasn't just talking about battlefields. This is the job offer you didn't answer in time, the deal that slipped to a faster competitor, or the "let's meet" text you sat on until the other person made other plans.

Sun Tzu knew the win often goes to the one who strikes fast and catches the enemy off-guard. Waiting for "perfect" usually means watching someone else seize it while you're still polishing your PowerPoint.

What it teaches us

- **Work smarter, not harder:** Leverage tools – AI, real-time data, rapid feedback loops – to help you think better and act faster..
- **Good enough beats ready**: Decisiveness gives you speed, and speed gets you a step closer to the finishing line.
- **Stack quick wins early:** Build credibility, trust, and momentum by identifying and securing quick wins.

> ***"A good plan violently executed now is better than a perfect plan executed next week."***
> **— George S. Patton**

The Dao Whispers: Am I waiting for perfect conditions, or just afraid to make the move I already know is right?

May 2

The First Step Is the Hardest

A journey of a thousand miles begins with a single step

千里之行，始于足下

qiān lǐ zhī xíng, shǐ yú zú xià

Translation: "A journey of a thousand miles begins with the first step."
— Laozi, Dao De Jing (道德经)

This well-loved proverb from Laozi is more than an ancient wisdom, it's a gentle nudge. Every goal, no matter how ambitious, begins with one ordinary step. ***And, we can start right where we are now.***

But let's be honest, the first step often feels like the hardest one. Not because of the long road ahead, but because of what's going on inside us.

- Worrying about the unknown.
- Fear of messing up, judgement, or rejection.
- Overthinking everything, leading to paralysis by perfectionism.
- Waiting until it's perfect, which never comes.

We can try this together today

- **Name what's holding you back:** Choose one thing you've been avoiding, something that lingers in your mind. Now, give it a name – is it a feeling, a situation, a person?
- **Break it down:** Jot down three tiny actions. Nothing fancy, just something simple and doable.
- **Take one step:** Just one. Doesn't matter how small. Once you move, the momentum will build, and the fear will start to lose its grip.

> ***"Life can only be understood backwards; but it must be lived forwards."***
> — **Søren Kierkegaard**

The Dao Whispers: What have I been avoiding out of fear, not impossibility, and can I take that first step anyway?

May 3

Leverage Well to Win

The skilled strategist reads the situation and turns timing, tools, terrain, and systems into an edge

善战者，求之于势，不责于人

shàn zhàn zhě, qiú zhī yú shì, bù zé yú rén

Translation: "The skilled strategist seeks advantage from the situation, not from individual effort."
— Sun Tzu, The Art of War (孙子兵法)

This verse from Sun Tzu's Art of War tells us that a clever strategy is not one in which you play the hero or go head-to-head with the problem. It's one in which you assess the situation and use it to your advantage.

势 (shì) is the art of momentum, positioning and influence. At its best, it multiplies the effect of every action you take. Think of it like surfing: you don't fight the wave, you ride it.

Leverage what you have at your disposal, including alliances, systems, timing, and tools, to extend your reach and amplify your results. Don't confuse strategy with doing more. It is about doing what counts and making what you do go further.

The meaning of 势 (shì)

- **Positioning:** Gain strategic advantage by securing high-leverage ground. This could mean being first to market, owning critical assets or creating a winner-takes-all dynamic.
- **Momentum:** Move with the current, not against it. Ride larger forces like policy shifts, economic trends, or changes in consumer behaviour to accelerate progress.
- **Influence:** Shape perceptions, narratives, or systems to align with your goals and shift the playing field in your favour.
- **Adaptability:** Respond quickly to change. Reposition when needed to sidestep risks and ride the next wave of opportunity.

What it teaches us

1. **Business**

- **Market positioning:** Identify and capture emerging trends or niches in which the organisation holds an advantage.
- **Resource allocation:** Double down in areas with high potential and a clear right to win, backed by core capabilities, or favourable timing.

2. **Strategy (Military, Political, Organisational)**

- **Geopolitical strategy:** Nations cultivate *shì* by forging alliances, securing critical resources, and shaping dominant narratives on the global stage.
- **Organisational strategy:** Leaders build *shì* by setting clear priorities, aligning teams around value-creating goals, and embedding strong operating rhythms, incentives, and decision-making models.

3. **Personal Life**

- **Career navigation:** Position yourself in rising fields. Proactively build the skills, networks, and reputation that generate pull.
- **Time key decisions:** Make the biggest impact by choosing the right moment to act. That might mean switching careers, starting something new, or learning new skills when the timing is right.

> ***"If you're not working hard on the right things, working hard will only make things worse."***
> — **Ray Dalio**

The Dao Whispers

- Are you actively leveraging your networks, capabilities, and timing to multiply your impact, or are you still relying on effort alone?
- Am I investing energy where it truly matters, or am I pushing hard in the wrong direction?

May 4

Take the Olive Branch Before It Turns into A Stick

Sometimes the first offer is the best one

敬酒不吃，吃罚酒

jìng jiǔ bù chī, chī fá jiǔ

Translation: "Decline the drink that came with a polite offer, and you'll be made to accept the drink that comes with a penalty."
— Traditional Chinese proverb

Every now and then, someone extends a hand – a gentle ask, an olive branch, or advice meant to save you trouble down the road. You can reject it, that doesn't necessarily make you strong or independent, it simply closes a door that may not open again.

It's not about being a pushover, overcompromising, or not asserting what's right for you. It's about recognising when grace, compromise, or a gentle nudge is your best option before things turn sour, especially when you have very few options on the table and working with the person is inevitable. Also, life has a funny way of circling back with lessons, often far less pleasant the second time.

What it teaches us

- **Take good advice early**: A mentor's tip today might save you from harsher judgement or consequences in the future.
- **Choose diplomacy early:** Accepting a respectful olive branch can avoid messy escalations later.
- **Read the room:** Sometimes, saying yes to a small ask preserves your ability to negotiate, or walk away on your own terms.

"Compromise is the best and cheapest lawyer."
— Robert Louis Stevenson

The Dao Whispers: Am I being strong, or just stubborn? Is this really about what's right, or about how it was offered?

May 5

Better a Turtle Than a Traffic Cone

It's fine to crawl, just don't stop dead

不怕慢，就怕站

bù pà màn, jiù pà zhàn

Translation: "Don't be anxious if you're moving slowly, but do worry if you're standing still."
— Traditional Chinese proverb

You might not be moving as quickly as you'd like, but that's okay. The real problem is stopping completely.

Saving money, getting healthier, or figuring out your next step in life is proof that momentum matters more than speed. Even if it's only one tiny little step forward, that still beats standing still.

You don't need to run the whole race today. Just keep putting one foot in front of the other.

What it teaches us

- **A slow start beats not starting:** A slow start still beats waiting for the "perfect time" to begin.
- **Small habits add up:** A 10-minute workout is better than none. It's about staying in motion, not being perfect.
- **Every skill is a stepping stone:** Updating your skills or exploring new interests can keep your career moving, even if change feels far off.

"What stands in the way becomes the way."
— **Marcus Aurelius**

The Dao Whispers

- Are you stuck not because of real obstacles, but because of fear or doubt?
- What's one small step you can take today, just to keep moving?

May 6

Stop Carrying Water in a Leaky Basket

Hard work means nothing if the setup's wrong

竹篮打水一场空

zhú lán dǎ shuǐ yī chǎng kōng

Translation: "If you use a bamboo basket to fetch water, you'll end up with nothing."
— Traditional Chinese proverb

Picture this: you're scooping water from a river, running hard to carry it home, only to watch every drop leak out through the holes in your basket. By the time you arrive, you've got nothing to show for all that sweat. This proverb is a reminder of what happens when we work hard on the wrong thing, with the wrong tools, in the wrong way.

Sometimes the smartest thing you can do isn't push harder, but pause and ask ***if this is even the right way.***

What it teaches us

- **Effort needs the right setup**: Hard work alone isn't enough. You need the right tools, timing, and foundation to see results.
- **Look beyond yourself**: If something keeps falling apart, don't rush to blame yourself. Step back and examine the system or approach.
- **Pause to pivot**: Know when to reassess and adjust your path. Taking a deliberate step back to weigh your options is what makes a pivot possible.

> ***"Insanity is doing the same thing over and over and expecting different results."***
> — Often attributed to **Albert Einstein**

The Dao Whispers

What if the problem isn't you, but the basket you're using?

May 7

Dream Big, But Keep Your Feet on the Ground

Castles in the sky look pretty… until gravity reminds you they were never real

脚踏实地

jiǎo tà shí dì

Translation: "Keep your feet firmly planted on the ground."
— Traditional Chinese proverb

Big dreams are wonderful but dreams alone won't build anything you can stand on. In the East, elders often tell ambitious young people to keep their feet planted and to stay grounded, not to crush their spirit, but to stop them from floating too high without a solid base to stand on.

To **脚踏实地** (jiǎo tà shí dì) does not mean that you have to think small. It simply means to balance big vision with wise, realistic pragmatism and persistence. Castles in the sky may look beautiful, but it takes one strong step after another to build something that lasts.

What it teaches us

- **Dream boldly but act steadily:** Big goals need pragmatic plans and consistent action. Without actions, a plan remains a plan.
- **Be here now:** Focus on the step in front of you, it's the only one that gets you closer to where you want to go.
- **Ground your plans in reality:** Vision without execution is just a fantasy with a nice paint job, or a pretty PowerPoint.

> ***"Many people admit that knowledge without experience is useless, but what is even more frustrating is that even if there is knowledge and wisdom but not action, everything is still empty talk."***
> — **John D. Rockefeller,** *Letters to His Son*

The Dao Whispers: Am I taking real, solid steps or stuck in wishful thinking? What's the next small action that turns my dream into something real?

May 8

Preparation Beats Panic

Hugging Buddha's feet in hope for last-minute miracles rarely works

临时抱佛脚

lín shí bào fó jiǎo

Translation: "Hugging Buddha's legs in hope for divine help at the eleventh hour."
— Traditional Chinese proverb

Some lessons only hit when it's already too late.

You skip the prep, tell yourself you'll get to it, and then suddenly it's go-time, and that familiar wave of panic sets in.

This proverb captures that moment when we reach for help at the last minute, hoping that a miracle can somehow make up for lost time.

Well, of course, sometimes we get lucky. But most of the time, we don't.

Preparation is not glamorous. It's invisible, often thankless...and it's lots of hard work. But when the pressure hits, it's what lets you breathe, focus, and show up strong.

> ***"Give me six hours to prepare a speech and I will spend the first four checking my email."***
> — Not Lincoln, but very real today

The Dao Whispers

- Am I trying to skip the boring part, and hoping it'll just work out?
- What small prep today could save me from panicking later?
- If I don't start now, will my future self regret it?

May 9

The Jade Was Once Just a Rock

Every cut, every grind brings you closer to yourself

玉不琢，不成器

yù bù zhuó, bù chéng qì

Translation: "The jade needs to first be carved, for it to become a gem."
— Traditional Chinese proverb

Have you ever felt worn down by the grind, wondering if all this effort will ever amount to anything real?

You're not alone. Even the strongest question the point of it all when progress feels invisible. Sometimes it feels like building IKEA furniture without the instructions, only later do you see what it was meant to be.

This saying tells us that raw jade, however precious, is still only a stone. Its true value stays hidden until it's carved, polished, and refined through pressure and friction.

In the same way, our struggles, mistakes, and daily efforts aren't meaningless. They mould us, they polish our rough edges, and they turn us into who we're meant to be.

Nietzsche once wrote, "**Become who you are.**"

Not as a gentle suggestion, but as a challenge to endure the sculpting process life demands. The shaping. The breaking. The becoming.

> ***"Nothing splendid has ever been achieved except by those who dared believe that something inside them was superior to circumstance."***
> — **Bruce Barton**

The Dao Whispers: What part of me is still unpolished? Can I trust the process, even when it feels slow or unclear?

May 10

Don't Count on Luck Twice

The story of a man who waited by the tree stump for a rabbit to run into it again

守株待兔

shǒu zhū dài tù

Translation: "Waiting by the tree stump for another rabbit."
— From the texts of Han Feizi

The Story

A farmer once saw a rabbit dash across a field, crash into a tree stump, and die. It was pure luck. A free meal.

Thrilled by his luck, the farmer stopped working and waited by the stump for another rabbit to come.

But no rabbit came. His crops went to waste, and he went hungry.

It's a funny story, but it reflects a very real mistake. When we rely on a lucky break to happen again without putting in effort, we set ourselves up for disappointment. Just because something worked once doesn't mean it will work again, especially if we stop doing the work that sustains us.

"Hope is not a strategy."
— **Vince Lombardi**

The Dao Whispers: Lightning rarely strikes the same spot twice, especially if we stand still. Luck plays a role, but it is no substitute for action. If nothing is showing up, maybe it's time to take the first step and make something happen.

May 11

The Wisdom of Wu Wei

Laozi thought stepping back can sometimes be the best move

无为而治

wú wéi ér zhì

Translation: "Govern by doing nothing (unnatural)."
— Laozi (老子), Dao De Jing (道德经)

Laozi's concept of wú wéi (无为) does not mean literally doing nothing; it is allowing things to unfold without force. It's the **art of non-interference:** stepping back, trusting the process, and letting things take their natural course.

In leadership, this means resisting the urge to control everything. A wise leader doesn't micromanage. Instead, they create the space for others to grow, take ownership, and rise on their own.

This principle makes practical sense as:

- Trying to control too much often backfires.
- Micromanaging kills creativity and motivation.
- Interfering too often makes others stop taking responsibility.

What it teaches us

- **Don't force it:** Work with your natural strengths and timing. If everything feels like a struggle, maybe you're pushing in the wrong direction.
- **In crisis, pause before reacting:** When things get tough, take a moment to breathe and think before jumping into action.
- **Leadership style is contextual:** Give direction when people are inexperienced, coach as they gain confidence, and over time provide autonomy and empowerment as they grow in skill and confidence. Delegate not just to show trust, but to scale impact. Resist the urge to micromanage.

"Music is the space between the notes."
— **Claude Debussy**

The Dao Whispers: Can I take a step back, stop trying to force things, and let life take its course?

Skill/Will Matrix: The Talent Management Cheat Sheet

Leadership is contextual. You can flex your style to match the individual needs of each team member – or design systems that support and unlock the full potential of everyone, from senior executives to interns.

High Will

High Will / Low Skill **Action:** Provide coaching, shadowing, and training to accelerate learning	**High Skill / High Will** **Action:** Mentor, empower and delegate for full unlock - then let them run
Low Skill / Low Will **Action:** Back-to-basics – clear goals, structured support, patient guidance	**High Skill / Low Will** **Action**: Uncover & remove motivation barrier – misaligned incentives, boredom, burnout

High Skill

The idea is simple: The goal is to help people grow into the top-right quadrant **(High Skill / High Will)**. Sometimes that means building skills; other times it means reigniting motivation. With the right coaching and context, you unlock the full potential of the talent, and the team.

What each talent archetype needs

- **High Skill, High Will:** Experienced and motivated. Give them mentorship, empowerment, and delegation. They are your scale levers.
- **High Will, Low Skill:** Enthusiastic but inexperienced. Provide coaching, training, and opportunities to learn quickly.
- **High Skill, Low Will:** Capable but disengaged. Investigate barriers – misaligned incentives, boredom, burnout – and address morale directly.
- **Low Skill, Low Will:** Lacking both capability and drive. Requires significant investment: structured training, clear expectations, and patient support.

(Adapted from the Skill/Will framework originally developed by Hersey & Blanchard.)

May 12

Sun Tzu's Five Pillars of Strategy

A timeless blueprint for making every move count: path, timing, terrain, leadership, and method

道、天、地、将、法

dào, tiān, dì, jiàng, fǎ

Translation: "The Art of War is governed by five elements: the Way, Heaven, Earth, the Commander, and the Method."
— Sun Tzu (孙子), The Art of War (孙子兵法)

Strategy isn't just one clever move, it's pulling together many moving parts that work in sync.

Sun Tzu, the master of strategic thought, laid out five universal principles that shape success in war, business, leadership, and life.

1. **道 (dào), The Way: The Vision**
   Refers to the shared purpose of the people, and their alignment with the leader's purpose When people are aligned, their collective will is stronger than any individual force, becoming the multiplier every great strategist needs.
2. **天 (tiān), Heaven: Timing and Seasons**
   This represents natural forces or external conditions such as climate, cycles, timing, and sometimes, fate. Like a farmer watching the weather, a strategist must sense the right moment; when to pause, shift, or strike.
3. **地 (dì), Earth: Terrain & Conditions**
   Know your environment – physical, geographical, emotional, or social – in other words, your terrain. Your surroundings shape your options, define your range of motion, and influence your strategic positioning: where to stand, retreat, lead, or lure. Position is leverage.
4. **将 (jiàng), General: Leadership**
   Great strategy needs great leadership that is built on wisdom, integrity, courage, discipline, and compassion. Good leaders inspire trust and bring people together through a shared vision, and lead with clarity and respect.

5. 法 **(fǎ), Law: Method, Discipline and Systems**

   Even the best intent fails without structure. Systems, logistics, training, and clear rules, i.e., your operating model; allow teams to move as one. Discipline builds consistency, structure builds scale, and scale leads to sustainability.

> ***"Everything in war is very simple, but the simplest thing is difficult."***
>
> — **Carl von Clausewitz, *On War***

The Dao Whispers: A move without the five elements checked is a gamble. Purpose, timing, terrain, leadership, structure... which is your weakest link right now?

May 13

You Don't Need Einstein to Fry an Egg

Use the right tool for the right problem

兵来将挡，水来土掩

bīng lái jiàng dǎng, shuǐ lái tǔ yǎn

Translation: "When soldiers come, send generals to block them; when water rises, use earth to contain it."
— Traditional Chinese proverb

When crisis hits, it's easy to panic and scramble... doing everything but the one thing that might actually work.

This old Chinese saying reminds us to match the response to the problem. If there's a flood, grab sandbags not a megaphone. If it's a battle, send a general not a marching band. In other words, pair the right tools with the right people for the problem at hand.

What it teaches us

- **Tackle crunch time at work strategically:** When facing a tight deadline, **prioritise** tasks that move the needle, leverage the right tools to accelerate delivery and **delegate** to scale your impact.
- **In execution:** Match the right people and tools to the tasks. A simple, fit-for-purpose tool often beats a complex one.
- **In communication:** Tailor the message to the audience. A board needs clarity, a team needs detail, the public needs reassurance.

> ***"It is essential to have good tools, but it is also essential that the tools should be used in the right way."***
> ***— Wallace D. Wattles***

The Dao Whispers: Am I solving the real problem with the right people and tools?

May 14

Your Strategy Laundry List

Ten timeless frameworks every strategist should know

谋定而后动

móu dìng ér hòu dòng

Translation: "Plan thoroughly before taking action."
— Classical Chinese Wisdom

This proverb is simple: don't act until you've thought it through. It echoes Sun Tzu's advice – calculate, assess, and prepare before engaging; and to only move when you have a sound plan.

What it teaches us:

- **Clarity of destination:** Strategy starts with knowing what you want to become when you grow up – aspirations, outcome. Without a clear 'what,' the 'how' is meaningless.
- **Choosing the right map:** Frameworks give structure to your thinking. They don't solve the problem, but they ensure you don't miss blind spots as you plan the route. The "Playing to Win" concepts are among my favourite.
- **Prioritising leverage:** Once you see the full picture, focus on the 20% of the levers that move 80%% of results. Strategy is less about doing more, and more about doubling down where it gives you the highest impact, or returns.

> ***"All models are wrong, but some are useful."***
> — **George Box**

> ***"Structure, structure, structure – structure your problem, structure your solutions... practise structuring everything in your life and it will become intuitive over time."***
> — **Former McKinsey Partner** (anonymous)

The Dao Whispers:
Now, we also hear: **"Which strategic framework do you use?"**
The answer is: **"It depends..."**
It depends on your context: **What are you trying to solve for?**

The Strategy Laundry List

While there's no one-size-fits-all framework, here are ten tools to add to your strategy toolkit.

Scan the Environment

1. **SWOT Analysis**
   Scan internal capabilities vs external conditions of an asset or project. Good first step before committing resources.
   - Defines Strengths, Weaknesses, Opportunities, and Threats
2. **PESTEL Analysis**
   Evaluates macro-environmental trends before making strategic decisions. Critical for global or regulatory-sensitive sectors.
   - Elements: Political, Economic, Social, Technological, Environmental, Legal
3. **Scenario Planning**
   Simulates multiple futures based on uncertainty. Used by S&P 500 companies and top strategists. Excellent in volatile contexts. (recessions, financial crises, trade wars.)
   - **Driving Forces:** Spot the big external trends shaping tomorrow. (Technology shifts, geopolitics, consumer behaviour, regulation)
   - **Critical Uncertainties:** Zero in on the high-impact unknowns. (Will regulation tighten or loosen, will we rebound quickly, or stagnate?)
   - **Scenario Framework:** Use those uncertainties to create a 2×2 map (e.g., Regulation (strict vs loose) × Economic Growth (high vs low))
   - **Narratives:** Give each future a name, storyline, and details to make it feel real.
   - **Strategic Implications:** Stress-test your choices against each world.
   - **Early Signals:** Track leading indicators of which path is emerging.
   - **Robust Responses:** Prepare actions that hold up across futures.

Understand the Market

4. **Porter's Five Forces**

   Best for market entry or expansion. Shows you who holds power in the industry and how tough the game really is.

   - Elements: Threat of **New Entrants**, Bargaining power of **Suppliers**, Bargaining power of **Buyers,** threat of **Substitutes**, and Competitive **Rivalry**

5. **4Ps of Marketing**

   The basics of market strategy: what you sell, how, where, and to whom.

   - **Product:** What you offer and how it creates value.
   - **Price:** How you capture value and signal positioning; customer willingness-to-pay (WTP).
   - **Place:** Where and how your product reaches customers.
   - **Promotion:** How you communicate and persuade.
   - **Positioning** (5th P - bonus): How you differentiate in the customer's mind.

Align the Organisation

6. **McKinsey 7S Framework**

   Helps you ensure that all parts of the organisation are working together, not against each other.

   - Elements: Structure, systems, skills, style, staff, strategy, and shared values

7. **The Strategic Planning Pyramid**

   Clarifies long-term direction before setting tactical actions. Aligns daily action with long-term purpose.

   - Vision → Mission → Goals → KPIs

Design, Choose, Execute

8. **McKinsey's "Rewired" Digital Playbook**

   A blueprint to turn digital ambitions into reality.

   - **A Clear Roadmap:** A clear path for where digital creates value.
   - **Organisation & Operating Model:** Cross-functional, agile teams that cut across silos.
   - **Talent & Capability model:** Build skills, hire right talent, and upskill for digital.

- **Technology:** Modern, scalable, secure tech stack with governance.
- **Data & Analytics:** Treat information as a strategic asset.
- **Adoption & Change management:** Make digital ways of working stick (most fail here).

9. **Playing to Win**
   A practical decision-making framework built around five key choices:
   - **What** is our winning strategy?
   - **Where** will we play?
   - **How** will we win?
   - **What capabilities** must be in place?
   - **What systems** must support those capabilities?
10. **Business Plan Canvas (BMC)**
    A simple **one-page framework** for describing the key building blocks on a single sheet.
    - **Customer Segments:** Who you serve – your target audience.
    - **Value Proposition:** The problem you solve, or the value you deliver.
    - **Channels:** How you reach customers – stores, website, distributors.
    - **Customer Relationships:** How you interact – self-service, community, personal.
    - **Revenue Streams:** How you earn money – sales, subscriptions, ads.
    - **Key Resources:** What you need – people, tech, IP, cash.
    - **Key Activities:** What you must do – manufacturing, marketing, R&D.
    - **Key Partnerships:** Who helps you - suppliers, collaborators, allies.
    - **Cost Structure:** What it costs to run – fixed and variable costs.

May 15

Making Grand Plans and Empty Promises

Drawing a pancake to satisfy hunger

画饼充饥

huà bǐng chōng jī

Translation: "Draw a pancake to satisfy hunger."
— Traditional Chinese proverb

The Story

During a time of political turmoil, the strategist **Lu Yu** served under the Wei or Jin regime, where leaders often made grand promises to calm subordinates without offering real solutions.

At one point, the soldiers were hungry, tired, and losing hope. A general tried to lift their spirits by promising future rewards to promotions, wealth, and comfort.

Lu Yu pulled him aside and said, ***"Making empty promises to tired soldiers is like drawing pancakes for the hungry. They look good, but they can feed no one."***

He made a clear point: words without action do not sustain people. Lu Yu urged the leaders to give real support, not just illusions.

The proverb continues to remind us of the gap that can exist between intention and impact. It highlights the importance of matching words with action, especially when people are looking for real support, not just comforting ideas. Examples of "the drawing of pancakes" in our time:

- Strategy decks with no clear roadmaps, goals, or resources to deliver on them.
- Leadership rhetoric that's yet to be brought to life.
- Corporate "transformation programmes" with no operational follow-through.

> ***"However beautiful the strategy, you should occasionally look at the results."***
> **— Winston Churchill**

The Dao Whispers: Strategy without execution is just ink on paper. To make it real, it needs resources, effort, and the courage to follow through.

May 16

When Plans Forget the World Moves

The man who marked the boat where the sword fell to find it later

刻舟求剑

kè zhōu qiú jiàn

Translation: "Marking the boat to find a lost sword."
— From the Annals of Lü Buwei

The Story

A man from Chu was crossing a river when his sword slipped and sank into the water.

"Don't worry," he said. "I'll find it." He carved a mark on the side of the boat where the sword had fallen.

When the boat reached the shore, he jumped into the river at that spot, forgetting that the boat had moved while the sword stayed behind.

The story pokes fun at rigid thinking: when we stick to one plan or idea even after the situation has completely changed.

What it teaches us

- **Don't freeze your strategy:** Plans need updating when facts change.
- **Match your approach to shifts:** If the environment changes, your approach should probably change too.
- **Beware of 'but this is how we've always done it':** Tradition is not a strategy. What worked before may not necessarily work again under different circumstances.

"No plan survives first contact with the enemy."
— **Helmuth von Moltke the Elder**

The Dao Whispers

- Does my plan assume that the river will always stay still?
- Where am I solving today's problem with yesterday's logic?
- What assumption do I need to test again now?

May 17

First Impressions: Appearance Matters

Appearances may not be everything, but they are the first thing

马靠鞍装，人靠衣装

mǎ kào ān zhuāng, rén kào yī zhuāng

Translation: "A horse relies on its saddle; a person relies on their clothing."
— Traditional Chinese proverb

This proverb reminds us that just like a good saddle makes a horse look even more impressive, the way we dress and carry ourselves shapes how others see us.

Appearances may not be everything, but **they are the *first* thing**. Like it or not, people form first impressions almost instantly.

Research shows that **first impressions form** in as little as **0.01 to 0.5 seconds.** That's why what people see first matters.

- A Princeton study (Willis & Todorov, 2006) found that we make snap judgements on trustworthiness and competence in just **100 milliseconds.**
- Insights from fashion psychology and nonverbal communication show that clothing, grooming, and posture can signal status and confidence in **under half a second.**
- Brain studies reveal that snap emotional responses can occur within **0.01–0.03 seconds**, forming instinctive impressions before thought even begins.

In high-status circles, this effect is amplified. People scan how you show up and silently decide whether you "belong." How you come across and your presence often speaks louder than words.

> ***"Clothes make the man. Naked people have little or no influence on society."***
> — Often attributed to **Mark Twain**

The Dao Whispers: What signals am I sending before I speak, and do they reflect the values I want to be known for?

May 18

The One-Trick Guizhou Donkey

In Guizhou, the donkey can bluff a tiger but only once

黔驴技穷

qián lǘ jì qióng

Translation: "The tricks of the Guizhou donkey are exhausted."
— Traditional Chinese proverb

The Story

Long ago, in the mountainous province of Guizhou, there were no donkeys. One day, a man brought one into the region and let it roam free.

A tiger, having never seen such a creature, was startled by the donkey's loud braying and kept his distance. But over time, the tiger observed and waited.

He realised the donkey had no strength, no speed, and no real defence. It had one trick; it made loud noises. Once the bray lost its magic, the tiger attacked and ate it.

You can fake it once, but you can't fake it forever. Sure, a clever trick or bold first impression might get you ahead early. But to stay ahead? That takes real skill, real value, and real work.

"What got you here won't get you there."
— **Marshall Goldsmith**

The Dao Whispers: If my go-to move stopped working, would I be ready with something new or just stuck repeating the past?

May 19

Five Traits That Win Wars and Hearts

According to Sun Tzu, they are wisdom, trustworthiness, benevolence, courage, discipline

将者，智、信、仁、勇、严也

jiàng zhě, zhì, xìn, rén, yǒng, yán yě

Translation: "A general possesses wisdom, trustworthiness, benevolence, courage, and discipline."
— Sun Tzu, The Art of War (孙子兵法)

Sun Tzu said the best generals share five immovable traits – wisdom, trustworthiness, benevolence, courage, discipline – which form a blueprint for enduring leadership and strategic strength:

- **Wisdom**, 智 (zhì): Seeing the bigger picture. The ability to judge clearly and think strategically.
- **Trustworthiness**, 信 (xìn): Being someone others can count on. Say what you mean and follow through.
- **Benevolence,** 仁 (rén): Leading with compassion. When people feel cared for, they stand by you.
- **Courage,** 勇 (yǒng): Daring to act when it's risky or uncomfortable, not just when it's easy.
- **Discipline,** 严 (yán): Setting the tone through your actions. Holding yourself and others to high standards, even when it's hard.

What it teaches us

These aren't leadership buzzwords, they're what make people trust you enough to follow you into the fire.

- **Wisdom:** Take a step back and see the whole field before making your move. A wise leader protects the team's energy and avoids wasting time on things that don't move the needle.
- **Trustworthiness:** Be someone your team can count on, especially when it matters most.
- **Benevolence**: Lead with care, not fear. Loyalty grows naturally when people feel seen, respected, and supported.
- **Courage:** If you only act when it's safe, you're not leading, you're waiting. Sometimes, you've got to make the tough calls,

speak up or defend what matters to your team, even when it's inconvenient or lonely.

- **Discipline:** Model excellence. Set the tone through action. Hold yourself and others to high standards, and don't cut corners.

> ***"Leadership is not about being in charge. It is about taking care of those in your charge."***
> — **Simon Sinek**

> ***"Only three things happen naturally in organisations: friction, confusion, and underperformance. Everything else requires leadership."***
> — **Peter Drucker**

The Dao Whispers

- Am I leading with strength and compassion?
- In difficult times, do I choose what's easy, or what's right?

May 20

The More You Hide, the More You Reveal

There are no three hundred taels of silver buried here

此地无银三百两

cǐ dì wú yín sān bǎi liǎng

Translation: "There are no three hundred taels of silver (buried) here."
— Traditional Chinese proverb

The Story

A man buries three hundred taels of silver in a secret spot to hide it. Worried someone might find it, **he places a sign at the location that reads:**

"There are no three hundred taels of silver here."

A passerby, seeing the sign, immediately became suspicious and started to dig. Lo and behold, his spade hit something solid, and a few scoops later, the buried silver gleamed in the light.

The man's attempt to hide his treasure only drew attention to it and ended up exposing his secret.

"Never miss a good chance to shut up."
— **Will Rogers**

The Dao Whispers

- **Self-sabotage:** Am I overcompensating to hide my flaws, and end up sabotaging myself?
- **Reflect before acting:** Do I take a step back and reflect before action, or react in a way that betrays my intent?
- **Reservation price:** Does my behaviour reveal my true intentions or reservation price (the point at which I'd walk away)?

May 21

How to Lose Even When You're Ahead

The ancient story of drawing legs on a snake and losing the prize

画蛇添足

huà shé tiān zú

Translation: "To draw a snake and add feet to it"
— Traditional Chinese proverb

The Story

During the Warring States period (475–221 BCE), a group of people in the state of Chu were holding a ritual to offer wine to their ancestors. After the ceremony, there was a jug of wine left, and they decided to share it among themselves. To make it fair, they agreed to hold a contest: each person would draw a snake on the ground, and whoever finished first would win the wine.

One man drew his snake quickly and finished first. Proud of his speed, he looked around and saw the others still working. To show off, he decided to embellish his drawing by adding feet to the snake, saying, **"I have time to make it even better!"**

But another man finished soon after, with a plain, proper snake.

"A snake doesn't have legs," he said, and claimed the wine. The first man lost not for being slow, but for doing too much.

> ***"The essence of strategy is choosing what not to do."***
> — **Michael Porter**

The Dao Whispers

- Am I adding value?
- Do I know when to stop, or do I keep going just to prove a point?
- Would the outcome be better if I did nothing?

May 22

The Rabbit Who Never Gets Caught

A clever rabbit always prepares three burrows. One to live in, one to escape predators, and one as a backup

狡兔三窟

jiǎo tù sān kū

Translation: "A cunning rabbit has three burrows."
— Traditional Chinese proverb

The Story

This idiom originates from the *Strategies of the Warring States* era and is famously associated with the strategist **Feng Xuan**.

To persuade Lord Mengchang of Qi to hire him, Feng Xuan said:

> ***"A clever rabbit always prepares three burrows. One to live in, one to escape predators, and a third as a backup. If you, my lord, have only one plan or path, how can you survive in a treacherous world?"***

Impressed, Lord Mengchang hired him. Feng Xuan later proved invaluable by helping him escape political danger and regain influence through strategic foresight.

What it teaches us

- Create multiple exits, don't rely on just one.
- Diversify your strategy. Always have a plan B... and a plan C.
- Create options: having choices strengthens your position.

> ***"The person with the most options often holds the most power."***
> — **Nassim Nicholas Taleb**

The Dao Whispers: Am I putting all my eggs into one basket, or do I also build a second and third way out?

May 23

Problem-Solving: Address the Root Cause

Don't steal bricks from one wall to save another

拆东墙补西墙

chāi dōng qiáng bǔ xī qiáng

Translation: "Tear down the east wall to repair the west wall."
— Traditional Chinese proverb

The Story

Once upon a time, a poor man lived in a house with crumbling walls. When the western wall began to collapse, he lacked the money to repair it.

So, he tore bricks from the east wall to patch the west.

For a moment, it looked fixed until a storm came and brought the east wall down. Now both sides were broken.

He hadn't solved the problem; he had only shifted it.

The man in the fable wasn't progressing, he was creating the illusion of progress by shifting resources, attention, or energy without resolving the root cause.

Contemporary equivalents:

- Taking on debt to pay debt.
- Reassigning budget from a critical function to plug another.
- Overloading high performers while avoiding systemic fixes.
- Prioritising firefighting over root-cause resolution.
- Taking supplements instead of changing a poor lifestyle.

> ***"If I had an hour to solve a problem, I'd spend 55 minutes thinking about the problem, and 5 minutes thinking about solutions."***
> — **Albert Einstein**

The Dao Whispers

- Don't just reallocate. Rearchitect and resolve the root cause.
- A short-term patch often creates long-term cracks.
- Is there a hole in your life that you are plugging, while creating another?

May 24

No Plan Survives First Contact

Rigid strategy risks shattering like glass

水无常形，兵无常势

shuǐ wú cháng xíng, bīng wú cháng shì

Translation: "Water has no fixed shape; warfare has no constant strategy."
— Sun Tzu, The Art of War (孙子兵法)

Sun Tzu reminds us that strategy isn't about rigid plans, it's about adapting like water. He compared it to water, which flows, bends, and reshapes itself to fit its surroundings. In the same way, soldiers and strategists must stay flexible and adjust to whatever the moment calls for.

Whether you're in battle, running a business, or navigating life, the message is clear... stick too firmly to one plan and you risk breaking it, or yourself. Stay flexible and adaptable, and you can move around obstacles and maybe even shape the path ahead.

What it teaches us

- **Strategy must be dynamic**: Anticipate shifts in markets, people, or relationships early, and adjust before you're cornered.
- **Structure should follow flow:** Design your operating model – structure, tools, resources, and ways of working – to enable agility and progress, not block them.
- **Act before things get stuck:** Trust your instincts. You don't need perfect information to make a move. Often, the earlier you act, the more influence you have.

> ***"To become an outstanding leader, we must make ourselves a strategic thinker, not just a designer of means. We also have to avoid confining ourselves to the established plans."***
> — **John D. Rockefeller** (Letter to His Son)

The Dao Whispers: Do I adjust my strategy based on the situation that merits the tweak, or do I cling to a plan that is no longer fit-for-purpose?

May 25

Looting a Burning House: Will You Grab or Give?

Is there such a thing as an ethical opportunist?

趁火打劫

chèn huǒ dǎ jié

Translation: "Loot a burning house."
— Thirty-Six Stratagems (三十六计)

The proverb literally means "to loot a burning house." It paints a vivid picture of taking advantage of chaos to get what you want. It sounds ruthless, and it can be. Originally, it referred to rival states attacking others when they were already in crisis.

But there's a deeper layer of meaning. In every crisis, there's also opportunity. When others are panicking or stepping back, those who stay calm and act smart can move ahead.

It doesn't mean you should exploit others unfairly. But it does mean that timing matters. In business, careers, and life, those who know how to spot weak moments such as a gap in the market, a change in leadership, a delay by competitors, can step in and win ground ethically.

What it teaches us

- **Support friends in need**: When a friend faces hardship, like job loss or heartbreak, offer to help rather than taking advantage of them.
- **Uphold integrity in crises:** During community emergencies, like a natural disaster, contribute to relief efforts instead of profiting, for example, price-gouging essentials or critical healthcare supplies.
- **Reflect on ethical choices**: When tempted to exploit a situation, like a coworker's mistake, perhaps choose to help or stay neutral and keep your moral compass intact.

"The time is always right to do what is right."
— **Martin Luther King Jr.**

The Dao Whispers: When have you seen someone exploit a crisis? How might compassion have changed the outcome?

May 26

Can Memory Lose Its Sting?

When you can remember without reliving the past

回首向来萧瑟处，
归去，也无风雨也无晴

huí shǒu xiàng lái xiāo sè chù, guī qù, yě wú fēng yǔ yě wú qíng

Translation: "Looking back at the desolate place I came from, I return, with neither wind nor rain, nor clear skies."
— Su Shi (苏轼)

Picture Su Shi, poet, and scholar (no, not the one with salmon and wasabi), stripped of everything he once held dear. Years of exile, loneliness so deep it laid beside him like an uninvited guest.

One day he turns back to those memories. The storm is gone, the rain has stopped, the wind is silent. Even the sunshine is nowhere to be found. No drama, no sting, no glory; just silence. There comes a point when you realise pain and joy are nothing more than passing weather. When the mind no longer protests "This is terrible" or "This is wonderful" and simply says "This is."

What it teaches us

- **Don't ride the emotional rollercoaster:** Life is full of highs and lows, but you don't have to ***become*** the rollercoaster. Take the small ride, but get off it when it stops and don't go on the next round.
- **Look back without getting stuck:** Hard times lose their power when you stop replaying them in a loop. Reflect, but don't overindulge. Reliving only keeps you trapped.
- **"This too shall pass" is your superpower:** Good or bad, nothing lasts forever. Ride the waves instead of resisting them, and you'll discover strength in the eye of the storm.

> ***"The real voyage of discovery consists not in seeking new landscapes, but in having new eyes."***
> — **Marcel Proust**

The Dao Whispers: Ever look back at your toughest times and realise you're still here, fully in the present? The past loses its hold on you when you stop calling it "good" or "bad." Just let the past ***be***.

May 27

A Featherless Phoenix Loses Its Magic

Don't lean on someone else's reputation to feel worthy

没毛的凤凰不如鸡

méi máo de fèng huáng bù rú jī

Translation: "A featherless phoenix is worse than a chicken."
— Traditional Chinese proverb

Sure, a phoenix is impressive with feathers on. But pluck them out and it's just another bird, maybe worse than a chicken. The same goes for titles, brands, or status symbols. They can make anyone look important, but remove them and you see what's real.

This proverb reminds us that sometimes, it's not the person who's impressive, but the title or brand they're wrapped in. Job titles, big-name logos, or fancy labels can make someone look powerful. But when the title is removed, what's actually left?

What it teaches us

- Looking impressive doesn't mean much if there's nothing real behind it.
- Titles come and go. What you can do and who you are underneath are what stay with you.
- Don't measure your own worth by borrowed status. Build something of your own.

> ***"It never ceases to amaze me: we all love ourselves more than other people, but care more about their opinion than our own."***
> **— Marcus Aurelius**

The Dao Whispers: Are you standing tall on your own or leaning on a borrowed identity, and if the image were stripped away would your confidence stay? And hey, maybe I am a featherless phoenix today. That's fine. I'll grow new feathers.

May 28

Confucius' Five Pillars of Character

Five habits that never go out of style: kindness, fairness, respect, wisdom, and trust

仁、义、礼、智、信

rén yì lǐ zhì xìn

Translation: "Benevolence, justice, propriety, wisdom, integrity."
— Confucius (孔子)

Trends change. Laws change. What's "acceptable" changes. More than two millennia ago, Confucius mapped out the Five Constants (五常, wǔ cháng). They remain a framework for character that works in life and leadership today. They're not just principles, but compass points to lean on when life presents you with difficult choices.

1. **仁 (rén): Benevolence, compassion, humaneness**
   The core of Confucian ethics: love and empathy for others.
2. **义 (yì): Righteousness, justice, moral integrity**
   Doing what is right, not what is convenient or self-serving.
3. **礼 (lǐ): Propriety, ritual, decorum**
   Respect for social order, customs, and appropriate conduct.
4. **智 (zhì): Wisdom, insight, understanding**
   Exercising discernment and making thoughtful and sound judgements.
5. **信 (xìn): Trustworthiness, faithfulness, integrity**
   Being reliable, keeping one's word, and acting with sincerity.

The Dao Whispers

- Have I treated others with compassion and empathy? (仁)
- Were my actions guided by justice and moral clarity? (义)
- Have I upheld respect and propriety in how I behaved? (礼)
- Have I been thoughtful and discerning in my choices? (智)
- Have I kept my promises and acted with integrity? (信)

May 29

Be at Peace with Who You Are

When you know your own worth, you don't need others to validate it

自知不自现，自爱不自贵

zì zhī bù zì xiàn, zì ài bù zì guì

Translation: "Know yourself without the need to flaunt; love yourself without needing to exalt yourself."
— Traditional Chinese proverb

The people who really know their self-worth are often secure and have no need to keep talking about themselves or showing off. They have nothing to prove.

This proverb reflects a subtle kind of confidence, one that doesn't chase likes, praise, or attention.

- 自知不自现 (zì zhī bù zì xiàn): Understand your strengths and weaknesses without needing to flaunt them.
- 自爱不自贵 (zì ài bù zì guì): Value and respect yourself without exaggerating your own importance.

What it teaches us

- **Self-awareness**: Pay attention to your thoughts and feelings throughout the day without judging them.
- **Spotting narcissism**: Notice when conversations revolve around self-importance, in others or in your own behaviour. Is someone constantly talking about themselves to feel important? Or do I sometimes fall into that pattern of self-glorification and self-grandiosity?
- **Stand firm in your worth:** You don't need others' approval to know your worth.

> ***"Humility is not thinking less of yourself, but thinking of yourself less."***
> — **C.S. Lewis**

The Dao Whispers

- In what ways do you still chase validation from others?

How can I develop a sense of self-respect that doesn't rely on approval or recognition from other people?

May 30

Don't Trim the Weeds, Uproot Them

Some problems need pulling out, not just a tidy trim

斩草除根

zhǎn cǎo chú gēn

Translation: "Cut the grass and remove the roots."
— Traditional Chinese proverb

This Chinese saying is blunt for a reason. If you only trim the surface, the weeds will grow back. If you want lasting peace, you have to deal with the root, not just the symptoms.

It applies to life too. Toxic habits. Messy friendships. Hidden resentment. The people and things that drain you little by little, until you don't even notice how tired you are. You can keep giving chances, making excuses, hoping for better. Or you can be honest and end what needs to end.

What it teaches us

- **Face what's draining you:** The situation you keep rationalising? Call it what it is, it's not going to magically get better.
- **Fix the root, not the symptoms:** Fixes are like duct tape, they hold things together for a while, but the real problem's still lurking underneath. It's best to stop slapping on band-aids and dig out the root, only then will the issue go away.
- **Know when it's done:** Letting go is hard. But sometimes you just ***know*** it's over, you're just not ready to admit it yet.

Charlie Munger, a legendary investor once said,

> "The toxic people, who were trying to fool you, aren't reliable or aren't meeting their commitments – **the great lesson of life is: get them the hell out of your life. And do it fast. Do it fast...** yes, yeah, I don't mind a little tact, or even a little financial cost, but the question is: getting them the hell out of your life..."

The Dao Whispers: When someone shows you who they are, ***believe it.*** Who are you still giving another chance, knowing they've already shown you who they are?

May 31

No Rivals Beside the Throne

Why survival requires vigilance and allies

卧榻之侧，岂容他人鼾睡

wò tà zhī cè, qǐ róng tā rén hān shuì

Translation: "By my bedside, how can I allow another to snore?"
— Attributed to Wu Zetian, China's only female emperor
Note: This may sound uncomfortable. One need not endorse the yang within the yin, but it is important to recognise that it exists.

Power rarely sleeps peacefully. This proverb, linked with Wu Zetian, captures the ruthlessness of defending one's domain. You cannot allow threats to linger at your side because they will eventually wake up and move against you.

But there is another layer to the lesson. Wolves do not hunt alone. They move in packs, first eliminating outside rivals, then turning on each other to fight for dominance. The strongest wolf is not always the fiercest. It is often the one who builds enough alliances to avoid being isolated and taken down first. In courts, corporations, or politics, the lone genius who ignores the need for allies often does not even make it to the final fight.

What it teaches us

- **Defend your turf:** A leader cannot afford to let dangerous rivals nest too close. Distance matters.
- **Allies matter:** The most talented without allies are often the first to fall. Strength without support rarely survives.
- **Beware the pack:** Eliminate your competitors too quickly, and you may find your allies turning on you. Strategy is as much about balance as it is about power. And if you are the lone wolf, beware the pack who will take you out, then fight among themselves to be the alpha.

"The ends justify the means."
— Niccolò Machiavelli

The Dao Whispers: Am I guarding my space wisely, building alliances while watching the pack, or am I the lone wolf, admired yet easily expendable?

JUNE

德

dé

Meaning of 德 (dé):

- Virtue
- Moral integrity
- Kindness
- Compassion
- Ethical conduct

In Chinese wisdom, 德 (dé) is not just about looking good on the outside, but about the core of who you are. It's the compass that guides your choices when no one is watching. It shows in how you treat others, how you carry yourself, and what you stand for. To live with 德 (dé) means doing what is right even when it is hard, especially when it goes unseen. 德 doesn't chase success alone; it seeks to lift the world a little higher.

Living with 德 (dé) means:

- **Lead with kindness:** Let compassion guide your actions. Small acts of compassion add up and it usually means a lot to the receiver – a kind word, a small gift, a helping hand.
- **Do the right thing:** Even if it's hard. And especially when no one notices, it's what you then choose to do.
- **Be real and honest:** Let your actions match your word.
- **Stay grounded:** Choose to stay calm, even when things get messy.
- **Lift others up:** Just as you have benefitted by being lifted by others, you can keep the ripple going by paying it forward.

June 1

When Darkness Feels Endless

Struggle cracks you open so you can grow

苦尽甘来

kǔ jìn gān lái

Translation: "After bitterness comes sweetness."
— Traditional Chinese proverb

Every rough season feels endless while you're in it. But life has a way of coming around, even if it takes longer than we'd like.

Hard times crack us open, strip away illusions, and teach things comfort never could.

Darkness is not the end of your story. Like seeds underground, we break apart before we grow. When you've gone through enough struggle, easier times often follow; not because you've earned it, but because that's how life flows. Seasons move on, but so do struggles.

What it teaches us

- **Stay hopeful in relationships**: Some bonds heal slowly, but time and care can change more than anger ever will.
- **In life's detours**: It's in losing your way that you'll begin to find yourself.
- **In struggle, keep going**: Even if it's in tiny steps, keep going, keep showing up. The hard work now will lay the ground for better days ahead.

> ***"Sometimes when you're in a dark place - you think you've been buried, but, actually, you've been planted."***
> — **Christine Caine**

The Dao Whispers: When you're knee-deep in the hard parts of life, can you trust that this season will pass?

June 2

Friends Who Tell You the Truth

Like bitter medicine, truthful words may sting but they can also heal

忠言逆耳利于行，良药苦口利于病

zhōng yán nì ěr lì yú xíng, liáng yào kǔ kǒu lì yú bìng

Translation: "Honest advice may be unpleasant to hear, but it benefits one's conduct; good medicine tastes bitter, but it cures the illness."
— Traditional Chinese proverb

Would you rather have a friend who tells you that you look silly in an outfit, or one who says you look fantastic only to find out later the outfit made you look ridiculous?

The people who genuinely care about you aren't always the ones patting you on the back. Sometimes, they're the ones putting down the sugar and handing you a spoonful of truth you'd rather push away. Like bitter medicine, their honesty might sting, but it's what helps you heal and grow.

The real danger isn't the friend who tells you what you don't want to hear. It's the ones who nod, smile, and let you march straight into a ditch without saying a word. Or someone who'd let you stroll into a black-tie event in Mayfair or Manhattan looking like a silly pumpkin.

> ***"Leaders who don't listen will eventually be surrounded by people who have nothing to say."***
> — **Andy Stanley**

The Dao Whispers

- Who in my life speaks hard truths with care, and do I listen?
- Am I surrounded by people who reflect my best self, or who help me avoid my blind spots?
- Do I resist truths that sting but could help me grow, or do I face them with courage?

June 3

The Mantis That Forgot to Check Its Back

Eyes on the prize is great, until you miss the predator on your tail

螳螂捕蝉，黄雀在后

táng láng bǔ chán, huáng què zài hòu

Translation: "The mantis stalks the cicada, unaware of the oriole behind."
— Traditional Chinese proverb

The Story

A hungry mantis spots a cicada on a branch and moves in for the kill. So focused on its prize, it doesn't see the orange-chested oriole right behind, ready to have it for lunch.

In the end, the hunter becomes the hunted.

This story reminds us that when we get so fixated on what we want, a goal, a win, or a person, we sometimes forget to look around. We stop paying attention to risks, people, or shifts around us. And sometimes, what's really creeping up on us is lost time, people we love, and the things that actually matter.

> ***"Sometimes that light at the end of the tunnel is a train."***
> — Unknown (Attributed to multiple thinkers)

The Dao Whispers: Am I so focused on chasing my prize that I've stopped watching my back?

June 4

Mencius on Human Nature

Why one of China's greatest thinkers believed goodness lives in us all

孟子之道

mèng zǐ zhī dào

Translation: "The Way according to Mencius."

Mencius (孟子 Mèngzǐ), the spiritual heir to Confucius, argued that **every person is born with a natural sense of goodness.** Not perfection or saintliness, but a built-in compass for right and wrong. If we act badly, he said, it's usually because life hardened us or led us astray, not because we were born bad.

Core philosophy: Human nature is inherently good

Mencius described **four moral instincts** that live in all of us:

- **Compassion** – which gives rise to **benevolence** (仁 rén)
- **Shame –** which gives rise to **righteousness** (义 yì)
- **Courtesy** – which gives rise to **propriety** (礼 lǐ)
- **Discernment** - which gives rise to **wisdom** (智 zhì)

When nurtured, these instincts grow into good character and ethical leadership. Mencius believed **great leaders lead by example, not force.** They win hearts with empathy, fairness, and care for the people; and not through fear or control.

Legacy

Mencius's teachings shaped the foundation of Confucian political and ethical thought for over two millennia. His belief in the moral potential of every person influenced **education**, **governance**, **civil service**, and the social values of many countries across East Asia.

Today, people still turn to the core principles that Mencius shared when talking about how to build good character, lead with heart, and understand others better.

Core Teachings of Mencius

Mencius championed four foundational principles for personal and political virtue:

- **Human nature is inherently good (性善 xìng shàn):** Mencius believed all humans are born with the capacity for goodness. When we see bad behaviour, it usually comes from neglect, hurt, or a broken environment; not because people are born bad.
- **Benevolent leadership (仁政 rén zhèng):** He believed rulers should lead by example, not by force. According to him, good leadership is grounded in empathy, justice, and care for the people.
- **Obligation to dissent:** When rulers abandon morality and harm the people, Mencius taught that it is not only a right, but a moral obligation to dissent. Staying silent is complicity in his view... a radical idea for his time.
- **Self-Cultivation and Education**: Becoming a good person or leader doesn't happen by accident. You build on your natural sense of right and wrong through learning, reflection, and discipline.

A Brief Note of Rebuttal

Not everyone agreed. Xunzi, another Confucian thinker, argued that people are born selfish and chaotic, and only strict laws and discipline make them good.

Two visions of humanity, one hopeful and one wary, still echo in today's debates about leadership, education, and politics.

> ***"Good people do not need laws to tell them to act responsibly, while bad people will find a way around the laws."***
> — *Plato*

The Dao Whispers

- Do my actions reflect what I stand for, even when no one is watching?
- Am I putting in the work to grow myself before trying to change others?

When it's uncomfortable, do I still speak the truth and live by it?

June 5

Like an Ostrich with Its Head in the Sand

If I can't see it, it's not there... right?

掩耳盗铃

yǎn ěr dào líng

Translation: "Covering your ears while stealing a bell."
— Traditional Chinese proverb

The Story

Once, there was a man named Fan who tried to steal a giant bell from a wealthy family. But the bell was heavy and noisy. Worried that the sound would draw attention, Fan came up with a plan: he covered his own ears, thinking that if *he* couldn't hear the bell ring, then no one else could either.

Of course, the bell rang, and he was caught.

This idiom became a classic example of self-deception, of pretending something isn't real simply because it's uncomfortable to face.

We all do it in some way. We ignore warning signs in a relationship, deny stress, or put off decisions we know are long overdue. But pretending not to see the truth doesn't make it disappear. It only gives it more time to grow bigger.

> ***"You can ignore reality, but you can't ignore the consequences of ignoring reality."***
> — **Ayn Rand**

The Dao Whispers: Ignoring reality doesn't make it go away, it only makes the wake-up call a little louder. What am I refusing to hear?

June 6

Why Bring a Bazooka to a Chicken Fight?

Not every problem needs the big guns. Save your energy

杀鸡焉用牛刀

shā jī yān yòng niú dāo

Translation: "Why use an ox cleaver to kill a chicken."
— Traditional Chinese proverb

Have you ever used way too much energy on something that really didn't matter? Or reacted so strongly to something small, it left you feeling a little foolish afterward?

Why bring a bazooka to a chicken fight?

It's funny, yes, until we realise that we do it all the time in life, work, or relationships.

Confucius once called out his disciple **Ziyou (子游)** for using overly elaborate rituals (like ceremonial music) to govern a small town. He implies that grand methods are unnecessary for small things, and tasks should be approached with tools or efforts proportionate to their scale.

What it teaches us

- **Don't overcomplicate simple tasks:** It reflects the idea that one shouldn't overcomplicate a simple problem or task.
- **Apply proportionality:** Don't escalate small conflicts into big battles. Match your response to the actual problem, don't turn a spark into a wildfire.
- **Use the right tool and effort:** Avoid unnecessary extravagance or overkill when solving for a simple task, as it wastes resources, talent, effort, and time.

> ***"Though proceeding from a good intention, an act may be rendered unlawful, if it be out of proportion to the end."***
> — **Thomas Aquinas**

The Dao Whispers: There's no need to burn your house down to kill a fly. Where might I be spending way too much energy on something that doesn't deserve it?

June 7

Let Them Find Their Own Way

The fastest way to lose friends? Start playing life coach

人之患，在好为人师

rén zhī huàn, zài hào wéi rén shī

Translation: "The trouble with people lies in their desire to act as teachers of others."
— Mengzi (孟子, Mencius)

Mencius highlights a tendency many of us fall into, which is **the habit of offering advice or trying to fix others, even when they haven't asked for it.** It can seem like care or concern on the surface, but often it's driven by our own ego, judgement, or discomfort.

Emotional intelligence isn't just about understanding others. It's also knowing when to speak, when to step back, and when to simply listen. Some people aren't ready to hear certain truths. Others may not want them. Sometimes the best move is to say less.

What this teaches us

- **Listen first:** Hold back the urge to advise, learn to hear what others have to say.
- **Respect their path:** Give people space to grow in their own time.
- **Focus on personal growth**: Perhaps we can first fix ourselves before trying to fix anyone else.

> ***"Never do for another what they can do for themselves, for it robs them of growth."***
> — Unknown

The Dao Whispers: Do I seek first to understand, or do I rush to correct, or impose my view?

June 8

Hang Out with Ink, and You Might Be Stained

The company you keep colours your character, for better or for worse

近朱者赤，近墨者黑

jìn zhū zhě chì, jìn mò zhě hēi

Translation: "Those who draw near to vermilion become red; those who draw near to ink become black."
— Traditional Chinese proverb

Spend time with kind, principled people, and you're more likely to rise. Spend too long among the bitter, the careless, or the self-serving, and their habits will start to rub off too. Your circle is your mirror, so choose with care.

This proverb isn't saying you should be snobbish or start cutting people out left and right. It simply asks you to notice who's in your circle, how they're shaping you, and whether their influence is turning you into someone you don't recognise.

What it teaches us

- **Choose your circle wisely**: Surround yourself with those who inspire growth; people who uplift you, live with integrity, and share your values
- **Avoid toxic influences**: Toxicity leaves a mark, so spend less time with those who drag you down or drain your energy. A little ink spreads fast if you stay too close for too long.
- **Pick your paint wisely:** If you want a brighter shade of life, stand closer to the colours you admire.

> ***"You are the average of the five people you spend the most time with."***
> **— Jim Rohn**

The Dao Whispers

- Who has the strongest influence on your thinking, your habits, or your values?
- Who's really in the driving seat, your environment or you?

June 9

You Don't Need to Agree to Get Along

The wise does not force others to be the same

君子和而不同，小人同而不和

jūn zǐ hé ér bù tóng, xiǎo rén tóng ér bù hé

Translation: "The noble pursue harmony without forcing others to be the same. The insecure demand sameness, even if it comes at the expense of peace."
— Confucius (孔子), Analects (论语)

You've probably been in a meeting where everyone nods along, but something feels off. In those meetings, there's often a quiet tension, the kind that makes people second-guess whether it's safe to speak up. It looks like agreement, but it's really discomfort... the kind that shows up when people are afraid to rock the boat.

People who are secure don't need everyone to agree with them. They're comfortable hearing different opinions, can disagree without taking it personally, and still find ways to work together.

What it teaches us

- **Pressure to conform:** You see it in boardrooms where only one tone is allowed. In families where disagreement feels like betrayal, or in friendships where you play along to "keep the peace," you may lose a bit of yourself each time.
- **Maintaining agency:** If you're feeling pressure to fit in just to stay included, pause. Fitting in should never come at the cost of your voice.
- **Learn to embrace diversity**: Respecting differences can take more strength than forcing uniformity.

> ***"It is the mark of an educated mind to be able to entertain a thought without accepting it."***
> — **Aristotle**

The Dao Whispers: Am I willing to respect others' views, or am I simply judging what I don't understand? When the chorus sings another tune, how do I keep my own voice?

June 10

Don't Corner People, Give Them a Way Out

A little grace today saves you a grudge tomorrow

给台阶下

gěi tái jiē xià

Translation: "Give (someone) a step to step down."
— Contemporary expression rooted in traditional values

It's not uncommon to see someone humiliate another person in public, burning bridges just to "win." In many disagreements, the focus shifts to proving a point so fiercely that the other person gets backed into a corner with no way out.

But here's the thing: ***when you leave people no escape, they often fight back harder,*** even if they know they're wrong. It's human.

This Chinese saying reminds us to leave people an exit. Instead of pushing them off the stage, offer a step down. The goal isn't to let them off the hook, it's to handle conflict in a way that keeps the door open for trust, respect, and future collaboration. Let them retreat with dignity.

What it teaches us

- **Don't force people to admit defeat in public:** Even if you're right, leave some space for pride.
- **Relationships matter more than proving a point:** Humbling someone might feel good now, but it can ruin things later.
- **Real strength is quiet:** Sometimes the most powerful move is letting someone walk away gracefully.

> ***"You can be right, or you can keep the relationship."***
> — **Dr. John Gottman**

The Dao Whispers: Am I giving others a way to back down, or am I cornering them? What matters more right now: being right, or staying kind? Would I want someone to offer ***me*** a way out if the roles were reversed?

June 11

Some Stories Should Stay in the Family

Don't air the family's dirty laundry in public

家丑不可外扬

jiā chǒu bù kě wài yáng

Translation: "Family issues should not be aired to the public."
— Traditional Chinese proverb

Not every frustration needs a stage and a spotlight. In Chinese culture, this ties back to *miàn zi* (面子), which literally means "saving face." It reflects the importance of loyalty and keeping the group strong. What happens inside a family, team, or country should be handled with care and respect.

Once private tensions spill into public drama, the credibility of the family, organisation, or even a nation can be damaged. Rebuilding that trust is generally far harder than protecting it in the first place.

What it teaches us

- **Sort things out respectfully:** Taking team issues public breaks trust and hurts morale. More often than not, discreet, respectful conversations solve more than blame or shaming ever will.
- **Think twice before venting about your partner:** Sharing relationship frustrations with outsiders can cause confusion and distance. Without context, even well-meaning friends can make things worse.
- **Handle family matters with care:** When family problems go public, they often get worse. Protect each other's dignity and talk things through in private.

> ***"Speak in anger, and you will make the best speech you'll ever regret."***
> — **Ambrose Bierce**

The Dao Whispers: Am I resolving this in a way that protects trust and dignity, or am I exposing what should stay private? Would I feel comfortable if someone shared my flaws in the same way I am sharing theirs?

June 12

When Old Systems Stifle Fresh Thinking

New wine in old bottles

旧瓶装新酒

jiù píng zhuāng xīn jiǔ

Translation: "Putting new wine in old bottles."
— Traditional Chinese proverb

Ever seen a "game-changing idea" presented in a deck that looks like it was made on PowerPoint 2003? Fresh thinking deserves fresh delivery. Otherwise, even brilliant ideas get buried in outdated packaging.

This old saying reminds us of what happens when fresh wine is poured into worn-out bottles. The wine might be excellent, but if the container is outdated or cracked, it could spoil or explode.

It's the same with ideas. When powerful content is delivered through outdated channels, it loses impact and can even backfire.

What it teaches us

- **Ensure you have up-to-date interfaces**: If your pitch feels like a policy paper from 2008, no one pays attention even if the idea is gold.
- **Outdated systems and structures**: You can't fund innovation with yesterday's mindset or keep talent excited with the same tired incentives.
- **Go beyond the new theories**: You can learn all the new frameworks in the world, but if you keep showing up in the same way, nothing truly shifts.

> ***"The world as we have created it is a process of our thinking. It cannot be changed without changing our thinking."***
> **— Albert Einstein**

The Dao Whispers

- Where in my toolkit is outdated and needs to be refreshed?
- Am I trying to grow while still clinging to the same old habits and systems?

June 13

With Me or Against Me

Why absolute power leaves no middle ground

顺我者昌，逆我者亡

shùn wǒ zhě chāng, nì wǒ zhě wáng

Translation: "Those who follow me will prosper; those who oppose me will perish."
— Attributed to Wu Zetian, China's only female emperor

Wu Zetian was willing to articulate something most leaders are too polite to say out loud. Power does not tolerate neutrality. You are either aligned, or you are a threat. This proverb expresses the ruthless binary of authority: submission brings survival, while resistance brings destruction.

For most of us, this level of absolutism feels uncomfortable, even tyrannical. But history shows how often it emerges. From emperors to dictators to corporate titans, many leaders impose a with-me-or-against-me frame because it simplifies loyalty. There is no space for ambiguity.

In today's world, this logic still shows up in politics, business, and even personal relationships. Some people cannot tolerate grey zones, so they push others into binary categories: friend or foe, ally or enemy, supporter, or saboteur. The risk is obvious. It breeds obedience through fear, but it also suffocates genuine trust.

What it teaches us

- **Recognise absolutists:** If someone operates in binaries, there are no grey zones. Adjust your expectations and strategy accordingly.
- **Beware false loyalty:** Fear-based obedience is fragile. The moment the power dynamic shifts, so will allegiance.
- **Find your line**: Decide where you draw boundaries. Sometimes compromise is survival, but resistance, though costly, is the only way to preserve your compass.

> ***"A prince never lacks legitimate reasons to break his promise."***
> **— Niccolò Machiavelli**

The Dao Whispers: Do I dare face the yang within the yin?

June 14

Filter the Filters

See it for yourself before believing the edited version

耳听为虚，眼见为实

ěr tīng wéi xū, yǎn jiàn wéi shí

Translation: "What you hear may be false; but what you see is real."
— Traditional Chinese proverb

Gossips tend to travel faster than a double shot of espresso. Everyone seems to "know" something, but few have actually seen anything for themselves.

In ancient times, the proverb acted as a simple reminder not to trust hearsay. Today, with curated feeds, viral posts, and information flying at us from all directions, it's a reminder to slow down when we see the WhatsApp forwards, LinkedIn humblebrags, and TikTok drama, and resist being swept away by second-hand stories.

What it teaches us

- **In relationships:** Want to know someone's real character? Watch how they treat people who can't offer them anything.
- **In leadership:** Don't rely solely on reports or pretty slide decks; get on the ground. Check the pulse yourself, not just the reports.
- **In institutions:** When someone gossips, ask yourself: ***what do they gain by telling me this?***

> ***"Believe nothing you hear, and only half of what you see."***
> ***— Edgar Allan Poe***

The Dao Whispers: Do I judge from gossip, or from what I've seen with my own eyes? Do I outsource my judgement?

June 15

Preparation Is Not a Waste of Time

Spend the time to sharpen your axe,
it will not delay the job of cutting the wood

磨刀不误砍柴工

mó dāo bù wù kǎn chái gōng

Translation: "Sharpening the axe will not delay the job of cutting wood."
— Traditional Chinese proverb

Ever rushed into a presentation, a pitch, or a tough conversation thinking you'll just wing it, only to flop?

This old proverb reminds us that taking time to prepare doesn't slow us down. It sets us up to succeed.

The one who swings a blunt axe may look busy, but gets nowhere fast. The person quietly sharpening their tools will finish the job faster, with less stress and fewer mistakes.

What it teaches us

- **In business:** Don't mistake motion for progress. Clarifying the problem, aligning the team, and planning properly helps you solve problems and move more effectively.
- **In personal growth:** Rest and learning may look passive, but they often drive the biggest transformation. A dull mind works harder, a clear one works smarter.
- **In management:** Taking time to sharpen your narrative, storyline, and rehearse ahead of a presentation helps you deliver your message with more confidence and impact.

> ***"An hour of planning can save you ten hours of doing."***
> ***— Dale Carnegie***

The Dao Whispers

- Am I rushing in before I'm ready?
- Could a little more sharpening today save us a lot of effort tomorrow?

June 16

Don't Judge the Message by Its Messenger

A good point is still a good point

不以人废言，不以言取人

bù yǐ rén fèi yán, bù yǐ yán qǔ rén

Translation: "Don't reject a message because of who says it; and don't accept a person just because of what they say."
— Confucius (孔子), Analects (论语)

Confucius reminds us not to throw out a good point just because we don't like the person saying it. Likewise, don't swallow a message whole just because it's delivered by someone impressive or wrapped up in clever words.

These days, a sharp suit, a slick LinkedIn post, or a shiny PowerPoint deck can make nonsense sound profound. Meanwhile, genuinely useful insights often get ignored because the messenger isn't glamorous, popular, or saying what we want to hear. Good ideas don't always arrive with good PR... they can be blunt, awkward, or come from unexpected voices.

What it teaches us

- **Look beneath the surface:** Don't be dazzled or bamboozled by eloquence. Listen for the real substance behind the words.
- **Value ideas, not status:** Don't dismiss an insight just because it comes from a junior or unpopular voice. The best insights can come from anyone, even a five-year-old.
- **If it feels too slick, stay alert:** When someone's pitch sounds too smooth, trust your gut, it probably is.

> ***"It's only when the tide goes out that you discover who's been swimming naked."***
> — **Warren Buffett**

The Dao Whispers

- Am I judging the message or the messenger?
- Can I look past the surface to find what's real?
- How often have I ignored something valuable just because it came in a plain wrapper?

June 17

Burnt, But Not Beaten

Flames don't mark the end of the story, but the beginning of the next chapter

野火烧不尽，春风吹又生

yě huǒ shāo bù jìn, chūn fēng chuī yòu shēng

Translation: "Though the wildfires may burn and destroy the grass, they can't wipe them out completely. When the spring breeze blows once more, they shall again rise."
— Poems from Bai Juyi (白居易)

Life has a habit of torching everything you've built… then casually expecting you to start over like it's no big deal. Spoiler alert: you can.

Bai Juyi describes that resilience with grass that is scorched by fire, yet never fully destroyed. With the return of spring, it grows back. It symbolises the ***indomitable spirit of life***...of people and things that endure hardship, recover, and even thrive in spite of adversity.

Resilience is found in that soul that has been forged in the crucible of pain, choosing to live with strength and with grace, even in the face of hardship, cruelty, or chaos.

What it teaches us

- **Resilience in adversity:** Like grass surviving fire, we too can recover from personal crises, job loss, or betrayal. The fire simply burnt away what you've outgrown.
- **Healing takes time:** With time and care, trust can be rebuilt, if both are willing to work for it.
- **Reinvention professionally:** Setbacks don't define your path. They clear the ground, and what feels like the end is often a beginning in disguise.

"That which does not kill us makes us stronger."
— **Friedrich Nietzsche**

The Dao Whispers: What has the fire taught me that the calm never could? Am I merely recovering or becoming something greater?

June 18

The Thucydides Trap of Power

One mountain cannot contain two tigers

一山不容二虎

yī shān bù róng èr hǔ

Translation: "One mountain cannot contain two tigers."
— Traditional Chinese proverb

Ever seen two strong personalities try to lead the same team? At first, it's polite. Then, it's politics. Eventually... it's personal.

This proverb reminds us that two powerful forces often can't share the same space, not because they hate each other, but because their **ambition, strength, or vision makes conflict structurally inevitable**.

Whether it's founders, co-leaders, business units, or global superpowers, when two actors seek control over the same domain, the friction isn't theoretical.

The Thucydides Trap

This dynamic isn't folklore, historians call this the **Thucydides Trap** – the idea that when a rising power threatens an established one, war often follows. Not because either side wants it, but because neither can afford to lose ground.

In companies, it shows up in leadership succession fights, in competing product teams, or in peers slowly edging each other out.

Historically, it plays out in trade wars, defence posturing, broken alliances, or loss of trust between empires.

> ***"There is nothing more difficult to carry out... than to initiate a new order of things. For the reformer has enemies in all who profit by the old order."***
> — *Niccolò Machiavelli*

The Dao Whispers

- Not all conflict is personal – some tension is systemic by design.
- If two tigers must survive, maybe they need two mountains.

June 19

Let Ducks Be Ducks, Cranes Be Cranes

Don't try to fix what's not broken

鸭有短腿，不可长也；鹤有长腿，不可短也

yā yǒu duǎn tuǐ, bù kě cháng yě; hè yǒu cháng tuǐ, bù kě duǎn yě

Translation: "A duck has short legs, don't try to lengthen them. A crane has long legs, don't try to shorten them."
— Zhuangzi (庄子)

Some people are ducks. Others are cranes. Both are doing just fine until someone decides to "fix" them.

Zhuangzi's point? Stop turning everyone into your version of "ideal." The duck doesn't need longer legs. The crane doesn't need trimming. When we try to change people, partners, kids, or colleagues into who ***we want*** them to be, we often end up hurting them... and ourselves. Sometimes, the thing you want to fix is the very thing that makes someone special.

What it teaches us

- **Let people be people:** Trying to force someone to become like you, or who you think they should be, rarely works. Acceptance gives people a sense of safety where people can be authentic and thrive.
- **Play to strengths:** Build teams around what people naturally do well, not what you wish they could do.
- **Speak their language of love:** According to Gary Chapman, we all express and feel love differently – through words, gifts, acts of service, time, or touch. If your language is gifts and theirs is quality time, you could be handing them diamonds and still miss the mark.

> ***"The shoe that fits one person pinches another; there is no recipe for living that suits all cases."***
> ***— Carl Jung***

The Dao Whispers: Can I love someone for who they are, not who I want them to be?

This week's exercise: If you haven't already, explore the Five Love Languages and find out how your partner, friend or family member truly feels loved.

June 20

Don't judge a fish by how it climbs a tree

How misjudgement hides talent and thwarts potential

别教鱼爬树

bié jiào yú pá shù

Translation: "Don't judge a fish by its ability to climb a tree."
— Modern Chinese Proverb

Trying to make a fish climb a tree isn't only unfair, but also, quite absurd. Or imagine telling an eagle it's a terrible swimmer. If you judge every creature by the same test, you'll miss what makes each one exceptional.

This proverb literally means don't try to teach a fish to climb. The fish is not stupid for failing. It was made to swim and it's probably brilliant at it.

Failure isn't always a sign of incompetence. Sometimes, it simply means the environment was wrong.

Good judgement in leadership, parenting, or self-reflection means recognising that talent is contextual. Great leaders don't just evaluate performance; they take responsibility for matching potential with the right role and environment.

What it teaches us

- **In teams:** Allocate tasks based on strengths, interests, and growth aspirations.
- **In self-talk:** Don't measure your worth by someone else's scoreboard. You're not playing the same game – and you didn't start from the same place.
- **In life:** Honour diversity of talent, temperament, and design. An eagle can't judge how well a dolphin swims and shouldn't try.

> ***"Do not let what you cannot do interfere with what you can do."***
> ***— John Wooden***

The Dao Whispers: Are you the eagle judging the fish, or the fish judged by an eagle? Perhaps, the real question is whether you're in the right place to use your talents.

June 21

When It's Risky to Stand Out

Feign madness but stay in control

假痴不癫

jiǎ chī bù diān

Translation: "Feign madness but stay in control."
— Thirty-Six Stratagems (三十六计)

Watch a poker table long enough, and you'll see this: someone plays the fool, lets everyone underestimate them, and then wins big at the end. Sometimes, that is the smartest move on the table.

This ancient stratagem is about doing just that in life. Acting simple or harmless can stop others from guessing your real abilities or intentions. It is not about dumbing yourself down. It is about knowing when to keep your cards close, when to avoid drawing unwanted attention, and how to navigate complex situations without showing your full hand.

What it teaches us

- **Stay in the game:** In competitive or political settings, letting people think less of you can sometimes keep you safe and free to make your real move later.
- **Avoid needless enemies:** Showing all your talent right away can stir jealousy or resistance. Playing it down gives you space to plan.
- **Spot hidden insight:** Those who act like fools often hide their insight. The quietest person, or the one pretending not to understand, may actually see the most.

"To be great is to be misunderstood."
— Ralph Waldo Emerson

The Dao Whispers: Is this the right time to speak up, or to blend in and observe? Have I ever held back my full capabilities to avoid attention or conflict? What happened as a result?

June 22

Not Every Problem Needs Your Paws

Sometimes the dog should leave the mice to the cat

狗拿耗子

gǒu ná hào zi

Translation: "When a dog catches mice, it's meddling in others' business."
— Traditional Chinese proverb

The Story

There was once a dog who had always done what dogs do. He barked at strangers. He guarded the gate. He chased the occasional bone.

But one day, he decided that wasn't enough. "I'm going to catch mice," he said proudly. "Cats do it. Why can't I?"

So he began sneaking through kitchens and creeping along rafters, trying to pounce like a cat. The mice, of course, got away. The house was a mess, and the cat looked on, baffled.

Some people were impressed by his ambition, while others just shook their heads.

As the old saying goes: 狗拿耗子，多管闲事. When a dog starts catching mice, it's meddling in what's not its place. Just because you can do something doesn't mean you should.

Sometimes, it's wiser to play to your strengths instead of chasing someone else's job, or someone else's life.

"He who is everywhere is nowhere."
— **Seneca**

The Dao Whispers: Sometimes, the wisest thing is to do less, not more. If you solve problems that aren't yours to begin with, would you risk creating more?

June 23

The Secret of Solitude

Solitude often reveals the truths we hide from ourselves

独善其身

dú shàn qí shēn

Translation: "Perfect yourself in solitude."
— Traditional Chinese proverb

Have you ever found yourself thinking more clearly when no one else is around?

Spending time alone can feel awkward at first; no noise, no one to impress, just you. But that's exactly when we start noticing things we normally ignore. Our habits, our thoughts, the things we're proud of… and the ones we're not. It's not about cutting people off. It's about stepping back just long enough to hear your own thoughts and doing some honest work on yourself while you're at it.

This proverb speaks to how solitude is not retreat, but refinement. Western philosophers have said the same. Many believed solitude was essential for self-understanding and real freedom.

> ***"A man can be himself only so long as he is alone; and if he does not love solitude, he will not love freedom; for it is only when he is alone that he is really free."***
> — **Arthur Schopenhauer**

The Dao Whispers:

- When no one's watching, what kind of choices do I make?
- How do I spend time with myself? Do I avoid it, or value it?

If solitude is a mirror, what is it showing me right now?

June 24

The Hidden Risk of Generosity

The dog that bit hands that healed it

狗咬吕洞宾，不识好人心

gǒu yǎo Lǚ Dòngbīn, bù shí hǎo rén xīn

Translation: "Even Lü Dongbin, a kind immortal, could be bitten by a dog that does not recognise his good intentions"
— Chinese Folk Saying, rooted in Daoist legend

The Story

In Chinese folklore, Lü Dongbin, one of the Eight Immortals, often wandered the world disguised as a mortal to test human nature.

In one tale, he found a sick, starving dog. Moved by compassion, he offered it food and medicine. But the dog, scared and confused, lashed out and bit him.

Unharmed, Lü remained kind, but the villagers remembered the moment.

Over time, the saying came to mean: some people bite the hand that feeds them, not because you were wrong, but because they couldn't recognise your goodwill. **Not all kindness is recognised**, and **not all recipients are ready to receive it**.

What it teaches us

- Kindness is powerful, but misplaced kindness can become a trap: the more you give, the more some take without ever giving back.
- In work and life, generosity without boundaries often gets mistaken for weakness.
- Not everyone is ready for help. Some react from fear, habit, or ego and bite back.

> ***"Gratitude is a duty which ought to be paid, but which none have a right to expect."***
> ***— Jean-Jacques Rousseau***

The Dao Whispers: Know when to walk away from those who mistake your help for harm or take you for granted. Where in your life are you helping someone who bites back?

June 25

The Power of Playing the Simpleton

The wisest often let others underestimate them

大智若愚，大忍若弱

dà zhì ruò yú, dà rěn ruò ruò

Translation: "Wisdom can be mistaken for foolishness, while patience can be mistaken for weakness."
— Traditional Chinese proverb

You know the person who sits through drama without saying a word, while everyone else is running in circles? People think they're clueless or passive, until they **decisively** take a step no one expected and change the entire game.

This proverb explains that the people with grit rarely show it on the outside. The toughest people often seem the gentlest because they've been broken and learned how to rebuild. Similarly, the wise may appear quiet, ordinary, or even a little naïve, making it easy for others to mistake self-mastery for nonchalance.

What it teaches us

- **Don't rush to prove yourself:** You don't need to post your pain or your comeback to the world to prove your strength, resilience, or grit.
- **Respond with grace:** It takes real maturity to handle being misunderstood without getting defensive. The wise don't waste energy on drama, and they're fine with being underestimated because they know their worth.
- **Let them underestimate you:** If it's harmless, then let people misjudge you if they must. Their assumptions can be a shield while you prepare your next move.

> ***"Wise men speak because they have something to say; fools because they have to say something."***
> — **Plato**

The Dao Whispers: Can you recall a time when someone's simple or unassuming behaviour hid their real potential until they acted in a way that surprised everyone?

June 26

A Story About the Weight We Choose to Hold

The two monks and a woman by the river

放下包袱，轻装前行

fang xià bāo fú, qīng zhuāng qián xíng

Translation: "Put down your burden and walk forward with lightness."
— Traditional Chinese proverb

The Story

Two monks, one old and one young, were travelling together. They came to a river with a strong current. A woman stood by the bank, unable to cross. She asked for help.

Without hesitation, the elder monk carried her across. The younger monk was bound by rules forbidding physical contact with women and was stunned, but silent.

Hours passed.

Unable to contain himself, the younger monk finally said, "How could you carry her? We're not supposed to touch women."

The elder monk replied: ***"I put her down at the riverbank. Why are you still carrying her?"***

We include this story not because it belongs to a single proverb, but because its message is universal. To walk free, we must learn to put our burdens down.

The past is not the present, unless we drag it with us.

But if we do, our future becomes our past.

The Dao Whispers

What weighs us down isn't always what we've done, but the thoughts we refuse to let go.

June 27

To Walk in Their Shoes, Start with the Heart

If you wish to persuade me, you must feel my feelings

将心比心

jiāng xīn bǐ xīn

Translation: "To compare your heart with someone else's heart (Put yourself in someone else's shoes)."
— Traditional Chinese proverb

Have you ever given great advice, only to watch it fall flat? Not because it was wrong, but because they weren't ready to hear it?

The truth is, people don't listen when they feel judged, misunderstood, or pressured. They listen when they feel seen.

This proverb reminds us that understanding must come before influence. To reach someone, we have to step into their shoes. See as they see. Speak as they speak. Feel as they feel.

Sometimes we forget that communication isn't about winning the argument or proving we're right. It's about building a bridge, one that connects to the other person's concerns, language, and interests. We need to learn about what makes them tick. Once you have the alignment, influence becomes the natural next step.

What it teaches us

- **Empathy builds trust:** It's the foundation of trust. Without it, even the best ideas rarely land.
- **Seek first to understand:** People listen best when they feel heard first.
- **Start with common ground**: Persuasion is not about pressuring someone to agree, it's about resonance. People are more open when they feel you're with them, not against them.

> ***"If you wish to persuade me, you must think my thoughts, feel my feelings and speak my words."***
> **— Cicero**

The Dao Whispers: Do I first seek to understand others, their concerns, language, interests, and goals, before I try to help, align, or influence?

June 28

Composure: Grace Under Fire

Reactivity is leverage... for the other side

处变不惊

chǔ biàn bù jīng

Translation: "Do not be startled by external changes."
— Traditional Chinese idiom

Few things are more uncomfortable than watching someone lose their cool and thinking, "Yikes, don't be that guy."

That's what this idiom is all about. Whether you're in a heated meeting, a messy breakup, or just dealing with delayed trains and back-handed compliments, staying calm can be a superpower.

For leaders, composure means more than staying cool. It is strength coupled with a confident, calm demeanour, and the ability to speak with authority and decisiveness. A steady tone, clear message, and measured delivery can mobilise a room more effectively than sheer volume. When others are losing their heads, your ability to project control and conviction becomes an anchor for the team.

What it teaches us

- **When things feel uncertain**: Don't rush to fill the silence or "do something." Pause. Breathe. Respond on your terms.
- **In confrontations**: You might *feel* justified blowing up, but staying cool gives you more control and credibility.
- **In negotiations**: A calm presence commands respect. It keeps your head clear and your position strong.

> ***"The ultimate measure of a man is not where he stands in moments of comfort, but where he stands at times of challenge."***
> ***— Martin Luther King Jr.***

The Dao Whispers: Composure under fire is the clearest signal of discipline and self-mastery.

June 29

The Flipside of Competence

Work is like a pizza eating competition. The better and faster you can eat, the more you get to eat

能者多劳

néng zhě duō láo

Translation: "Those who are capable should do more work."
— Traditional Chinese proverb

Someone once said that work is like a pizza-eating competition. The faster and better you finish your pizza, the more pizza you get. This proverb reflects the same spirit, and a deeply rooted social expectation: capable people often get loaded with more work. In Chinese culture, it comes from a place of duty, contribution, and collective responsibility. But there's a flipside...ability earns trust, yes, but it can also invite exploitation.

What it teaches

- **More responsibility**: If you're good at what you do, people lean on you. This can grow you, but only if paired with agency, support, and respect.
- **Burnout risk:** Without clear boundaries, the "go-to" person silently absorbs disproportionate burdens, stretched thin and risks exhaustion.
- **Social Dynamics**: Exceptional performance can trigger envy, isolation, or resentment, especially in fragile team environments.

The idiom reminds us that just because someone ***can,*** doesn't mean they ***should...***not endlessly, and not without fairness or care. A healthy system honours talent not by exhausting it, but by respecting, protecting, and placing them with care.

> ***"Burnout is not a personal failure. It's a sign that the system was never built to support you."***
> — **Anne Helen Petersen**

The Dao Whispers: Competence is a strength, not a sentence to self-sacrifice. Do you always rush to carry the heaviest load, or do you wait for when your strength serves you best?

June 30

The Phoenix Can Only Be by Being Burnt

When you walk through the fire, you can be reduced to ashes, or choose to transform

凤凰浴火，非死即生

fèng huáng yù huǒ, fēi sǐ jí shēng

Translation: "The phoenix bathes in fire; it either dies or is reborn."
— Attributed to Wu Zetian, China's only female emperor

For thousands of years, people in China and the West have told the story of the phoenix, a bird that burns and then rises again. To be reborn, it must first burn. There is no safe way through the flames.

This proverb goes beyond polishing jade or being slowly shaped by hardship. It is about the moment of rupture, when the fire either consumes you or transforms you. Some trials you endure. Others annihilate you. And a rare few, if you survive them, make you into something entirely new. Leadership theory speaks of "crucibles," the defining tests that forge character. The phoenix reminds us that the crucible is not only about endurance, but about transcendence. You must pass through fire, risk the death of who you were, and only then emerge different.

What it teaches us

- **Not every trial is survivable**: Some battles will destroy you, and wisdom lies in knowing which fires to enter.
- **Survival is not the same as renewal:** Endurance is necessary, but rebirth requires letting go of who you were.
- **Transformation has a cost**: To transcend the fire, part of you must die.

> ***"When we are no longer able to change a situation, we are challenged to change ourselves."***
> — **Viktor Frankl**

The Dao Whispers: What part of me must I let die in the fire so that the rest of me can rise? Sometimes clarity doesn't come *while* you're in the fire – it comes in the **aftermath, when you look back and say, "Never again."**

JULY

信

xìn

Meaning of 信 (xìn):

- Trust
- Trustworthiness
- Reliability
- Sincerity

In Chinese philosophy, 信 (xìn) is the invisible thread that holds together relationships, leadership, and society. It goes beyond honesty; it is living in a way that others can depend on, whose word carries weight.

The character 信 combines "speech" (言) and "person" (人), and serves as a reminder that trustworthy speech comes from the person behind the words. People with 信 don't just talk about values; they live them.

Those who live with 信 (xìn):

- **Keep their word,** even when no one's keeping a scorecard.
- **Speak with care because** words affect trust.
- **Act with consistency,** showing up as promised.
- **Align actions and values,** guided by a healthy inner compass.
- **Build bridges, not just reputations,** nurturing mutual trust in relationships.

July 1

To Be Credible – *Be* Credible

Action speaks louder than words

行胜于言

xíng shèng yú yán

Translation: "Actions trump words."
— Confucius inspired philosophy

Have you ever trusted someone's words, only to realise they never followed through? Or been promised the world and then ghosted? We've all met a flaky person or two.

This idiom reminds us that credibility isn't built on words, talk alone is cheap. What counts is what you do. Often used in leadership, relationships, or personal goals, it calls for reliability and accountability; and avoiding empty promises.

This cannot be emphasised enough: credibility is earned only through follow-through.

What it teaches us

- **Show Up**: People judge us by our actions, not our intentions. Following through in relationships, friendships, or family is how we build trust. Sometimes, it starts as simply as showing up or returning a call when you said you would.
- **Lead by example:** Speeches can inspire, but real impact comes from what we do. Great leaders earn respect by following through and setting the tone through consistent action.
- **Don't be flaky:** If we can't commit, just say so. Being honest upfront is far better than leaving others hanging or wasting their time.

> ***"What you do speaks so loudly that I cannot hear what you say."***
> **— Ralph Waldo Emerson**

The Dao Whispers

- Do I consistently show up when I say I will?
- Am I surrounding myself with people who honour their word, or those who often flake?

July 2

When Time Runs Out, Only Kindness Stays

What we hold back in life, mortality compels us to speak

鸟之将死，其鸣也哀；
人之将死，其言也善

niǎo zhī jiāng sǐ, qí míng yě āi;

rén zhī jiāng sǐ, qí yán yě shàn

Translation: "A dying bird tends to sing with melancholy, while a dying man tends to speak with compassion."
— Traditional Chinese proverb

There's something about knowing time is limited that stirs the heart. People speak more kindly, forgive more easily, and say what matters.

This ancient proverb reminds us that, in the face of death, all pretence fades. Birds sing with grief. People, aware of their mortality, often speak with rare sincerity...shedding ego, resentment, and noise. What's left behind is often wisdom, regret, or love as mortality strips away illusion.

What it teaches us

- Live and speak with the honesty death might inspire – be kind and truthful *now*, not later.
- It's never too early to forgive, to reconcile, or to say what must be said.
- Regret often comes not from what we did, but from what we didn't say in time.

> ***"Remembering that I'll be dead soon is the most important tool I've ever encountered to help me make the big choices in life."***
> — **Steve Jobs**

The Dao Whispers

What would I do differently, if today were my last day?
Perhaps, we can choose kindness, while we still have the choice.

July 3

When Kindness Comes with a Catch

When the weasel wishes a chicken Happy New Year, it's probably up to no good

黄鼠狼给鸡拜年，没安好心

huáng shǔ láng gěi jī bài nián, méi ān hǎo xīn

Translation: "When a weasel wishes a chicken Happy New Year, it's up to no good."
— Traditional Chinese proverb

This old saying is a cheeky reminder that not every friendly face has good intentions. If someone shady suddenly turns sweet, they're probably not there to help, they're there to hunt. Think of it like your office rival bringing you coffee out of the blue… right before a big meeting. Or someone who's ignored you for months, now suddenly calling you 'bestie.'

What it teaches us

- **Pause before trusting:** If someone with a track record of self-interest suddenly shows generosity, ask yourself: ***Why now? What do they want?***
- **Protect yourself:** Be cautious of compliments or favours that come with strings attached. "You're amazing" might really mean "Can I borrow your deck and take credit for it?"
- **Watch the pattern, not the pitch:** Words can charm, but actions tell the truth. If someone's kindness always ends in a request, that's not kindness. That's strategy.

> ***"Political language is designed to make lies sound truthful and murder respectable."***
> — **George Orwell**

The Dao Whispers

If a weasel wishes you Happy New Year, you might want to show it the 'Exit,' or perhaps, your claws.
Otherwise... run?

July 4

Bloom Where You Are Planted

Since you're here, settle in, grow, and thrive

既来之，则安之

jì lái zhī, zé ān zhī

Translation: "Since you are here, be at peace."
— Traditional Chinese proverb

There are times in life when we cannot change the situation we're in – a job that isn't ideal, a city that doesn't feel like home, or a chapter we didn't choose. When that happens, this proverb offers a gentle nudge to stop resisting what's already here.

It's not about giving up. It simply asks one to take a breath, make peace with the present, and figure out how to move forward from where you are. When we stop resisting reality, we reclaim the energy we've been using to fight it, and we can learn to grow again. To that point, an American philosopher and psychologist, **William James,** once said,

> ***"The art of being wise is the art of knowing what to overlook."***

So much of life lies not in forcing solutions but in consciously choosing where to invest or withhold your energy, and releasing what drains you. Letting go demands strength, and that strength begins in the mind. To find that strength, Stoic philosopher Marcus Aurelius shared,

> ***"You have power over your mind, not outside events. Realise this, and you will find strength."***

The Dao Whispers: Perhaps, we can learn to accept the present situation with grace. Make yourself at home in whatever place or circumstance you've arrived. And then, start thriving.

July 5

To Know and Not Do is to Not Know

To appreciate what we learn in theory,
we must put it in practice

纸上得来终觉浅，绝知此事要躬行

zhǐ shàng dé lái zhōng jué qiǎn, jué zhī cǐ shì yào gōng xíng

Translation: "What is learned from books is shallow; true understanding comes from personal experience."
— Traditional Chinese idiom, from Song Dynasty poet Lu You

Ever heard of someone who read a book on swimming, then jumped in and nearly drowned? That's this proverb in action. Lu You, a poet from the Song Dynasty, reminds us that no matter how much theory we absorb, its meaning won't sink in until we actually ***do*** the thing.

Whether it's love, leadership, healing, or humility, learning lives in practice, not in perfectly highlighted pages. The proverb acts as a gentle nudge for us to get off the page and bring what we know into life.

What it teaches us

You can...

- ... study leadership philosophy, but until you lead through conflicts and crisis, it remains a theory.
- ... read about empathy, but only shared struggle brings it to life.
- ... memorise negotiation frameworks, but until you're across the table under pressure, your knowledge is untested.
- ... speak of compassion, but until you show up for someone, it's just talk.
- ... study presence and mindfulness, but it means little until you practise it when you're overwhelmed.

> ***"In theory, theory and practice are the same. In practice, they're not."***
> — **Benjamin Brewster** (commonly attributed)

The Dao Whispers: To know, and to not do, is to not know.

July 6

When Holding Your Ground Costs Everything

Better a shattered jade than a perfect tile

宁为玉碎，不为瓦全

nìng wéi yù suì, bù wéi wǎ quán

Translation: "Better to be a shattered jade than a whole tile."
— Traditional Chinese proverb

This proverb speaks to the courage of upholding one's integrity, even when it comes at a steep cost. Jade represents virtue — rare, precious, and strong. Tile, though intact, is cheap and easily replaced.

The proverb comes from a tale that speaks of a man caught between betraying his principles to survive and holding true to them at great cost. He chose integrity over survival, explaining that it was better to break with honour than live by bending into something unrecognisable.

Across cultures, this value echoes:

- Socrates chose death over betraying his philosophical principles.
- Mandela endured decades in prison rather than compromise on justice.
- In business and politics, whistleblowers often choose to pay dearly to protect what matters to them.

> ***"You have enemies? Good. That means you've stood up for something, sometime in your life."***
> **— Winston Churchill**

The Dao Whispers: What's the real cost of survival if you no longer recognise yourself?

Reflection: This is not a call to martyrdom but a reminder that not all survival is equal. Some costs are simply too high. Some things are worth breaking for, while others are not worth keeping intact. The difference is everything.

July 7

Close the Gaps Before They're Exploited

Flies don't land on eggs without cracks

苍蝇不叮无缝的蛋

cāng yíng bù dīng wú fèng de dàn

Translation: "Flies do not usually land on seamless eggs (eggs with no cracks or flaws)."
— Traditional Chinese proverb

Ever left a lid off your rubbish bin and found a swarm of flies having a party? Life can be like that. Trouble finds its way in through gaps, be it a loose boundary, a weak spot, or a crack in our character.

A flawless egg that is smooth, whole, and sealed doesn't attract pests. In the same way, when we work on our inner cracks, others have fewer ways to take advantage of us.

The proverb isn't asking for perfection. It simply asks us to see our own cracks and to take steps to fix them.

What it teaches us

- **Do the work:** Fix the cracks before someone else finds them and uses them.
- **Integrity is armour:** Resist pressure to cheat or cut corners. Integrity is a surprisingly good shield.
- **Project strength:** Confidence, clarity, and boundaries can deter manipulative people from drawing close.

> ***"Man is condemned to be free; because once thrown into the world, he is responsible for everything he does."***
> **— Jean-Paul Sartre**

The Dao Whispers: As Sartre said, we're responsible for everything we do. That includes patching our own cracks so that flies don't find a way in.

July 8

When a Softer Approach Works Better

Diplomacy can soften the hardest metal

柔能克刚

róu néng kè gāng

Translation: "Softness overcomes hardness."
— Traditional Chinese proverb

We're often taught to be tough, to stand our ground, fight back, and stay firm. And sometimes, that is exactly what's needed. But there are moments when a softer, more flexible approach works better.

This proverb reminds us that force isn't always the smartest tool. In certain situations, calmness, tact, and emotional control open more doors than pressure or power ever could. It doesn't mean you fold – it means you know when to shift gears, especially when pushing harder might only make things worse.

What it teaches us

- **Growth:** Real growth happens when you're open with yourself, not when you fight against what you need to learn.
- **Negotiation:** The best deals aren't about 'winning,' they're about finding solutions where everyone walks away happy.
- **Feedback:** Constructive feedback can land better when it's delivered with care, not harsh criticism.

> ***"The best revenge is to be unlike him who performed the injury."***
> **— Marcus Aurelius**

The Dao Whispers: Could a softer approach work better than going head-on with the challenge at hand now?

July 9

The Discipline of Less

Master yourself through calm and simplicity

夫君子之行，静以修身，俭以养德

fū jūn zǐ zhī xíng, jìng yǐ xiū shēn, jiǎn yǐ yǎng dé

Translation: "The noble person cultivates oneself through calmness, and nurtures self-discipline and moral integrity through simplicity (frugality)."
— Zhuge Liang (诸葛亮), legendary statesman, strategist, and scholar of the Three Kingdoms period (220–280 CE)

Ever noticed how we say things we regret when agitated, or buy things we don't need just to fill a gap we cannot explain?

This proverb comes from a letter Zhuge Liang wrote to his son. Amid chaos and conflict, he encouraged him to stay centred. Calm composure, he believed, was important for self-mastery. Simplicity and living a frugal life, meanwhile, can help guard against greed and distraction. A wise leader, he said, must first be able to lead himself.

What it teaches us

- **Thinking clearly under stress:** Staying mindful in stressful moments helps us clear mental clutter, so we can think straight and respond, not just react.
- **Composed communication:** In high-stakes conversations, staying composed lets us speak with clarity and respect, rather than lash out emotionally.
- **Needing less makes us stronger:** The more content you are with less, the harder you are to corrupt, and the less power others have over you.

> ***"It is not the man who has too little, but the man who craves more, that is poor."***
> — **Seneca**

The Dao Whispers: Would having less give me more life, or am I still enslaved by wanting more?

July 10

Start Where You Are

Change yourself, and the world around you will begin to change

修身齐家治国平天下

xiū shēn qí jiā zhì guó píng tiān xià

Translation: "Cultivate the self, harmonise the family, govern the state, and bring peace to the world."
— Confucian Classic: The Great Learning (大学)

Want to make the world better? Start with your morning, your mindset, or how you treat people at home.

This ancient Confucian teaching outlines a ladder of influence: start with the individual, then the family, and finally society. Real change doesn't begin with catchy slogans or grand speeches at the podium. It starts with cleaning your room, making amends with loved ones, or doing the right thing when no one is watching.

What it teaches us

- **Don't skip steps:** Trying to fix the world without first tending to our own life is like pouring water into a cracked glass.
- **Set the tone at home:** How we show up at the dinner table matters more than what we post online.
- **Personal growth creates stability:** When we focus on our own growth, we become stronger and steadier, and better able to lead and uplift others.

> ***"Put your house in perfect order before you criticise the world."***
> **— Jordan Peterson**

The Dao Whispers: If I can't lead myself, why should anyone trust me to lead them?

July 11

Before You Win, Calculate the Cost

Every prize comes with a cost. Don't just ask what you'll gain; ask, what it takes to win

欲思其利，必虑其害；
欲思其成，必虑其败

yù sī qí lì, bì lǜ qí hài; yù sī qí chéng, bì lǜ qí bài.

Translation: "To weigh the benefits, you must weigh the harm. To plan for success, you must also prepare for what could go wrong."
— Traditional Chinese proverb

It's easy to get excited by the upside... a new role, a business deal, a big opportunity. But we rarely stop to ask what it might cost us.

This old saying is a reminder to think fully. Before we jump in, we should weigh not just the rewards, but the risks, trade-offs, and possible setbacks. Smart decisions go beyond dreaming big. They require knowing what you're willing to lose, the lines you won't cross, and how you'll respond if things don't go your way.

What it teaches us

- **Weigh the cost, not just the prize:** Even the best minds can be seduced by upside if they forget to ask what it really takes to win.
- **Plan for things to go sideways:** Aim high, but build in buffers, backups, or exit plans.
- **Be ready to walk away:** If your red lines are crossed, courage may mean knowing when to leave.

> ***"The wise man bridges the gap by laying out the path by means of which he can get from where he is, to where he wants to go."***
> — **J. P. Morgan**

The Dao Whispers: Am I clear about both the benefits and the costs of my decisions?

July 12

Have Faith the Path Will Show Itself

When it all seems foggy, take the first step anyway

车到山前必有路

chē dào shān qián bì yǒu lù

Translation: "When the cart reaches the mountain, there will be a way through."
— Traditional Chinese proverb

Ever faced a challenge so big you wondered how you could possibly get through it? This proverb reminds us that you don't need to see the entire road before you start. Take the next step, and the path often reveals itself once you have the courage to move forward. That's the hope, at least.

> ***"I have always believed that an opportunity comes from another opportunity...As long as you are willing to take active actions, you will be closer to success."***
> — **John D. Rockefeller** (Letter to His Son)

And if you need more strength, find your ***why***... your reason. It will carry you through almost anything.

> ***"He who has a why to live can bear almost any how."***
> — **Friedrich Nietzsche**

The Dao Whispers: You don't need all the answers to take the first step. Have faith that the next step will become clear once you start walking. Just keep going, don't stop and don't look back.

July 13

The Temptation of Tit-for-Tat

A tooth for a tooth leaves both sides toothless

以牙还牙

yǐ yá huán yá

Translation: "A tooth for a tooth."
— Traditional Chinese proverb

When someone wrongs us, the instinct to strike back can feel justified. They land a blow, and your brain instantly queues the comeback. Why is it so tempting to return harm for harm?

Retaliation feels good in the moment, but what comes after? The urge to hit back is deeply human.

This old proverb speaks to that. If someone knocks out your tooth, you knock out one of theirs. Fair is fair, right?

It taps into something deep in us, the need to restore balance by returning harm. But if both sides keep swinging, soon no one has teeth left. Some fights settle things, while others just drag on and drain us.

In game theory, there's a famous idea called Tit-for-Tat. You mirror what the other person does, but you're also willing to forgive if they stop. That version actually works. The goal isn't revenge. It's resolution.

> ***"If a man puts out the eye of another man, his eye shall be put out."***
> — **The Code of Hammurabi** (Babylonian Law)

> ***"An eye for an eye leaves the whole world blind."***
> — **Mahatma Gandhi**

So, the real question isn't just whether to strike back. It's whether doing so will solve the problem, or keep you stuck in it.

The Dao Whispers: If you must respond, respond to end the conflict, not to fuel it. But hit back *(only if you really must)* only if it restores balance, not just your pride. Not every insult deserves a comeback. Not every opponent deserves your energy.

July 14

What You Cling to May Be Holding You Back

To gain something new, you often have to let something go

舍得，舍得，有舍才有得

shě dé, shě dé, yǒu shě cái yǒu dé

Translation: "Give up to gain...give up and gain again. It shows that only by letting go, that you can begin to gain something (new)."
— Traditional Chinese proverb

If you try holding sand in a clenched fist, the tighter you grip, the more slips through.

A wise professor from the National University of Singapore once said, ***"When you clench your fist tightly, it's closed. Only when you open your palm can something new fall into it."***

We often hold on out of fear, to jobs, people, pride, or old habits, thinking that if we let go, we'll lose everything. But this ancient Chinese saying reminds us that only when we release what no longer serves us, can life offer something new in return.

Of course, it isn't always easy. Letting go isn't easy. It can feel like failure, especially when we've poured in time, energy, or hope. But holding on to what we've outgrown often keeps us stuck in places we were meant to move on from.

> ***"To dare is to lose one's footing momentarily. To not dare is to lose oneself."***
> — **Søren Kierkegaard**

The Dao Whispers: What we refuse to release may be the very thing holding us back. We grip so tightly, we forget what we're even holding on for.

That's when we lose our way.

But sometimes, it is by becoming lost that we find ourselves again.

July 15

The Echo of Our Deeds

What we plant today shapes tomorrow's inheritance

积善之家，必有余庆；
积不善之家，必有余殃

jī shàn zhī jiā, bì yǒu yú qìng; jī bù shàn zhī jiā, bì yǒu yú yāng

Translation: "A family that accumulates good deeds is sure to have abundant blessings; a family that accumulates bad deeds is sure to have lingering misfortunes."
— Zuo Zhuan (左传, Spring and Autumn Period Classic)

What seeds are you planting not just for yourself, but for those who come after you?

According to Zuo Zhuan, what we do doesn't end with us. Every choice, every action, even every silence, becomes part of the inheritance we hand over; an invisible chain linking one generation to the next.

In his view, we are always planting seeds of protection, or of pain. Doing good becomes a form of intergenerational guardianship. And if we inherited thorns instead of flowers, perhaps the greatest strength is to break the cycle, not pass it on.

What it teaches us

- **Moral legacy:** Consistent ethical behaviour can create a positive legacy, shaping not just our lives but those of our families and communities for generations.
- **Long-term consequences**: Daily choices pile up. Be mindful of what you're stacking for the future.
- **Collective responsibility**: Our actions are not just personal. Talking openly as a family about values can help keep everyone pointed toward a better "north star."

> ***"The greatest burden a child must bear is the unlived life of the parents."***
> — ***Carl Jung***

The Dao Whispers: Are my daily choices sowing blessings or burdens? Could I be the one to break the chain to change what is passed forward?

July 16

Less Wrong is Still Wrong

When you point a finger at others, three are pointing back at you

五十步笑百步

wǔ shí bù xiào bǎi bù

Translation: "The one who flees fifty steps laughs at the one who flees a hundred."
— From Han Feizi (韩非子)

Ever judged someone for slipping up, then realised you did the same thing, just a little less?

That's the spirit of this old Chinese idiom.

It comes from a parable where a soldier who ran fifty steps from battle mocked another who ran a hundred. But both had still run away. The point? Don't act superior when you've done the same thing, even if just a little less.

We're often quicker to point fingers than to look in the mirror. But judgement without reflection turns into hypocrisy. Being slightly "less wrong" doesn't make you right.

In other words, before we judge, we must admit that we too are flawed.

What it teaches us

- **Lead with humility**: When we remember our own flaws, it's easier to be kind when others slip up.
- **Let's not confuse less with better:** A small difference in mistakes doesn't put us on higher moral ground.
- **Look in the mirror first**: It's easy to spot faults in others, but harder to admit our own.

"You too are not blameless."
— **Seneca**

The Dao Whispers: Being "less wrong" doesn't make you right. People who live in glass houses shouldn't throw stones, they'll only shatter their own.

July 17

I Look in the Mirror, Reflect, Then Become

Every day, I examine myself thrice

吾日三省吾身

wú rì sān xǐng wú shēn

Translation: "Each day, I examine myself thrice."
— Confucius (孔子), Analects (论语)

We all get swept up in the day. Emails, errands, opinions flying everywhere. But a few quiet questions at the end of it all can bring us back to who we really are.

Long before Descartes, Confucius reminded us that reflection shapes how we live. The phrase comes from Confucius' *Analects*. The original phrase was longer:

> 吾日三省吾身：为人谋而不忠乎？
> 与朋友交而不信乎？ 传不习乎？
>
> wú rì sān xǐng wú shēn, wèi rén móu ér bù zhōng hū?
>
> yǔ péng yǒu jiāo ér bù xìn hū? chuán bù xí hū?
>
> It translates to: "Every day, I examine myself three times: Have I been unfaithful in planning for others? Have I been insincere in my interactions with friends? Have I failed to practice what I have learned?"

Centuries later, **Descartes** would famously say,

"Cogito, ergo sum – I think, therefore I am."

The Dao Whispers: We don't have to figure everything out at once. Sometimes, just noticing what feels off is enough to begin.

A few honest questions, asked with real intention, can help more than chasing the perfect answer. Very often, it's not the answer that changes us, but the courage to finally ask what's really going on.

July 18

Don't Ignore the First Red Flag

When someone shows you who they are, believe them the first time

一朝被蛇咬，十年怕井绳

yī zhāo bèi shé yǎo, shí nián pà jǐng shéng

Translation: "You need only be bitten by a snake once, to end up fearing the rope for ten years."
— Traditional Chinese idiom

Have you ever ignored a red flag… only to wish later you hadn't? Have you ever given someone a second chance… and ended up regretting both the first and the second?

This idiom captures the lingering sting of betrayal. After being bitten by a snake, even a harmless rope can trigger fear. One act of disloyalty can change how or if we trust again.

When someone shows you who they are, you don't need to wait for a second bite. The signs are usually obvious from the start... we just often choose to ignore it.

> ***"Forgive your enemies, but never forget their names."***
> — Often attributed to **John F. Kennedy**

The Dao Whispers: They say, "Who betrays you once will betray you a thousand times; you don't need to drink the whole sea to know it's salty."

July 19

When Dreams Become Daily Life

Celebrate what we have, don't take for granted what you once prayed for

知足者常乐

zhī zú zhě cháng lè

Translation: "One who knows contentment is always happy."
— Traditional Chinese proverb

We work, plan, and hustle, always onto the next thing. A better job, a nicer flat, more recognition. But once we get there, do we pause… or just move the goalpost again?

This old proverb reminds us that happiness doesn't only come from chasing the next thing. Sometimes, it's about knowing when to pause and take in what's already here, the very things we once dreamed of.

> ***"Do not spoil what you have by desiring what you have not; remember that what you now have was once among the things you only hoped for."***
> — **Epicurus**

Ambition matters, but if it blinds us to what's already here, we risk overlooking the joy, and the very life, we once worked so hard to create.

The Dao Whispers: Gratitude doesn't just happen; it's a choice we renew again and again. Sometimes, just imagining life without what we have is enough to remind us how lucky we already are.

- What do I have today that I once wished for?
- What blessings do I take for granted, that I would grieve if they were taken away from me?

July 20

When Now is Too Late

Why the best time to dig a well is before you're thirsty

临渴掘井

lín kě jué jǐng

Translation: "Digging a well when you're thirsty."
— Traditional Chinese proverb

Ever waited until the very last minute to deal with a problem, only to find it's now ten times harder to handle? We've all done it, whether it's cramming for an exam, starting a work project the night before, or saving money only after an emergency strikes.

This 2,000-year-old saying points exactly to that issue. Waiting until disaster strikes to get your act together usually backfires. A little preparation upfront could've saved you a world of stress and headaches.

> ***"By failing to prepare, you are preparing to fail."***
> — **Benjamin Franklin**

The Dao Whispers: What am I neglecting today that could turn into tomorrow's crisis, and how can I prepare now instead of panicking later?

July 21

When Holding On Holds You Back

Forgiveness isn't forgetting, it's choosing to walk free

一笑泯恩仇

yī xiào mǐn ēn chóu

Translation: "A single smile can erase all grudges and hatred."
— Traditional Chinese proverb

That old anger you're holding on to? It's heavy. It colours how you see the world long past its expiry date. Strange how we keep feeding grudges long after they've stopped feeding us.

This saying reminds us that even deep wounds can dissolve in a single act of grace. Choosing to smile instead of stew, to release instead of ruminate – is how the chains of resentment finally break. Forgiveness may feel like a gift to others, but in truth it's the greatest gift you give yourself.

So, what will you choose?

- Hold on to the weight or drop it?
- Feed the bitterness or starve it?
- Let the past define you or decide for yourself what comes next?

> ***"If we only forgive what is forgivable, then forgiveness no longer exists. Forgiveness must address the unforgivable or it is not forgiveness at all."***
> — **Jacques Derrida**

People often say, "forgive but not forget." At first it can sound bitter, even vindictive. But seen differently, it makes sense. Forgive fully so you can let go, and remember the lesson so you don't walk into the same injury twice. Forgiveness creates space for healing, while memory protects you from repeating the same hurt.

The Dao Whispers: Forgiveness doesn't mean forgetting or trusting blindly. It means you're no longer trapped by betrayal and free to walk away.

July 22

Confident...and Completely Wrong

Being wrong is fine. Being sure you're right when you're not... that can end up being a costly illusion

自以为是

zì yǐ wéi shì

Translation: "To assume that one is always right (and others are not)."
— Traditional Chinese idiom

Ever met someone completely confident…and completely wrong? You'll see this everywhere, from loud voices in meetings to overconfident opinions at dinner tables. And let's be honest, most of us have been that person at least once.

Ancient Chinese wisdom recognised this long ago. It's not the questioners who are lost in translation, but rather, the ones who've stopped questioning because they think they've got it all figured out. Psychologists call this the Dunning–Kruger effect: the less we know, the more likely we are to overestimate what we do know. Why? Because the insight needed to spot our own mistakes is often the very thing we're missing.

What it teaches us

- **False certainty can close doors**: You stop listening, people stop trusting, and teams start making poor calls based on your overconfidence. The cost isn't just mistakes, but the loss of credibility.
- **The danger is not only being wrong – it's staying wrong:** When you think you already know, you rob yourself of the chance to learn, improve, or see a bigger picture.
- **Overconfidence can hurt trust**. When you insist you're right and dismiss others, people quietly stop sharing what you most need to hear.

> ***"The greatest enemy of knowledge is not ignorance. It is the illusion of knowledge."***
> — **Stephen Hawking**

The Dao Whispers: The more certain you feel, the more carefully you should reflect. Just because the smoke alarm didn't go off doesn't mean you cooked well.

July 23

Learning with Your Feet

To know the world, you must walk it as well as read it

读万卷书，行万里路

dú wàn juàn shū, xíng wàn lǐ lù

Translation: "Read ten thousand books and walk ten thousand miles."
— Dong Qichang

Wisdom isn't only found in libraries and books. It's also found on dodgy bus rides, lost luggage, and awkward translation fails abroad. ***"Eine frango mit kartoffel, err, popol fur eingang, und blanco wein bitte, obrigado? Mucho kartoffel please, merci."***

Books open our minds to ideas, patterns, the perspectives of great minds and the lessons of history. But to really appreciate those lessons, we must also venture out to see, feel, and challenge our assumptions. One deepens our understanding of patterns, the other reveals how those patterns actually play out ***in real life.***

What it teaches us

- **Broadened perspective:** Only through travel and exposure can we truly appreciate diverse cultures, challenge our assumptions and be more empathetic. Stay open, eat what the locals eat, the way they eat. That's usually a good start.
- **Better judgement**: Only with time can you gather sufficient data points to make meaningful comparisons. And with that experience, you can sharpen your ability to read context, navigate ambiguity, and make wiser choices.
- **Practical learning:** Learning sticks best when you pair theory with practice. It's one thing to understand an idea but applying it in real life is what helps you navigate all the grey areas.

> ***"The world is a book, and those who do not travel read only one page."***
> — **Saint Augustine**

The Dao Whispers: Which parts of life demand experience, not just theory?

July 24

Life Doesn't Have a Pause Button

Time doesn't wait around for us

时不我待

shí bù wǒ dài

Translation: "Time does not wait for me."
— Traditional Chinese proverb

Sometimes, it feels like time's racing ahead while I'm still fumbling for my to-do list, or staring blankly into the ether. Ever felt that way too?

This old proverb gives a gentle nudge: life moves on, whether or not we're ready to live it. Moments slip past, chances slip away, and that "perfect time" we're waiting for often disappears while we're still deciding what to do.

What it teaches us

Time is our most precious resource. Once it's gone, you can't get it back. Don't waste it on things or people that drain your energy or keep you from doing what truly matters. Living with intention, courage, and presence means fewer regrets down the road.

> ***"Life is what happens when you're busy making other plans."***
> — **John Lennon**

The Dao Whispers

- Am I really living my life, or just watching the days blur together on autopilot?
- What am I trading my precious hours for? Mindless distractions, people who don't appreciate my time, doomscrolling, or things I won't even remember tomorrow?

July 25

Knowing What We Don’t Know

The wise know what they do not know

智者知其所不知

zhì zhě zhī qí suǒ bù zhī

Translation: “The wise person knows what they do not know.”
— Traditional Chinese proverb

Ever been caught off guard by a question and felt the pressure to say something, even when you weren’t sure?

It’s tempting to pretend we know; to nod, guess, or blurt something that sounds right. Sometimes it even feels expected. But there is strength in saying, "I don’t know."

We have all met people who always seem to have an answer, even when they clearly don’t. Their confidence can be oddly persuasive. But this old proverb reminds us that wisdom isn’t about always being right; it’s about being honest when we’re not.

Funny thing about wisdom, it often shows up right after we admit we don’t have all the answers. That kind of humility opens the door to learning, growth, and everything that comes after.

> ***“The only true wisdom is in knowing you know nothing.”***
> — **Socrates**

The Dao Whispers

- When was the last time I said ***“I don’t know”*** and meant it?
- Do I sometimes judge others for not having the answer, even when it takes guts to say so?
- When I pretend to know, who am I really trying to impress?

July 26

The Only Sober One in the Crowd

The strength to think clearly when no one else will

举世皆浊我独清，众人皆醉我独醒

jǔ shì jiē zhuó wǒ dú qīng, zhòng rén jiē zuì wǒ dú xǐng

Translation: "When the world is cloudy, I alone am clear; when everyone around me is drunk, I alone remain sober."
— Traditional Chinese proverb

The Story

Qu Yuan, exiled and heartbroken, wandered to the banks of the Miluo River. When a fisherman asked why he grieved, he replied: ***"All the world is muddy, only I am clear. All men are drunk, only I am awake."*** He could not bear the corruption of his kingdom. When Qin conquered Chu, despair finally overcame him, and he drowned himself in the river.

To this day, his sacrifice is remembered through the Dragon Boat Festival, throwing rice dumplings into the river to keep fish from eating his body; a tribute to the poet who chose death over compromise. His words still echo today and act as a defiant cry for the courage to hold your ground in a world clouded by lies.

What it teaches us

- **Think for yourself:** Don't let Twitter tantrums, TikTok trends, or groupthink do your thinking for you. Your gut knows more than the algorithm.
- **Resist the pull of the crowd:** If the crowd's rushing toward a cliff, you don't have to follow.
- **The rarity of A+:** Excellence is never the majority. It's the exception. By sheer volume, their voices will be drowned. Just as in any classroom, perhaps only 5-10% of students achieve an A+, the same applies to ideas. Most will be ordinary, some below par, and only a small minority truly excellent. Our job is to tell the difference.

"To thine own self be true."
— **William Shakespeare**

The Dao Whispers: Have the courage to question illogical norms and notice subtle deviations in patterns. If something feels off, trust your judgement even if it's unpopular. Protect your agency.

July 27

The Power of One Focus

You can do anything, but not everything at once

一心不可二用

yī xīn bù kě èr yòng

Translation: "A single heart cannot do two things well at once."
— Traditional Chinese proverb

Ever tried replying to a text, eating lunch, and joining a Zoom call at the same time, only to realise you clicked on a scam link by accident?

This proverb is a reminder that no matter how good we think we are at multitasking, our brains were built for focus, not for juggling.

What it teaches us

- **Prioritise effectively:** Pick one thing that matters most right now and give it your full attention rather than spreading efforts thinly across multiple tasks.
- **Avoid multi-tasking:** Multitasking usually leads to doing everything worse, not better.
- **Mastery through focus:** If you want to get really good at something, you need to focus deeply and stick with it for a while.

> ***"He who is everywhere is nowhere."***
> — **Seneca**

The Dao Whispers: What deserves my full attention right now? Am I spreading myself too thin?

July 28

Win Hearts, Not Just Battles

Winning people beats seizing cities

攻心为上，攻城为下

gōng xīn wéi shàng, gōng chéng wéi xià

Translation: "Winning hearts is the highest strategy; conquering cities is the lowest."

—Sun Tzu (孙子), The Art of War (孙子兵法, **sūn zǐ bīng fǎ**)

Here's why this 2,500-year-old advice still works today:

- Yelling at your kids? They'll obey...but resent you.
- Boss demanding respect? He gets fake smiles, not loyalty.
- Trying to "win" a fight? You might end up losing the relationship.

The strongest wins are those earned through trust, not demanded through fear. And Zhuge Liang knew this well.

When the Shu Kingdom faced rebellion in the south, he led a series of campaigns against the tribal leader Meng Huo. Each time he defeated Meng Huo, he let him go.

Seven times, Meng Huo was captured. Seven times, Zhuge Liang released him without harm.

At last, Meng Huo surrendered willingly. He said, ***"Your mercy has won my heart. The southern tribes will never rebel again."*** There was no need for more war. Peace lasted for decades.

What it teaches us

- Build trust first, people follow those who listen.
- Inspire, don't control; shared goals work better than orders.
- In conflict, seek understanding instead of forcing your way through.

> ***"A leader is a dealer in hope."***
>
> — **Napoleon Bonaparte**

The Dao Whispers: Win hearts first, the rest will follow.

July 29

Form Allies Beyond Your Immediate Circle

Win close battles with faraway friends

远交近攻

yuǎn jiāo jìn gōng

Translation: "Make alliances with distant states, while attacking those who are nearby."
— Traditional Chinese proverb

Help sometimes comes from people we least expect, not the ones closest to us.

Sometimes, the ones nearby are too involved, too familiar, or too caught up in their version of you. This classic strategy reminds us that support, insight, and momentum often come from outside the inner circle.

It teaches us that to resolve nearby conflict, sometimes you need to strengthen your position elsewhere. Alliances across distance, whether geographic, political, or emotional, can give us the space and leverage to better deal with what's close, messy, and personal.

What it teaches us

- **Build long-range alliances:** Connections beyond your circle can offer fresh insight and future leverage.
- **Career reinvention:** If you're stuck, try networking across sectors, industries, or geographies. This may unlock new paths.
- **Bring in a neutral voice:** Sometimes a mentor, coach, or distant friend can help shift what those close to you cannot.

Paraphrased from **Herminia Ibarra**, a professor at LBS:

> ***"When you're reinventing yourself, your current network may unconsciously anchor you to who you've been, not who you're becoming."***

The Dao Whispers: Don't rely only on your inner circle. Expand your network before you need it. Distant allies often become powerful bridges. Who outside my circle could shift the game for me?

July 30

When the Wind Shifts

He who can read the room knows when to act, and when to wait

识时务者为俊杰

shí shí wù zhě wéi jùn jié

Translation: "He who knows when to act is the real winner."
— Traditional Chinese proverb

The right move at the wrong time is still the wrong move. This proverb says that we not only need to know what to do, but also, know when to do it.

The most effective leaders don't just charge forward with conviction. They **read the room**, sense subtle shifts, and know when to pivot. They see **not just what *is*, but what's *coming*.** They recognise the invisible forces at play – is this the right moment to push? Are people leaning in or checking out? Are they anxious and not convinced, or have they fully bought into an idea?

The difference between good and great requires not just IQ, but EQ too. Strategic intelligence means knowing when to...

- Speak or hold back.
- Push or pivot.
- Lead from the front or guide from behind the scenes.

> ***"It is not the strongest of the species that survives, nor the most intelligent, but the one most responsive to change."***
> **— Charles Darwin**

The Dao Whispers: Read the room. Notice the silence, the glance, the weight. Then decide whether it's the right time to act, or to wait.

July 31

The Verdict Was Decided Before the Trial Began

The facts don't matter when the outcome's fixed

欲加之罪，何患无辞？

yù jiā zhī zuì, hé huàn wú cí

Translation: "If you want to condemn someone, you can always find a charge."
— Traditional Chinese proverb, Attributed to Zuo Zhuan

Sometimes the verdict comes before the evidence.

This proverb reminds us of stories we've seen everywhere, from Netflix dramas about ancient kingdoms to prime-time news, modern offices, and boardrooms. When someone is determined to make someone a target, the reason becomes secondary. Facts are twisted, words reframed, narratives invented because the outcome was decided long before the inquiry even began.

And it's not just imperial courts or political thrillers. It can still happen today:

- A friend justifies distancing by rewriting the past.
- A boss who never liked you finds fault in what you say or do.
- A colleague frames your boundaries as "not a team player."

What it teaches us

- **Spot rigged dynamics:** When facts and logic don't land, bias or agenda is likely steering the room.
- **Protect your energy:** Don't waste your energy arguing with a story that's already written. Stick to what you know is true.
- **Lead wisely:** When you're in a position of power, don't just look for faults, try to see ***why*** people act the way they do. And, at the end of the day, trust your gut.

> ***"Someone must have been telling lies about Josef K., for without having done anything wrong, he was arrested one fine morning."***
> — **Franz Kafka**

The Dao Whispers: Don't exhaust yourself fighting twisted logic. Step back. The truth has a way of surfacing in its own time.

AUGUST

明

míng

Meaning of 明 (míng):

- Clarity
- Inner knowing
- Strategic discernment
- Illuminated perception
- Insight

明 (míng) is the lantern that lights the path ahead. It is not merely intelligence, but an awakened sort of understanding, the kind that emerges only after deliberate reflection, and lived experience.

Mastering 明 (míng) allows us to:

- **Read between the lines:** See what others miss. Not just what is presented to us, but also what lies hidden in between the lines.
- **Separate what matters from what doesn't:** Separate signal from false positive, opportunity from mirage, and truth from untruths, to cite a few.
- **Master the art of timing:** Know when to speak, when to act, when to let go, and when to wait.
- **Stay true to core values:** Make decisions that are aligned with values, relationships, and long-term direction; not just what looks good today.
- **Stay hungry to learn:** Stay teachable, humble, and open to better ways. The smartest people know they don't know it all.

August 1

When a Shark Grins, Count Its Teeth

There is a dagger behind the smile

笑里藏刀

xiào lǐ cáng dāo

Translation: "To conceal a dagger behind a smile."
— Thirty-Six Stratagems (三十六计, sān shí liù jì)

Some people use charm as cover. They seem warm, helpful, even friendly. But behind the smile might be something sharper – envy, ambition, or quiet resentment. This proverb is a reminder to trust slowly and to pay attention. Not everything that looks kind is kind. Some of the biggest betrayals come wrapped in friendliness.

What it teaches us

- **Guarding trust**: Be careful of excessive charm from new acquaintances. Watch their actions, not just their words.
- **Office politics**: Don't be disarmed by flattery. Ask yourself: ***Why now? What's at stake?***
- **Negotiating**: A handshake and smile may hide sharp terms. Read both contracts and intentions with equal care.

> ***"Men are so simple and so subject to present necessities that he who seeks to deceive will always find someone who will allow himself to be deceived."***
> — **Niccolò Machiavelli**

The Dao Whispers

- A sudden smile can sometimes unsheathe a knife.
- Free gifts come with invisible price tags.
- Trust should be earned in teaspoons, not poured in gallons.
- When a shark grins, count its teeth.
- The sweetest fruits grow nearest the thorns.
- Being polite doesn't mean they have your best interests at heart.
- There is no free lunch.

August 2

The Weight of Promises

If broken promises added weight, the world would be obese

食言而肥

shí yán ér féi

Translation: "Growing fat from eating one's own words."
— Zhuozhuan, Duke Ai of Lu, Year 25(《左传·哀公二十五年》)

The Story

During the **Spring and Autumn period**, the **State of Lu (鲁国)** was engaged in diplomatic talks with the neighbouring **State of Zou (邾国)** to form an alliance. The delegation from Zou arrived as planned but at the last minute, **Duke Ai of Lu (鲁哀公)** backed out of the agreement and **refused to meet them**, effectively betraying the trust established between the two states.

His loyal and upright minister, **Guo Chong (郭重)** known not only for his integrity but also for his rather large build, was deeply offended by the breach of honour. In a moment of bold, moral clarity, Guo Chong **publicly scolded the Duke**, saying: ***"My lord, you are growing fat just from eating your own words!" (君食言而肥!)***

To this day, the idiom is used to call out those who:

- Break promises for personal gain.
- Say one thing and do another.
- Keep up appearances while betraying trust when it pays.

> ***"A business model that relies on trickery is doomed to fail."***
> **— Charlie Munger**

The Dao Whispers: Do I keep my promises?

August 3

The Polite Assassin: Duplicitous by Design

Not all harm comes from enemies

两面三刀

liǎng miàn sān dāo

Translation: "Two faces, three knives."
— Traditional Chinese idiom

This idiom describes someone who is duplicitous and treacherous, pretending to be friendly or neutral while secretly wielding multiple layers of deceit or harm. "Two faces" represent hypocrisy and double-dealing, while "three knives" symbolise complex, hidden betrayal. It serves as a reminder that not all harm comes through open conflict. Some of the most dangerous people conceal their intentions behind charm, smiles, and carefully chosen words.

What it teaches us

- **Protect personal boundaries**: Watch out for those who flatter you in person but undermine you behind closed doors.
- **Watch out for manipulators**: If they deceive others, they will eventually deceive you too.
- **Read duplicity as a pattern, not a tactic**: Those who play both sides in conflicts are often hardwired to serve only themselves. These are the ***nefarious personalities*** that modern psychology sometimes describes under the "**Dark Triad**" – narcissism, Machiavellianism, and psychopathy.

> ***"I'm not upset that you lied to me, I'm upset that from now on I can't believe you."***
> — **Friedrich Nietzsche** (Beyond Good and Evil)

We cannot control others. But recognising the dual nature of people, their capacity for both good and malice, is the beginning of understanding the true nature of humans. That awareness is not cynicism; it is where naivety begins to mature into wisdom.

The Dao Whispers: In a just world, only mildly harmful people would exist. The good news is, in our world, they do exist. And the bad news is, so do the deeply malicious. The trick is learning to tell the difference. ***Not all darkness announces itself loudly; some smiles are masks of control.***

August 4

The Danger of Being Too Agreeable

The horse without resistance is ridden; the person without boundaries is used

人善被人欺，马善被人骑

rén shàn bèi rén qī, mǎ shàn bèi rén qí

Translation: "A kind person shall be bullied; while a tame horse shall be ridden."
— Traditional Chinese proverb

This saying strikes a chord because it shows how being too nice can backfire. People often mistake kindness for weakness and suddenly you find yourself being walked over. Being too agreeable doesn't earn respect, it only invites exploitation. Even the gentlest soul needs boundaries. The horse metaphor is spot on – the more you let people ride you, the more they will treat you like a doormat.

What it teaches us

- **Kindness with boundaries**: Generosity without limits often invites exploitation, especially when you run into someone malevolent. Compassion includes self-respect.
- **Skip the superhero cape:** In high-pressure workplaces, competence gets punished with more work – not more rewards. Learn to set boundaries, and if possible, find a manager who actually notices and advocates for you.
- **Leading with confidence:** Lead with your heart, but never waver. Good leaders balance empathy with conviction. People respect you when you listen and understand, but they trust you when you make the hard calls. Good leadership is soft skills anchored by a strong backbone.

> ***"It is better to be feared than loved, if you cannot be both."***
> — **Niccolò Machiavelli**

The Dao Whispers: Being too agreeable doesn't earn respect, it invites exploitation.

August 5

Rich, Broke, or Powerful – Still You?

Do you lose yourself while chasing comfort?

富贵不能淫，贫贱不能移

fù guì bù néng yín, pín jiàn bù néng yí

Translation: "Great is the one whom wealth cannot corrupt, poverty cannot sway, and power cannot bend."
— Mencius (孟子)

Money changes people. So does struggle. Both tempt you to trade pieces of yourself for some form of comfort, or reward.

- **The Newly Rich** who forget their old values.
- **The Desperate** who justify "just this once."
- **The Powerful** who start believing their own narratives.

Mencius' words are not a rejection of ambition, but a challenge. ***Can we stay true to ourselves while climbing, or surviving?***

The three anchors in stormy seas

- **The Mirror Rule:** If your younger self saw you today, would they approve or look away?
- **The Poverty Test:** What would you still refuse to do, even if it meant eating plain bread tomorrow?
- **The Power Audit:** Would you say this to someone who couldn't help your career?

> ***"Live so that when your children think of fairness, caring, and integrity, they think of you."***
> **— H. Jackson Brown, Jr.**

The Dao Whispers

- What is the price of my morality, and what is the cost of my ambition?
- When tempted by comfort or status, where do I draw the line?
- Can I still say "no" when the cost of honesty is high?

August 6

There is No One Right Way

We must adapt our thinking based on the context

因时制宜

yīn shí zhì yí

Translation: "(One must) Adapt measures to suit the time (and context)."
— Traditional Chinese proverb

What worked last year may fail today. What was wise in one culture can backfire in another. There's no eternal playbook, only timing, judgment, and awareness.

This old Chinese saying reminds us that wisdom isn't about having fixed answers. It's about knowing how to adjust, understanding the context, and knowing when to shift course.

Some strategies work beautifully in one situation and fall flat in another. What seems unwise today may be strategic tomorrow. Even traits we admire, such as honesty or boldness, can land very differently depending on the time, place, or people involved.

There is no one-size-fits-all answer to most things, just as

- **Leadership is contextual**: Directive leadership may work well with inexperienced teams but can frustrate seasoned ones.
- **Strategy is contextual:** Expansion during a downturn may make sense for companies with a strong balance sheet, but risky for others with cashflow issues.
- **Character traits are contextual:** Silence is revered as wisdom in the East; but often misread as meekness in the West. Think ***"quiet"*** and ***Wall Street.*** Doesn't quite work, does it?

> ***"Foolish consistency is the hobgoblin of little minds."***
> — **Ralph Waldo Emerson**

The Dao Whispers: Am I forcing a rigid framework based on my own culture, past experiences, or outdated assumptions, onto a situation that plays by different rules?

August 7

Remember Who Helped Your Rise

Don't forget who dug the well

吃水不忘挖井人

chī shuǐ bù wàng wā jǐng rén

Translation: "When you drink water, don't forget the one who dug the well."
— Traditional Chinese proverb

The invisible ladder

Every success stands on sacrifices that are not visible.

- The mentor who answered emails at midnight.
- The generations before us who built the infrastructure and systems we now have.
- The parents who skipped meals for your education.

The three anchors in stormy seas

- **The Name Test:** Can you list five people who made possible your current position? (Not just bosses, think teachers, rivals, janitors)
- **The Mirror Question:** Would the 10-year-old you be proud of how you treat helpers today?
- **The Inheritance Audit:** What advantages did you luck into? (Language, timing, passport, safety)

> ***"If I have seen further, it is by standing on the shoulders of giants."***
> — **Isaac Newton**

The Dao Whispers

- Do I honour the people who helped me rise?
- Who made my success possible, and have I thanked them?
- Have I recognised and honoured the invisible work behind my success?

This week's challenge

Find one "well-digger" from your past, and send a specific memory, not just thanks.

August 8

Small Things Matter More Than You Think

A single match can start a fire; a single decision can change your life

一粒米可以倾覆整个船

yī lì mǐ kě yǐ qīng fù zhěng gè chuán

Translation: "A single grain of rice can capsize a ship."
— Traditional Chinese proverb

The physics of collapse

History's greatest disasters often began with something that seemed small, almost invisible.

- **A loose bolt** doomed the Challenger shuttle.
- **A missed comma** can cost a company $10M in legal fees.
- **Sleeping less** than five hours a night doubles your risk of dementia and of early death.

This proverb explains that even the smallest detail, left unchecked, can trigger outsized consequences. What seems trivial today may become the fault line tomorrow. And when the load is heavy, even a single grain can tip the balance.

What it teaches us

- **Tend to what matters**: Small daily choices shape long-term health, habits, and integrity.
- **Maintain relationships**: Small resentments left unspoken grow into distance.
- **Mind your finances:** Track seemingly small expenses (daily coffee purchases, unused subscriptions), small leaks can sink big plans.
- **Protect your peace:** Minor stressors unattended can wear resilience out.
- **Build with micro-actions:** One page a day, one honest word, one intentional step. Each builds momentum.

> ***"The chains of habit are too light to be felt until they are too heavy to be broken."***
> ***— Samuel Johnson***

The Dao Whispers: Is there anything that looks trivial today that may tip the scale later?

August 9

Don't Suffer More Than Life Asks of You

Hold steady when life's highs and lows try to pull you apart

不以物喜，不以己悲

bù yǐ wù xǐ, bù yǐ jǐ bēi

Translation: "To not be excessively overjoyed by external gains, nor overly distressed by personal loss."
— Yueyang Tower Record (岳阳楼记) by Fan Zhongyan, Song Dynasty

The idiom advocates for emotional equanimity – a mind unshaken by fortune or misfortune. It invites steadiness and detachment, not reacting excessively to success or sorrow, gain or loss.

It is not indifference, but the clarity to know what is within your control and refusing to let your peace be held hostage by what isn't.

What it teaches us

- **Cultivate equanimity and inner stability**: Life will throw highs and lows at you, but you don't have to ride every emotional rollercoaster. Stay anchored.
- **Be kind to yourself**: It's okay to admit when things are hard, but don't get lost in it. Treat yourself as kindly as you would someone you love.
- **Not every opinion carries equal weight, practise the art of weighted credibility:** Some criticism says more about the critic than about you. A piglet judging Mozart says more about the piglet than the music.

> ***"Who then is invincible? The one who cannot be upset by anything outside their reasoned choice."***
> — **Epictetus**

The Dao Whispers

- When good things happen, can I stay grounded?
- When disappointment hits, do I suffer more than I should? Ask, ***"Will this matter in 10 years? 10 months? 10 days?"***

August 10

Not Every Fire Needs You to Jump In

Watch the fire from across the river

隔岸观火

gé àn guān huǒ

Translation: "Watch the fire from across the river."
— Thirty-Six Stratagems (三十六计, sān shí liù jì)

We all want to be helpful. But not every situation needs our bucket of water. Some fires burn hotter when more people rush in. Others fizzle out if left alone.

Instead of rushing in to fix a mess that isn't yours, sometimes it's best to take a step back, observe, and wait. This doesn't mean you don't care. It means you value timing, perspective, and self-preservation.

Originally from classical Chinese strategy, this idiom teaches us to hold back until the picture is clear, the risk is understood, and the moment is right.

What it teaches us

- **Steer clear of pointless fights**: Skipping family or work drama isn't being indifferent, sometimes it's how we keep peace.
- **Think before jumping in**: Holding off to figure out a messy situation is usually better than rushing in and making things worse.
- **Protect your own stability:** Helping someone who's knee-deep in their mess without boundaries can drag you down. Know where to draw the line.

"Silence is the sanctuary of prudence.
The cautious seldom err."
— **Baltasar Gracián**

The Dao Whispers: Maybe the next time you face a messy situation, ask, "Can I give it time before deciding if it really needs me?"

August 11

If the Roof Leaks, the Floor Floods

When leaders drift, so does everyone else

官风不正，民风必邪

guān fēng bù zhèng, mín fēng bì xié

Translation: "If the conduct of the officials is corrupt, the morals of the people will not be otherwise."
— Traditional Chinese proverb

Leaders are like parents in a household.

They don't just give orders, they set the tone. When leaders cut corners, show favouritism, or bend the rules for personal gain, they normalise that behaviour for everyone else.

This proverb speaks to that ripple effect. When those at the top act without integrity, it shapes the culture beneath them. This is not just true in government, but in businesses, schools, and families. Over time, corruption at the top cascades through the system as it becomes normalised.

What it teaches us

- **Ethical decay spreads quickly:** When leaders bend rules for personal gain, it sends a signal to others that integrity is optional.
- **Culture mirrors leadership.** Self-serving leaders create an ***"every person for themselves"*** mindset, disengaged teams and cutthroat environments.
- **Rule-bending becomes habit:** When misconduct is accepted at the top, it soon becomes routine below. Once it takes root, it is difficult to undo.

Plato observed that when society is unjust by design, it sows further injustice as people come to see corruption as normal.

The Dao Whispers

- Does the conduct of those above me shape how I act?
- Do I mistake power for correctness, or am I brave enough to question it?
- What kind of leader am I, and what kind of leaders do I choose to follow?

August 12

The Trap of False Urgency

The emperor is not anxious, yet the eunuch is in a panic

皇帝不急，太监急

huáng dì bù jí, tài jiàn jí

Translation: "The emperor is not anxious, but the eunuch is in a hurry."
— Traditional Chinese proverb

Ever met someone who's pacing, fretting, overthinking, while the person at the centre of it all is sipping coffee like it's Sunday morning?

This old Chinese proverb captures that dynamic perfectly. A lower-ranking official (the eunuch) is in full panic mode, while the emperor, the one actually in charge, stays calm.

It's a reminder that anxiety doesn't always equal importance. Sometimes we panic not because it's needed, but because we don't know what else to do. Other times, we confuse motion with progress.

What it teaches us

- **Stay grounded at work:** Creating false urgency may signal poor judgement, not dedication.
- **Balance personal priorities**: Learn to tell the difference between what ***feels*** urgent and what **actually** is urgent.
- **Avoid emotional overreaction:** One unread message does not mean abandonment, or sidelining; let's not catastrophise.

> ***"Take time for all things. Great haste makes great waste."***
> — ***Benjamin Franklin***

The Dao Whispers

- Am I rushing to fix what no one else sees as broken?
- Why am I sprinting when no one fired the starting gun?
- Am I stressing my team out unnecessarily with false urgency?

August 13

Trust Grows and Breaks from the Little Things

It's the little things we do, or don't do, that people remember

小信诚则大信立

xiǎo xìn chéng zé dà xìn lì

Translation: "Keeping small promises adds up, it builds trust over time."
— Traditional Chinese proverb

We often think that trust comes from big milestones, grand gestures, or grand declarations of loyalty. But more often than not, trust is built over time and in the shadows of daily life; that's the message behind this proverb.

It's showing up when you said you would. Following through on the small stuff. Keeping your word even when no one is watching. These little acts stack up. Over time, they form your reputation, the version of you that others learn to rely on.

What it teaches us

- **Be someone people can count on:** Be punctual. Follow through. Do what we say, even when it seems minor.
- **In relationships, the small stuff matters:** Saying "I'll call you later" and actually doing it builds more trust than one big speech.
- **Reliability is steady:** Trust isn't built in a day. It's built in dozens of "I've got you" moments that you actually show up for.

> ***"Character may almost be called the most effective means of persuasion."***
> **— Aristotle**

The Dao Whispers

- Do I follow through on the little things I say?
- Do I show up for others and do they consistently show up for me?
- What do my daily actions say about who I really am?

August 14

When the General Lies, the Team Pays

An untrustworthy leader cannot be trusted to lead well

将无信，不可使也

jiàng wú xìn, bù kě shǐ yě

Translation: "A general who is not trustworthy cannot be employed."
— Traditional Chinese proverb

If a leader's word means nothing, neither do their strategy, promises, or vision. Their social contract with you will surely be voided, it's only a matter of time before the cracks show.

The proverb calls out that *good* leadership is impossible without trustworthiness.

And when someone breaks trust repeatedly, it's not an accident, it's a habit.

Red flags of an untrustworthy leader:

- Quick to take credit, and quicker to shift blame.
- Makes promises they never intend to keep.
- Throws the team under the bus for self-preservation.
- Silent in the face of wrongdoing is complicity in disguise.
- Uses flattery or charm to manipulate trust.
- Undermines colleagues privately, while posturing publicly.
- Gaslights others to deny accountability.
- Repeatedly bails on commitments.
- Consistently fails to show up physically or emotionally.

> ***"We look for three things when we hire people: intelligence, energy, and integrity. And if they don't have the last one, the first two will kill you."***
> — **Warren Buffett**

The Dao Whispers: With people of integrity, contracts are courtesy. With the untrustworthy, no contract can protect you, and the terms are likely full of traps.

August 15

Those Who Pull Others Down Won't Lift You Up

Like crabs in a net, some only climb by dragging others down

狗嘴里吐不出象牙

gǒu zuǐ lǐ tǔ bù chū xiàng yá

Translation: "You can't get ivory from a dog's mouth."
— Traditional Chinese proverb

Ever found yourself waiting for kindness from someone who only ever tears others down? Or hoping for wisdom from someone who gossips more than they listen?

This proverb is a gentle reminder that not everyone is capable of giving what you're hoping for, not because they're cruel but because they may simply not have it in them. Expecting insight from someone who's never learned to reflect, or softness from someone hardened by their own pain, will only leave you frustrated.

Instead of judging or resenting them, maybe it's time to protect your peace. Don't waste energy searching for gold where it never existed.

What it teaches us

- **Adjust your expectations:** If someone's always negative or harsh, don't expect a sudden burst of empathy. It's not personal – it's just who they are.
- **Protect your energy:** Don't keep opening up to people who drain or criticise you. Some just climb by dragging others down, like crabs in a net. Not everyone earns access to your inner circle.
- **Watch what they do:** People who speak poorly often act poorly too. Pay attention to what they do, not just what they say.

"They muddy the water to make it seem deep."
— Friedrich Nietzsche

The Dao Whispers: It's best not to expect wisdom from where it cannot exist.

August 16

One Rule for the Monk, Another for You?

When rules bend for some, they must bend for all

和尚摸得，我摸不得

hé shàng mō dé, wǒ mō bù dé

Translation: "If a monk can touch it, why can't I."
— Traditional Chinese proverb

Rules are rules… until someone decides they're optional. Ever noticed how some people seem to play by a different set? They bend them, break them, or get a free pass, while the rest of us are held to the letter.

This proverb calls that out. With humour but a sharp edge, it challenges us to see through the double standards we're often told to accept. Traditionally, it pokes fun at hypocrisy. Why should someone supposedly bound by stricter codes – like a monk – get away with more? Beneath the satire is a timeless reminder that justice only works when rules apply equally.

What it teaches us

- **Think critically:** Just because a rule exists doesn't make it just. Once in a while, we have an obligation to question it.
- **Call out inconsistency:** When rules are enforced for some but not for others, call it out. Fairness only means something if it applies to everyone. Selective rule enforcement is like a small crack; it spreads until it fractures the whole system.
- **Hold authority accountable:** Leaders demonstrate integrity when they live by the same standards they set.

> ***"All animals are equal, but some animals are more equal than others."***
> ***— George Orwell***

The Dao Whispers

- Do I hold myself to the same standards I expect of others, or do I look away when I see double standards?
- Do I have the courage to speak up, especially for those who cannot?

August 17

There's Room for Others to Be Different

The vastness of the ocean comes from its ability to accept a hundred rivers

海纳百川，有容乃大

hǎi nà bǎi chuān, yǒu róng nǎi dà

Translation: "The sea accepts a hundred rivers; its greatness lies in its capacity."
— Traditional Chinese proverb

The ocean doesn't complain that one river is too muddy or another flows too fast. It just takes them in, and that's how it became vast. This proverb reminds us that power doesn't always come insisting on doing things our way. Sometimes it comes from making space for different views, different people, and even a bit of mess. You don't have to agree with everyone. But if you can't tolerate difference, your world becomes smaller than it needs to be.

What it teaches us

- **Stay open**: You don't have to agree with every opinion, but hearing it won't harm you. It might even teach you something.
- **Lead by creating space for others:** It's not just about who's at the table, but who's really being heard.
- **Inclusivity has limits**: Making space for others doesn't mean tolerating bad behaviour. Boundaries still matter.

> ***"I have always believed that a nation is built by bringing together diverse talents and letting them thrive."***
> — *Lee Kuan Yew*

> ***"Our challenge, our generation's unique challenge, is learning to live peacefully and sustainably in an extraordinarily crowded world."***
> — *Jeffrey Sachs*

The Dao Whispers: Am I shutting out ideas simply because they challenge me? Do I harbour conscious or unconscious biases about people or ways of life – and who says different has to mean inferior?

August 18

The Bill for Ignoring the Wise Comes Fast

Hard-earned wisdom is the cheapest insurance you'll ever buy

不听老人言，吃亏在眼前

bù tīng lǎo rén yán, chī kuī zài yǎn qián

Translation: "If you do not listen to the advice of elders, you will surely suffer losses before your very eyes."
— Traditional Chinese proverb

Ever brushed off advice from someone older, thinking ***"Times have changed, what do they know?"*** only to end up learning the exact same lesson but with more pain and less money in your wallet?

Those who have walked ahead of us have weathered seasons of hardship, success, regret, and renewal. Their advice may not always sound flashy or 'modern,' but it's often been paid for in scars and second chances. This ancient proverb reminds us not to be too quick to dismiss elders as outdated or irrelevant. We may end up finding ourselves retracing their missteps.

What it teaches us

- **Learn from the mistakes of others:** It's easy to assume that we're the exception. Many before us thought they knew better, only to pay dearly for the same mistakes.
- **Prevent unnecessary losses:** Heeding seasoned counsel can save you time, money, and heartbreak.
- **Treat elder advice as a gift**: Every warning carries the echo of a scar. Every encouragement holds a memory of pain endured and hope reclaimed. It's like buying a ticket for the same journey they've taken but paying only a fraction of the cost.

> ***"It's good to learn from your mistakes, it's better to learn from other people's mistakes."***
> — **Warren Buffett**

The Dao Whispers: Do I insist on learning everything the hard way, or can I borrow wisdom from those who've already paid the price?

August 19

The Only Way Out Is Through

With experience, comes wisdom
Every scar carries a lesson

不经一事，不长一智

bù jīng yī shì, bù zhǎng yī zhì

Translation: "One cannot gain wisdom, without first gaining experience."
— Traditional Chinese proverb

No matter how many books we read or lectures we attend, our understanding only crystallises when life tests us. Whether it's a difficult decision, a painful mistake, or an unexpected turn, every challenge is the price we pay for perspective.

This proverb reminds us that there is no shortcut to wisdom, we earn it by walking through it ourselves.

What it teaches us

- **Learning from mistakes:** Errors or failures aren't just setbacks but stepping stones to better judgement.
- **Value experience:** Being in the thick of things, from hands-on tasks to crisis management, sharpens our instincts and strengthens our toolkit.
- **Growth through adversity:** Life's hard knocks don't just build grit, they teach you how others struggle too. It's the messy stuff that helps us understand the complexity of life more deeply.

> ***"Good judgement comes from experience, and experience comes from bad judgement."***
> — **Rita Mae Brown**

The Dao Whispers

- What hardship have I survived, and what did it teach me that nothing else could?
- Am I ***actually living,*** or just watching life happen to me from the sidelines?

August 20

The Loudest Accuser Is Often the Guilty One

Deflection as the oldest trick in the book

贼喊捉贼

zéi hǎn zhuō zéi

Translation: "The thief shouts, 'Catch the thief!'"
— Traditional Chinese proverb

The one raising the alarm is sometimes the one who set the fire. This proverb captures that perfectly. The thief causes a distraction by yelling, "Look, a thief!" and avoids getting caught himself.

We see this everywhere. In politics, at work, in group chats, and family dinner tables. Someone messes up, but instead of owning it, they deflect. They blame others, shift the spotlight, and stir confusion until no one knows what really happened.

It might work in the short term. But over time, people catch on. Trust fades, reputations get ruined, and finger-pointing starts to feel more like guilt than innocence.

What it teaches us

- **Character is shaped by accountability:** Owning your mistakes shows strength and earns respect.
- **Deflection repels the right people:** Blame games cost you real friends and leave you surrounded by those ready to also shove you under the bus when it suits them.
- **Reputation follows patterns:** If one always deflects blame or throws others under the bus, eventually no one will believe them even when they tell the truth.

> ***"When you place blame on others, you give up your power to change."***
> — **Robert Anthony**

The Dao Whispers: Do I take responsibility for my part, or do I just point fingers? Have I ever thrown someone under the bus to protect myself? And if I've been thrown under one, what's the most constructive way forward?

August 21

We Can't Plan a Life Together If We Want Different Things

No strategy survives if your principles are irreconcilable

道不同，不相为谋

dào bù tóng, bù xiāng wéi móu

Translation: "When our core values are irreconcilable, we likely cannot make plans together."
— Traditional Chinese proverb

Not all disagreements are negotiable. If you and your partner, co-founder, or organisation are on completely different pages about what truly matters, it doesn't matter how detailed the plan is or how polished the contract looks. You can't fake alignment. To build anything meaningful – a relationship, a company, or even a long-term career – everyone has to be aiming in the same direction from the start. Otherwise, no strategy, contract, or charm will bridge that gap.

What this teaches us

- **In relationships**: When your views on trust, commitment, or life priorities clash, it often leads to disconnection and eventually, a breakdown, no matter how strong the chemistry is.
- **In career:** If your values are at odds with those of your organisation, for example purpose-driven leadership versus profit-at-all-costs, burnout and disillusionment are often just a matter of time.
- **In partnerships:** If you and your co-founder or teammate are misaligned on the future or the rules you play by, things will eventually fall apart. It's less a matter of fault than of fit.

> ***"Friendship is impossible among those who do not share values."***
> — **Aristotle**

The Dao Whispers: Do I actually know what the people I'm building with stand for, and are we heading in the same direction? Are our differences irreconcilable or can we find a way forward? What's the cost of staying misaligned?

August 22

The Only Silly Question is the One Not Asked

The smartest people aren't afraid to ask 'obvious' questions

敏而好学，不耻下问

mǐn ér hào xué, bù chǐ xià wèn

Translation: "Be quick to learn, never be embarrassed to ask those junior to you."
— Confucius (孔子), Analects (论语)

Kids will ask ***why* a** hundred times before breakfast. Adults? We'd rather stay confused than risk looking silly. Somewhere along the way, we traded curiosity for pride. (*And someone says... thank goodness for ChatGPT!*)

Confucius reminds us that there's nothing embarrassing about asking or learning from someone younger, junior, or seen as "less important" than us. Smart people know they don't have all the answers, so they stay curious, ask questions freely, and learn from anyone willing to teach them.

And honestly, it's a sign of real intelligence to ask without worrying about looking silly. The "I've got this" act might save face for a minute, but it rarely makes you smarter.

What it teaches us

- **Good ideas don't care about titles:** Great ideas can come from anywhere – an intern, a stranger, a kid. If you only listen to "experts," you might miss the best insight.
- **Growth = asking:** Every time you ask, you get closer to knowing. Staying silent just keeps you stuck.
- **Pride slows learning:** The moment you care more about looking smart than becoming smart, you stop growing.

> ***"He who asks a question is a fool for five minutes; he who does not ask remains a fool forever."***
> *(问是一时之耻，不问是一世之耻;*
> *wèn shì yī shí zhī chǐ, bù wèn shì yī shì zhī chǐ)*
> — Modern Chinese saying

The Dao Whispers: The only silly question is the one we never asked. Are you willing to let go of pride to learn and get smarter?

August 23

When Standards Become Self-Destructive

King Chu loved slender waists, and so his courtiers starved themselves to lose weight

楚王好细腰，宫中多饿死

chǔ wáng hào xì yāo, gōng zhōng duō è sǐ

Translation: "The King of Chu loved slender waists, and many in his court ended up starving to death."
— Han Feizi (韩非子)

The Story

During the Spring and Autumn period in ancient China, King Ling of Chu (楚灵王) loved slender waists so much that his courtiers and concubines began to starve themselves to win his favour.

They ate sparingly. Some even resorted to extreme diets, tightening their belts, or wrapping themselves to appear thinner. Over time, many weakened, fell ill, and some died of malnutrition.

This saying captures the destructive impact of blind conformity and the harm caused when leaders impose personal whims as standards.

> ***"We are never so ridiculous through what we are as through what we pretend to be."***
> — **François de La Rochefoucauld**

La Rochefoucauld's line captures the absurdity of pretending to be something we're not. That is exactly what those courtiers did.

The Dao Whispers

- **Health and body image**: Are you chasing ideals of beauty, status or success that risk your peace or well-being?
- **Workplace pressure:** Are you overworking or bending your ethics just to meet unreasonable demands?
- **Relationships:** Are you bending yourself into a pretzel just to fit someone else's idea of "perfect?"
- **Leadership responsibility:** If you're in power, are your standards inspiring growth or causing harm to your followers?

August 24

The Perfectionist's Pitfall

To look for bones in an egg

鸡蛋里挑骨头

jī dàn lǐ tiāo gǔ tou

Translation: "Picking bones out of an egg."
— Han Feizi (韩非子)

You say "perfectionist."
They say, "You missed an Oxford comma on page 89."

This saying highlights the absurdity of hypercritical behaviour, where people zoom in on tiny flaws in otherwise good work and lose sight of the bigger picture.

In love, at work, or in your head, constant nitpicking is like death by a thousand cuts. That kind of nitpicking usually stifles the very thing it tries to perfect. (And perfect is a myth...)

What it teaches us

- **Workplace dynamics**: Being fixated on minor flaws in an otherwise successful project demotivates teams and redirects energy toward details that don't move the needle.
- **Relationships:** Nitpicking a partner's harmless habits strains intimacy and erodes goodwill.
- **Personal growth:** Ruminating on small missteps gets in the way of growth and ends up undermining your own self-confidence.

> ***"You have your way. I have my way. As for the right way, the correct way, and the only way, it does not exist."***
> — **Friedrich Nietzsche**

The Dao Whispers: There are many ways to skin the cat. Before nitpicking, ask: Is this useful, or just me looking for bones in an egg? Will this change the answer?

August 25

Nepotism is Human Nature

When one rises, even their chickens and dogs tag along

一人得道，鸡犬升天

yī rén dé dào, jī quǎn shēng tiān

Translation: "When one attains enlightenment, even their chickens and dogs rise to heaven."
— Traditional Chinese proverb

The proverb conveys the idea that when an individual gains power or success, those around them, even the unqualified or incidentally present, are lifted along with them.

Historically, it was often used with irony, pointing to nepotism, favouritism, or the unearned rewards of proximity. In modern terms, it reflects both uplift and unfairness, a reminder that influence can lift others, but also bend the rules of fairness.

What it teaches us

- **Use influence wisely:** Success gives you the power to lift others. It also helps you enable freeloaders; the choice is ultimately yours.
- **Proximity over merit:** Success can compound bias when rewards go to those nearby and not those most deserving.
- **The effect on meritocracy**: When someone's inner circle gets ahead without earning it, people lose trust, meritocracy declines and the whole system suffers in the long run.

> ***"The first method for estimating the intelligence of a ruler is to look at the men around him."***
>
> **— Friedrich Nietzsche**

The Dao Whispers: Nepotism feels unjust only when you are not the one favoured. The truth is, people often prefer to work with who they like or trust, and that is simply human nature.

- Influence is a multiplier. Am I amplifying merit, or enabling mediocrity?
- And if I've been the chicken in someone else's ascent... what did I learn? *(Always make sure you're someone's chicken?!)*

August 26

The Hidden Cost of Keeping It All

The CEO paradox: hoard profits and lose the best talents, or find a win-win?

财聚则民散，财散则民聚

cái jù zé mín sàn, cái sàn zé mín jù

Translation: "The ruler who hoards wealth scatters his people; the ruler who shares it unites them."
— Guanzi (管子), Warring States period

People don't stick around when everything's kept at the top. When leaders hoard power, money, or credit, resentment builds, trust fades, and motivation quickly dies.

But when success is shared through fair pay, real opportunities, or equitable access, people show up with more energy, loyalty, and purpose. Because deep down, we all work harder for something we feel part of, and that's exactly what the proverb alludes to.

What it teaches us

- **Leadership and trust**: Hoarding resources (money, power, opportunities) breeds disengagement and disloyalty. CEOs who cling to stock options may end up with talent quietly quitting, while those who share equity have better odds of building armies of innovators.
- **Wealth and society:** Equitable, meritocratic systems build thriving societies, Singapore being a case in point. When everyone has a real chance to get ahead based on talent and hard work, the whole society does well. But when a society becomes too unequal, talent gets wasted, mediocrity dominates, and decline sets in. History shows this pattern again and again.

> ***"We make a living by what we get, but we make a life by what we give."***
> — **Winston Churchill**

The Dao Whispers: Is the person leading you sharing the pie or just the crumbs? And are you lifting those who work hard to make you succeed along with you?

August 27

In the Place You Least Expect

We search endlessly, only to find what we seek hiding in plain sight

众里寻他千百度，蓦然回首，
那人却在灯火阑珊处

zhòng lǐ xún tā qiān bǎi dù, mò rán huí shǒu,

nà rén què zài dēng huǒ lán shān chù

Translation: "A thousand times I searched for him in the crowd. Suddenly, I turned, and there he was, where the lights were dim."
— Xin Qiji, Song Dynasty

We chase meaning in crowded rooms and imagined futures, thinking purpose lives under spotlights. We search for love, identity, and truth through noise, ambition, and projection.

But what we seek isn't always obvious. Some truths are subtle, some souls stay quiet, and some callings only whisper.

Whether it's a soulmate, a vocation, or a part of ourselves long forgotten, some of the most profound things reveal themselves when we stop chasing and turn inward.

> ***"Sometimes when you're looking for something, you look right past it."***
> — **George Moore**

The Dao Whispers: The rarest encounters reveal themselves when we stop chasing. What's meant for you won't pass you by. Follow your heart – what's real will always find its way home.

August 28

No Ctrl + Z in Real Life

The wood has already been made into a boat,
it is what it is

木已成舟

mù yǐ chéng zhōu

Translation: "The wood has already been made into a boat."
— Traditional Chinese proverb

Some choices cannot be undone.

Once you had a forest of possibilities. You cut the tree. You carved the planks. You hammered the nails.

And now? You've got a boat.

You can't un-chop the tree. You can't put the sawdust back. So whether it floats or leaks, this is what you've got to work with.

This old saying reminds us that some things in life are irreversible. The project was launched. The words were said. The relationship changed. The time has passed. There's no Ctrl + Z. But that doesn't mean there's no way forward. You can still learn to sail.

What it teaches us

- **Letting go of remorse:** Obsessing over ***what-ifs*** won't change the outcome. Let go, learn what you can, and shift your energy forward.
- **Leadership and accountability:** Good leaders acknowledge and own irreversible changes. Rather than regret them, they realign their teams and lead forward.
- **Heal and grow:** Whether it's a misstep, a loss, or a closed chapter, they're part of life. Coming to terms with them can help us grow stronger.

"It is what it is, and that's why it's beautiful."
— Seen on a hotel check-in sign in Switzerland

The Dao Whispers: Instead of crying over spilt milk, why not look for a paper towel and start cleaning up the mess. Some doors close for a reason, and that reason often reveals itself only later, once you stop staring at the closed door.

August 29

Obligation to Dissent

Find your voice. Once you do, use your voice

千人之诺诺，不如一士之谔谔

qiān rén zhī nuò nuò, bùrú yī shì zhī è'è

Translation: "A thousand yes-men are worth less than one who dares to speak the truth."
— Han Feizi

In ancient China, this proverb honoured the courageous advisors who challenged emperors, not to provoke, but to prevent harm. It honours the courage to dissent, the discernment to speak when silence feels safer, and the responsibility to speak truth to power.

Nuò nuò (诺诺) implies blind, submissive agreement. È è (谔谔) describes bold, principled dissent, often from a gentleman-scholar (士) who speaks out despite risk.

What it teaches us

- **Moral responsibility:** Silence in the face of injustice can be a form of complicity.
- **Resist groupthink:** One rational voice can save many from harmful consensus and collective failure. Don't mistake popularity for truth.
- **Evaluate advice:** When receiving input, prioritise quality over quantity. Just because the majority calls a piglet a lion, does not make the piglet a lion.

> ***"The only thing necessary for the triumph of evil is for good men to do nothing."***
> ***— Edmund Burke***

The Dao Whispers

When many agree blindly, your doubt might be the only light.
Find your voice.
And once you do, may you have the courage to use it.

August 30

Get to the Point, Say What You Mean

We all say 'let's circle back' when what we really mean is 'no'

开门见山

kāi mén jiàn shān

Translation: "(Let's) Open the door and see the mountain."
— Han Feizi

Imagine you open your front door, and BAM! There's a huge mountain right in front of you. That's the image behind this idiom: no fluff, no detours, just say what you mean.

What it teaches us

- **Speak plainly**: Don't send your audience on a verbal treasure hunt and definitely, don't send them on a runaround.
- **Get to the point:** Land your core message fast, without detours.
- **Solve what counts:** Don't treat symptoms; tackle the root.
- **Stop dancing around it:** Being vague might feel polite, but it's rarely kind.
- **Keep it short:** Don't waste time with long stories if a short one works.
- **Cut to the chase**: Be open with concerns, asks, or the terms and conditions. Avoid being evasive or stop dodging what has to be said.
- **Say it while it still matters:** Delayed honesty is often too late to help.
- **And one more thing:** Don't forget tact.

"Clear is kind. Unclear is unkind."
— **Brené** Brown

The Dao Whispers

- Am I being clear or beating around the bush to be polite?
- If I strip away the fluff, would anyone get the point without a decoder ring?

Try it this week: Before your next message, email, or meeting, ask, ***"If I only have 30 seconds, how would I say this?"***

August 31

Information Is Power, Especially When It's Missing

Power plays hide in the information they don't share

一人藏，百人寻

yī rén cáng, bǎi rén xún

Translation: "When one person hides, a hundred must seek."
— Han Feizi

Ever feel like you're chasing answers while someone else holds all the cards? That's the imbalance this proverb points to. One person keeps something hidden, and suddenly, everyone else is stuck guessing, chasing, and stressing.

Information asymmetry is one of the most primal strategies to preserve power.

And sometimes, all it takes to hold power is knowing something others don't… and keeping it that way.

What it teaches us

- **Secrecy = Control:** Withholding information makes others ask, appease, or depend – reinforcing the influence of the gatekeeper.
- **Effort imbalance:** A single act of concealment creates disproportionate work for others and turns hidden knowledge into powerful leverage.
- **A timeless strategy:** From merchants hiding prices to generals obscuring plans, the formula is ancient: the fewer who know, the more who obey.
- **Power through gatekeeping:** Access to data, decisions, and opportunities is often hoarded not for safety, but to preserve hierarchy.

"The oldest power is knowing what others do not."
— **Robert Greene**

The Dao Whispers: Who is benefitting by keeping you in the dark? Is anyone making you do the runaround, just to keep you in place? How different would the game look if everyone had the same information?

SEPTEMBER

敬

jìng

敬 (jìng) encompasses:

- Being respectful
- Reverence for life and others
- Respect for boundaries and roles
- Having respect for truth and integrity
- Upholding dignity

The word 敬 (jìng) means respect. It represents a deep kind of inner reverence for life, people, and principles. 敬 (jìng) urges people to respect boundaries, roles, wisdom, and dignity both in ourselves and others.

Mastering 敬 (jìng) helps us:

- **Be respectful of others:** Treat others with respect and dignity, even in disagreement.
- **Lead with humility:** Value others' contributions and perspectives, regardless of rank.
- **Guard your energy and boundaries:** Respect your own limits and set boundaries unapologetically.
- **Practise discernment:** Recognise that sometimes silence, patience, or restraint is the most respectful choice.
- **Uplift others:** Let your words and actions tell others: "*You matter.*"

September 1

The Race Goes Not to the Swift

The right time, the right place, the right people

天时地利人和

tiān shí dì lì rén hé

Translation: "The right time, the right place, the right people."
— Mencius

Have you ever met the right person… at the wrong time? Or had a brilliant idea… just before the market shifted? Life's not just about good plans. It's about good timing, the right setting, and the right people in the room.

This proverb reminds us that success isn't just about what you do, but **when, where, and with whom** you do it.

- 天时 (tiān shí): favourable timing
- 地利 (dì lì): advantageous location or circumstances
- 人和 (rén hé): harmony among people

On timing:

> ***"The race is not to the swift or the battle to the strong,***
> ***nor does food come to the wise or wealth to the brilliant,***
> ***or favour to the learned;***
> ***but time and chance happen to them all."***
>
> — The Bible, Ecclesiastes 9:11

The Dao Whispers: Wisdom is not just knowing **what** to do but **when**, **where**, and **with whom**. Often, that's the difference between failure and success.

September 2

When You Think You Know, Look Again

Seeing the sky through a straw

以管窥天

yǐ guǎn kuī tiān

Translation: "Looking at the sky through a bamboo tube."
— Chinese Idiom

Some people are so confident in their opinions you'd think they've seen the whole sky. In reality? They're peeking through a straw and calling it a telescope; they just may not know it.

This idiom **exposes the limits of our perception**, even when we feel certain. We can be constrained by the tools, experiences, and senses available to us. It applies to situations when we judge a complex issue based on incomplete information, like assessing a person's character from one action or understanding a situation without considering all factors. Even in science and nature, our limits are clear. Sharks navigate using electromagnetic fields. Bats 'see' through sound. In cosmology, dark matter remains "unseen," yet profoundly significant. What's invisible to us may still shape our world. So too in life: there are many truths beyond what we are equipped to perceive.

What it teaches us

- **On empathy:** We can never fully understand the suffering of another or know the depth of it.
- **On worldview:** Our upbringing defines what we consider "normal." It's difficult to see the world through the lens of someone who grew up in **radically different environments or beliefs.**
- **On knowledge**: What is "discovered" has always existed, we were simply unaware. Just because you've never seen it, doesn't mean it's not real.

> ***"The eye sees only what the mind is prepared to comprehend."***
> **— Henri Bergson**

The Dao Whispers: Truth is rarely absolute. The forces that define your world are often the ones you cannot see.

September 3

The Leader's Prerogative

To lift or to hide

不掠人之美，不隐人之恶

bù lüè rén zhī měi, bù yǐn rén zhī è

Translation: "Don't steal others' glory; don't hide others' wrongs."
— Traditional Chinese proverb

This proverb embodies two key Confucian virtues:

1. Integrity (**不掠人之美**) – Don't claim credit for others' achievements.
2. Righteous Courage (**不隐人之恶**) – Don't cover others' faults.

Good leadership often requires both recognising effort and dealing with failure with a clear head.

> ***"There are two kinds of people: those who do the work, and those who take the credit."***
> — **Indira Gandhi**

The Tension: Power before morality

And yet, a deeper dilemma lingers: **What if speaking up costs you power, before you've even earned the chance to use it for good?** Machiavelli thought morality was a luxury. In *The Prince*, he wrote:

"A prince must learn how not to be good."

In other words: secure power first, then decide what kind of person to be.

The Dao Whispers

- The proverb says: "Lead with virtue, and power follows."
- Whereas Machiavelli counters: "Seize power first, then pretend to have virtue."
- So where do you stand? Be noble now, or wait until you can do more?

In the end, every leader walks that line between principle and strategy. Just make sure the path you choose is one you can live with.

September 4

Huey's Law

Good things can happen, even if it's against the odds

吉人自有天相

jí rén zì yǒu tiān xiàng

Translation: "Fortune protects the virtuous."
— Traditional Chinese proverb

We've all heard of Murphy's Law: if it can go wrong, it will. But what about when things ***go right?*** When the plan unfolds, the stranger shows up, the message lands at just the right moment? Why expect only the rubbish, and not the good?

Let's call that Huey's Law, the yang to Murphy's yin:

> ***"If something good can happen, it just might, especially when you're not trying to force it."***

This ancient Chinese proverb, 吉人自有天相 (jí rén zì yǒu tiān xiàng), suggests that **those with good intentions, clear hearts, or honest spirits are quietly protected by the universe**. Not always in flashy ways, but through good timing, narrow escapes, and unlikely allies.

It doesn't mean bad things never happen to good people. But it suggests that goodness often creates its own momentum, **the kind that draws help, opens doors, or nudges events in your favour**. Not by chance, but by alignment.

The Dao Whispers

- Don't underestimate the power of kindness, good energy, and good will.
- What if things don't go wrong? What if they go beautifully right?
- We've heard of Murphy's law. Just as there is yin, there is also yang.

So here we go, Huey's Law – a law we write into the world simply by using the creative licence life has granted us. Believe in it, and you help bring it to life.

September 5

The Hues of a Leader

Insight, reflection, clarity, discernment, wisdom

智、慧、思、明、悟、识

zhì, huì, sī, míng, wù, shí

Translation: "Strategic wisdom, intuitive insight, reflection, clarity, realisation, and discernment."

Before reading on, let's try something different: **look up the YouTube clip 'Tywin & Tommen – What makes a good king (Game of Thrones).'**

In this scene, a seasoned elder challenges a young prince with a simple question: What makes a good king? Is it holiness? Justice? Strength? One by one, these traits are shown to fail. One starved himself in devotion. Another ruled justly but was murdered. A third won battles, then wasted his reign in indulgence.

Eventually, the answer becomes clear. Wisdom. Not the wisdom of clever tricks or technical know-how but the deeper kind – the kind that knows when to act and when to wait, when to trust, and when to listen to dissent. The kind that sees past appearances to real consequences.

Reflections: Leadership is contextual

Every leadership trait, no matter how noble, can become a liability if used at the wrong time or in the wrong way. Justice without awareness can be exploited. Strength without foresight can lead to recklessness. Even compassion, if unchecked, may result in poor decisions that harm the greater good. Like a conductor guiding an orchestra, a wise leader knows when to amplify strength, when to hold back, and when to lead by empowering others.

> ***"It is not enough to have a good mind.***
> ***The main thing is to use it well."***
> — **René Descartes**

The Dao Whispers: What kind of leader am I? Holy, but naïve? Just, but at the cost of survival? Brave, but blind to consequences? Or do I lead with wisdom?

September 6

Fix the **Roots, Not the Leaves**

If the roots are chaotic, the branches cannot thrive

其本乱而末治者否矣

qí běn luàn ér mò zhì zhě fǒu yǐ

Translation: "If the roots are in a mess, it is impossible for the branches to be in order."
— Confucian Classic: The Great Learning (大学)

Trying to fix a struggling plant by polishing the leaves is like putting perfume on a dirty shirt. It might smell nice and look better for a moment, but the real problem is still there.

This Confucian classic reminds us that if the foundation is a mess, no amount of surface-level masking or tidying will fix things. What you build is only as strong as what you build on it. If the foundation is weak, whether in character, structure, or intent, the results will likely be suboptimal.

In this metaphor:

- The roots are your values, mindset, and preparation.
- The branches are your actions, results, and relationships.

What it teaches us

- **Get your basics right**: In anything, from cooking to maths to coding, it's your core skills that carry you through, not fancy shortcuts.
- **Don't wing it:** Great execution starts with clear thinking and solid prep. If you build on chaos or unclear thinking, expect chaos and muddled results.
- **Address causes, not symptoms:** If your health keeps failing, a relationship feels strained, or work keeps stalling – it's rarely about the surface issues. It usually traces back to deeper roots like habits, trust, clarity, or alignment.

> ***"A house built on sand cannot stand."***
> — **Jesus of Nazareth**

The Dao Whispers: Am I trying to fix the symptoms while ignoring the real issue? Do I surround myself with people who have deep roots, or just shiny branches?

September 7

Once is a Slip. Twice, a Pattern.

To make a second mistake trying to cover the first

一错再错

yī cuò zài cuò

Translation: "To make one mistake after another."
— Chinese Idiom

Made a mistake, then told a little lie to cover it up… and suddenly you're juggling three more to keep the story straight? Or doubled down on a bad decision because backing out would be embarrassing? One mistake is human. But stack more on top, and suddenly you're not just stumbling – you're digging your own pit and jumping right into it.

This proverb gently calls out the slippery slope of denial and pride. The first error is forgivable. The second and third? That's on us.

The proverb alludes to being honest with yourself, to learning, correcting, and moving on before things spiral out of control and get messier.

What it teaches us

- **Cut your losses:** Don't throw good money, time, or energy after bad. Admit to the mistake, reset and move on.
- **Don't dig deeper:** If you're stuck in a failing relationship, in debt, or watching a project unravel, stop before you make things worse.
- **Learn from mistakes:** Reflect on past mistakes to avoid repeating them.

"To err is human; to persist in error is diabolical."
— **Seneca**

The Dao Whispers: Sunk costs are sometimes irrecoverable, it's best to cut losses. It's also helpful to remember that the first mistake teaches while the second exposes our ability and willingness to learn from our past. That said, the only real mistake is one from which we have learnt nothing.

September 8

History Is Written by Winners

The one who wins becomes king.
The loser? The "problem."

成者为王，败者为寇

chéng zhě wéi wáng, bài zhě wéi kòu

Translation: "The victor becomes king, the loser – the enemy."
— Chinese Idiom

Funny how it works: you win a battle, and suddenly you're a "visionary leader." But if you lose? You're a "dangerous traitor," or simply, erased from history. This proverb says it simply. The one who wins gets the mic, the crown, and the pen that writes history. The loser gets edited out...or blamed.

We should strive to be good, but not naïve. In war, politics, or leadership, success tends to legitimise, while failure makes nuance and context easy to forget.

What it teaches us

- **In leadership:** Legitimacy isn't a given. It's built, sometimes seized, and needs to be defended.
- **In life:** Don't confuse being moral with being immune. The world doesn't hand out awards for kindness or good intentions. Do what's right but stay alert to how the world ***really*** works.
- **Read with a critical mind:** Whether it's a headline, an article, or a history book, consider the storyteller's angle. Who's writing and what do they want you to believe?

> ***"Who controls the past controls the future. Who controls the present controls the past."***
> — **George Orwell**

The Dao Whispers: Sometimes, behind an official story, lies a shadow version; less told, but closer to the truth.

- Who has been cast as the villain around me, and more importantly, why?
- Wisdom lies in discerning not only what happened, but in asking: ***who benefits from the telling.***

September 9

Caveat Emptor: The Seller's Advantage

The seller always knows more

买的不如卖的精

mǎi de bù rú mài de jīng

Translation: "The buyer is not as shrewd as the seller."
— Chinese Idiom

You know the feeling when you're trying to make a deal and something feels... off? That's because it's rarely a fair exchange. One side always knows more about the product, the pitch, the psychology, while the other is guessing. That's the key message of this proverb. The seller almost always has the upper hand. It's a reminder that in business, negotiations, or any relationship, information is power. If you don't do your homework, you're not at the bargaining table, you're on the menu.

What it teaches us

- **Self-Protection**: Trust is good, but due diligence is better.
- **Commercial Savviness:** The best deals are often made ***before*** the sale through insight and leverage.
- **Negotiations:** Never reveal your floor as the first offer is rarely the real one.
- **Posture ≠ truth:** Confidence and the appearance of sincerity from the seller do not mean the offer is fair or the image is true. Be mindful of posturing.

A Line Borrowed from Wall Street

> ***"If you don't know who the sucker is at the table... it's probably you."***

A Reminder on Value by Oscar Wilde

> ***"The market is full of people who know the price of everything, and the value of nothing."***

The Dao Whispers: Before major decisions, study the terrain, the general at the other end of your table, their interests, and what they think yours might be. Assume the other side is better prepared – then out-prepare them. Cultivate your seller instinct, know your value, and frame it well. *Caveat emptor: buyer beware.*

September 10

What If You're Wrong?

Ever thought you were absolutely right… then realised you were completely off?

庸讵知吾所谓知之，非不知邪？
庸讵知吾所谓不知之，非知邪？

yōng jù zhī wú suǒ wèi zhī zhī, fēi bù zhī yé?
yōng jù zhī wú suǒ wèi bù zhī zhī, fēi zhī yé?

Translation: "How can one be sure that what I call knowledge is not ignorance? How can one be sure that what I call ignorance is not real knowledge?"
— Zhuangzi, Qiwulun (齐物论)

In this proverb, Zhuangzi pulls the rug out from under our intellectual pride. What if what we ***think*** we know is just ignorance in disguise? And what if what we dismiss as ignorance is actually an insight we're not yet wise enough to comprehend?

It's almost like a philosophical mic drop – one that echoes the ancient Greek sceptics, like Pyrrho, who taught that suspending judgement (epokhē) is a mark of wisdom, not weakness. Withholding judgement doesn't mean you're indecisive. It means you're wise enough to see that certainty may just be pride in disguise.

> ***"The trouble with the world is that the stupid are cocksure and the intelligent are full of doubt."***
> **— Bertrand Russell**

The Dao Whispers

- Are you judging too quickly without checking if you fully understand what you're judging?
- Are you certain, or just too proud to challenge your own assumptions?
- Can we sometimes admit: "I don't yet know enough to have an opinion."

September 11

Learn by Teaching

When I learn, I understand my ignorance
When I teach, I discover where I'm unclear

学然后知不足，教然后知困

xué rán hòu zhī bù zú, jiào rán hòu zhī kùn

Translation: "Through learning, one realises their inadequacy; through teaching, one uncovers their confusion."

— The Book of Rites (礼记, lǐ jì)

You were feeling pretty smart until someone asked a follow-up question. Now you're standing there, frozen like ChatGPT on dodgy Wi-Fi.

This proverb speaks to self-awareness and humility born of both learning and teaching. It suggests that:

- **Learning** shows us how much we don't yet know and gives us an opportunity to learn more and improve.
- **Teaching** challenges us to make the abstract understandable and simple, exposing gaps in our own clarity and communication of the subject matter.

What it teaches us

- **Embrace lifelong learning**: The more we learn, the more we realise what we ***don't*** know. Humility opens the door to growth because it keeps us curious, open, and aware that every stage of mastery reveals new depths still to explore.
- **Teaching reveals blind spots:** If you can't explain it clearly, you might not understand it well enough.
- **Mentor to grow**: Teaching deepens your mastery while lifting others.
- **Practise communicating difficult ideas**: Making the complex simple is the real test of your understanding.
- **Close the loop**: Learning completes its cycle when passed on.

"To teach is to learn twice."

— **Joseph Joubert**

The Dao Whispers: Can a child understand my explanation? If not, perhaps I do not yet know it well enough.

September 12

On Learning to Be Responsible

I shall not blame the Heavens
Nor shall I blame those around me

不怨天，不尤人

bù yuàn tiān, bù yóu rén

Translation: "Do not blame the Heavens, nor other people."
— The Book of Rites (礼记, lǐ jì)

Stuck in traffic? Blame the weather. Forgot your deadline? Blame your boss. Feeling unhappy? Blame your parents. Jeans too tight? Must be the dryer... definitely not the chocolate ice cream.

Blaming is easy, but it doesn't get you anywhere.

This Confucian proverb reflects the virtue of personal responsibility. It calls us to resist blaming fate or others for our misfortunes. To resent Heaven is to waste energy on the uncontrollable, while to blame others is to surrender our agency. By refusing to externalise blame, you reclaim your power to respond, to adapt, and to grow.

What it teaches us

- **Own your agency:** Focus on what you can influence and actually influence it, including the chocolate ice cream.
- **Build your toolkit:** Redirect energy from blame into growth, problem-solving, and taking action.
- **Embrace adulthood:** At some point, our story becomes our own. Parents, mentors, or systems may have shaped us, but they don't define us.

"It is not the situation that makes the man, but the man who makes the situation."
— Frederick William Robertson

The Dao Whispers: Who or what am I still blaming for where I am? Am I ready to let that go and be the steward of my own ship?

September 13

Are We Really Thinking Clearly

The mind at its best is like a mirror – clear, impartial, and free of attachment

至人之用心若镜，不将不迎，应而不藏

zhì rén zhī yòng xīn ruò jìng, bù jiāng bù yíng, yìng ér bù cáng

Translation: "The mind of the perfect person is like a mirror: it neither initiates nor resists and responds without holding on."
— Zhuangzi (庄子)

Some people meditate. Others journal. But for most of us, the mind is a noisy room with bad lighting where past regrets, future worries, and unspoken comebacks all talk over each other.

Zhuangzi offers a different model, through the metaphor of a mirror:

- **Clarity**: It reflects the world as it is, without distortion from pride, fear, or desire.
- **Does not chase or resist (不将不迎):** It doesn't run after what feels good, nor push away what feels bad.
- **Responds but doesn't cling (应而不藏):** It allows thoughts and emotions to pass through without clinging on to them, or ruminating. Like a mirror, it holds on to nothing.

> *"A man has free choice to the extent that he is rational."*
> — **Thomas Aquinas**

A cluttered and reactive mind isn't really free, it's like a mirror that captures every reflection that has ever gotten into it, and can never truly reflect what's right in front of it.

The Dao Whispers

- **Detach from obsession**: Am I clinging to outcomes, ideas, or narratives that distort how I see people or situations?
- **Judgement bias**: Do I judge before listening? Have I already written someone's script before they speak?
- **Reclaim mental freedom**: Am I thinking clearly or am I reacting through the lens of pride, prior beliefs, or external influence?

September 14

Stick to the Golden Mean

The path between extremes

允执厥中

yǔn zhí jué zhōng

Translation: "Be steadfast and hold on to the golden mean."
— Shangsu (尚書, Book of Document)

Started the week all disciplined and clean… then ended up binge-watching five shows and demolishing three tubs of ice cream by Friday? Balance may not be fun or sexy, but it's what keeps the wheels turning.

The phrase, first spoken by Yu the Great to Emperor Shun, reflects the heart of wise leadership and grounded living: avoid extremes, and stick to integrity, fairness, and emotional balance, avoiding all extremes.

Though rooted in governance, this idea of the "golden mean" applies just as much to our personal lives today, from regulating emotions to decision-making and avoiding burnout.

What it teaches us

- **Decision-making**: Avoid knee-jerk extreme or polarised actions. Aim for thoughtful, balanced choices that stand the test of time. Perhaps, let's go with half a tub instead of three.
- **Personal growth**: Don't swing between overdoing and underdoing. Discipline is in finding the middle, steering clear of excess, anger, or indulgence.
- **Emotional resilience:** Staying centred can protect us from being hijacked by highs and lows.

> ***"There is a mean in all things; and moreover, certain limits on either side of which right cannot be found."***
> **— Horace**

The Dao Whispers: Do I steer my own ship or am I at the mercy of my highs and lows? What does the 'mean' look like today in the way I live, speak, think, act, and decide?

September 15

Sometimes, It Has to Hurt Before It Heals

Only when we stop denying can healing start

病入骨髓，方可下猛药

biàn bìng rù gǔ suǐ, fāng kě xià měng yào

Translation: "When a disease reaches the bone marrow, only then can potent medicines be administered."
— Traditional Chinese saying

Putting off the dentist until the toothache hits your brain? Telling yourself your job's "fine" while dying inside by Thursday? It works until it doesn't. Avoiding the truth buys time, but not without a cost.

This proverb reminds us that meaningful change begins only when we face the full depth of a problem without self-deception or evasion. When something feels wrong in our body, our work, our relationships, or even the world around us, it takes courage to stop pretending and deal with the real issue. The first act of healing is to see things plainly and call it what it is.

What it teaches us

- Confront personal shortcomings head-on as avoidance only delays growth.
- In conflicts, have the courage to face uncomfortable realities including your role in the conflict, not just others' faults.
- When stuck in work or life, stop rationalising the situation and start thinking about how best to move forward.
- Acknowledge global or social realities. Change begins when we name problems for what they truly are.

> ***"The truth does not change according to our ability to stomach it."***
> — **Flannery O'Connor**

The Dao Whispers: Never underestimate the ability of an intelligent person to deceive himself. Where might I be kidding myself, if I'm really honest?

September 16

Hurry Slowly

Haste makes waste

欲速则不达

yù sù zé bù dá

Translation: "If you are too focused on speed, you might not arrive where you want to be."
— Confucius (孔子), Analects (论语)

You started a project and are eager to get it done. So you dive in, skip the thinking and planning, and push for speed. But halfway through, you're backtracking, fixing mistakes, and wondering why it feels harder than it should. Sometimes, you push your team too, working past 5am, beyond breaking point – only to end up with something rushed and lacklustre.

This proverb reminds us that rushing rarely gets us to where we want to go.

Why Hurry Backfires

- **Master pace**: If life is moving too fast to think, it's already moving too fast for you to grow.
- **Problem-solving:** A rushed answer may address surface symptoms but miss the root cause. Worse, it can trap you defending a shaky Day One hypothesis simply because you anchored to it too soon.
- **Health and well-being:** Quick-fix diets or extreme workout plans often fail and are not sustainable.

> ***"The more haste, the less speed."***
> **— John Heywood**

> ***"The straight path is not always the shortest."***
> — Stalker (a character in the film 'Stalker')

The Dao Whispers: The fastest path may not necessarily be the best path. Often, the more you force to get to an outcome quickly, the longer you'll spend untangling the mistakes.
Can slowing down now actually get you there faster?

September 17

Simplify Complexity

The best solutions or principles are often the simplest

大道至简

dà dào zhì jiǎn

Translation: "The Great Way (best principle) is often simple."
— Laozi, Dao De Jing (often attributed)

Tired of 10-tab spreadsheets, 40-page decks, and meetings about meetings? Sometimes it feels like we complicate things just to look smart. But the real genius? Making it simple. Einstein thought so too.

This proverb reminds us that what really matters or what really works is rarely complicated. Even if the process to get to the answer feels messy, the solution should feel clean and simple. Simple isn't the same as easy. But it's usually right.

What it teaches us

- **Decision-making:** When we over-analyse, it can lead to confusion or paralysis. Focusing on our core values, goals or needs can help us make clearer choices and prioritise better.
- **Lifestyle choices:** A minimalist approach focused on health, purpose, and meaningful relationships can often bring more contentment in life, than going after excess.
- **Leadership management**: Great leaders often simplify. They align teams with clear goals, and define OKRs and KPIs succinctly. They are artful in keeping the teams focused, cutting through ambiguity and red tape to make sure that what the teams do actually move the needle.

"Make everything as simple as possible, but not simpler."
— **Albert Einstein**

The Dao Whispers

- **Simplicity reveals mastery:** If they can't explain it clearly, they probably don't understand it.
- **Clarity in thought:** A bullshitter often knows when another bullshitter is bullshitting them.
- ***"If you can't convince them – confuse them."*** Who around you is doing this?

September 18

The Paradox of Morality

When sages create villains

圣人不死，大盗不止。
故绝圣弃知，大盗乃止。

shèng rén bù sǐ, dà dào bù zhǐ
gù jué shèng qì zhì, dàdào nǎi zhǐ

Translation: "As long as sages live, the thieves will not cease to steal. Therefore, abolish sages and discard knowledge, and great thieves will cease."
— Zhuangzi (庄子)

These sharp lines from Zhuangzi aren't just a jab at Confucian moralism; it's a radical challenge to **the entire idea of moral authority**. In classical Chinese thought, this tension wasn't a fluke. It was the point: wisdom requires discernment, not blind obedience. Zhuangzi invites us to consider whether institutions designed to promote virtue can, over time, become vehicles for hierarchy, control, or moral rigidity.

What it teaches

- **Reject absolutism:** There is no universal "right" or "wrong," only context, intention, and outcome.
- **Beware moral posturing:** Appeals to justice or virtue can just as easily be used to justify cruelty or coercion.
- **Read the fine print:** What is legal may still be unjust. Contracts, rules, and 'codes of ethics' may hide coercion beneath formality.

> ***"There are many contracts that are immoral...in a deep sense, and should be forbidden and not enforced through courts of law."***
>
> — **Joseph Stiglitz** ("The Road to Freedom")

The Dao Whispers: There comes a day when no 'sage' can tell you what is right. You'll have to trust your own judgement. Once in a while, we can even ask, ***"Who is the real sage, and who is the real villain?"***

September 19

Not Everyone Has a Voice

A person who cannot speak and eats a bitter herb must suffer in silence

哑巴吃黄连，有苦说不出

yǎ ba chī huáng lián, yǒu kǔ shuō bù chū

Translation: "Those who cannot speak and have eaten bitter herbs must suffer in silence – they cannot express their pain."
— Traditional Chinese proverb

You know that face someone makes when they've clearly had a day, but insist they're "fine"? This proverb is for them.

Sometimes people can't say what's wrong, not because they don't feel it, but because saying it might cost too much – their livelihood, relationship, or reputation. So, they stay quiet, even while chewing life's metaphorical bitter herb.

This saying speaks to the silent grief of those who endure hardship or injustice without the freedom to voice it. Silenced by fear, norms, or power dynamics, they carry their pain alone.

What it teaches us

- **School bullying:** Students may keep quiet to avoid backlash or shame. Schools must create spaces where they feel protected, not punished, for speaking up.
- **Personal empowerment:** Avoiding conflict at all costs can sometimes worsen suffering. Resilience matters, but so does knowing when to speak up, set boundaries, or seek help.
- **Workplace advocacy:** A quiet team isn't always a healthy one. Silence can signal fear, not harmony. Good leaders look out for those signals before damage sets in.

> ***"In the end, we will remember not the words of our enemies, but the silence of our friends."***
> — **Martin Luther King Jr.**

The Dao Whispers: Even the voice of the wise can be drowned out by the thunder of ignorance. When others are silenced, your voice becomes their echo. And if one day ***yours*** is drowned out too, know you tried. That's all that matters.

September 20

Taking Things for Granted

Riding a donkey to look for a donkey

骑驴找驴

qí lǘ zhǎo lǘ

Translation: "Riding a donkey while looking for a donkey."
— Traditional Chinese proverb

The Story

This idiom comes from a folk tale about a man so intent on finding his donkey that he fails to notice he's already riding it. Humorous on the surface, it reminds us that we often overlook what we already have in our grasp.

In our pursuit of more – more success, more love, more meaning – we risk missing what is already present in our lives.

What it teaches us

- **Personal relationships:** We search for ideal partners or friends, yet ignore the loyalty beside us.
- **Personal growth:** We chase the next self-help trend, forgetting the strength, wisdom, and progress we've already made.
- **Career choices:** In pursuit of the next shiny role, we may miss the growth, impact, or community in our current role.

> ***"We never know the worth of water till the well is dry."***
> — **Thomas Fuller**

The Dao Whispers

- Name three people or things you've been overlooking. Perhaps, you can consider thanking one today.
- Before chasing the next 'thing,' ask yourself: ***Do I already have what I'm looking for?***
- Write down one resource, one person, and one strength you already have, and appreciate them with conscious gratitude.

September 21

Clarity Requires Distance

The bystanders see clearly, while the protagonist is confused

旁观者清，当局者迷

páng guān zhě qīng, dāng jú zhě mí

Translation: "The onlooker sees clearly, while the person in the situation is confused."
— Traditional Chinese proverb

Isn't it amazing how everyone else's mess is so easy to solve? When we're too close to our problems, we lose perspective. Once in a while, the most logical move is to step outside the frame. Detachment can help give clarity.

That's what this proverb is getting at. When we're right in the middle of something, emotions, ego, or sheer overwhelm can cloud our judgement. We may lose the plot, and the perspective.

What it teaches us

- **At work:** When you're knee-deep in a project or conflict, it's easy to miss the obvious. Ask someone outside the situation. They might spot what you can't.
- **In relationships:** Arguments can feel all-consuming in the moment. A friend or therapist may help you reframe things with a cooler head.
- **With yourself:** Self-reflection is hard when you're in the thick of it, while self-assessment can be distorted by your pride or insecurity. Journaling, coaching, or even just taking a walk can give you the distance needed to think more clearly.

"The fish does not know it is wet."
— Often attributed to **Marshall McLuhan**

The Dao Whispers

- When emotions cloud your view, ask yourself: ***what advice would I give my best friend in this exact situation?***
- When you feel stuck, ask: ***Who do I trust to see what I can't?*** Then call them.

September 22

The Cost of Misplaced Kindness

Kindness is a gift, don't waste it on the wrong people

狼心狗肺

láng xīn gǒu fèi

Translation: "Heart of a (vicious) wolf, lungs of a (vicious) dog."
— Traditional Chinese proverb

Ever gone out of your way to help someone... only to be ignored, blamed, or worse...turned into the bad guy?

Yep. That's the feeling behind this old Chinese saying.

It refers to someone who may seem polite or thankful on the surface, but underneath, they're entirely self-serving, and quick to turn on those who helped them. That's putting it mildly, the original phrase is far more brutal.

While the phrase often comes across as harsh, it points to something many of us learn the hard way. Not everyone will appreciate your kindness, and some will take advantage of it. This doesn't mean you stop being generous. It simply means being more selective about where your energy goes and whom you keep close.

What it teaches us

- **Kindness is powerful, but it needs boundaries:** Don't pour yourself out for someone who only takes.
- **Pay attention to actions, not just words:** Trust isn't built on compliments, it's built on consistency.
- **Some people are good at pretending:** Just because someone's charming doesn't mean they're kind.

> ***"Men are ungrateful, fickle, false, cowardly, covetous...as long as you succeed, they are yours entirely; but when the time comes, they turn against you."***
> — **Niccolò Machiavelli**

The Dao Whispers: Have you been giving more than you're receiving? Are you investing in someone who wouldn't do the same for you?

September 23

The Thing About Preference...

Tastes differ, and that's the point

萝卜青菜，各有所爱

luó bo qīng cài, gè yǒu suǒ ài

Translation: "Radishes and greens, each will have someone who'd appreciate their uniqueness."
— Traditional Chinese proverb

Some people like pineapple on pizza. Others think coriander tastes like soap.

This proverb reminds us that taste is personal. There's no one-size-fits-all when it comes to what people value, enjoy, or believe in. It's a very gentle nudge for us to stop judging others for being different, and for you to stop apologising for your own quirks too.

What it teaches us

- **Diverse viewpoints:** Recognising that people have unique preferences can nurture tolerance and reduce conflict in personal and professional spaces.
- **Personal freedom:** People should feel free to pursue their interests without pressure to conform, as long as it doesn't infringe on others.
- **Avoiding judgement**: When we accept others' tastes and paths, we ease the urge to impose our own. Just as someone thinks it's a good time to buy Tesla stock, someone else is selling it at the same time.

"There are no facts, only interpretations."
— Often attributed to **Friedrich Nietzsche**

The Dao Whispers

- Do I respect my own agency?
- Must others value what I value for it to be valid?
- Am I at peace with differences, or threatened by them?

September 24

Fortune Favours the Bold

Courage is sometimes choosing the harder path on purpose

明知山有虎，偏向虎山行

míng zhī shān yǒu hǔ, piān xiàng hǔ shān xíng

Translation: "I know there are tigers in the mountain, and still, I head toward it."
— Traditional Chinese proverb

You know that uneasy feeling in your stomach when you open an email marked "urgent," knowing full well that it might not be a good read? That's the spirit of this proverb. You don't pretend the tiger isn't there...you see it, take a deep breath, and walk toward it anyway.

The proverb celebrates real courage, not bravado or foolishness, but the kind of boldness that comes from purpose, clarity, and guts. Sometimes you face the tiger because no one else will. Or sometimes, because the path to growth goes right through its territory.

What it teaches us

- **Real courage**: Sometimes, you have to face something hard, like a tough conversation, a risky move, or a big decision; and it can be daunting. You do it anyway, trusting it will build your resilience and character.
- **Growth beyond comfort zones**: When things are easy, growth doesn't come quite as easily. Fear and discomfort are often the doorway to the next version of you.
- **Strategic risk-taking**: Bold doesn't mean that you should be reckless. Smart risk-takers often weigh the odds, then take a step forward when the time is right.

"When most people complain about problems, entrepreneurs see opportunities in problems, and they look for solutions and develop them into businesses."
— **Professor Wong Poh Kam**

The Dao Whispers: Am I risk-averse, or do I take calculated risks? Do I mistake comfort for safety? What 'tiger' stands between me and the life I seek?

September 25

Seasons Change, So Do We

Nothing in the world stays immutable

天下事未有一成不变之理

tiān xià shì wèi yǒu yī chéng bù biàn zhī lǐ

Translation: "There is nothing in the world that remains unchanged."
— Traditional Chinese proverb

Nothing stays the same. Hairlines recede. Fashion trends come back (sadly, even low-rise jeans). Robots making my coffee, lunch, and dinner *every day*...one can always dream.

This proverb captures the Daoist idea of impermanence (无常 wú cháng). Life, nature, emotions, leadership, and even your local coffee shop menu are always shifting.

When we accept that change is part of the circle of life, and nothing lasts forever – not success, not failure, not even that weird phase you're in – it becomes less threatening. In fact, change is often the very thing that allows us to grow, adapt, and stay relevant.

What it teaches us

- **Stay grounded in the present**: Since nothing lasts, presence is the wisest use of time. Nostalgia and anxiety would only serve to cloud our judgement.
- **Reframe loss as transition**: Letting go of fixed identities or outcomes helps us evolve and reinvent ourselves.
- **Stay open to opportunities**: When things fall apart, new doors open, if we're willing to see them.

> ***"What's dangerous is not to evolve."***
> — **Jeff Bezos**

> ***"Intelligence is the ability to adapt to change."***
> — **Stephen Hawking**

The Dao Whispers: What am I holding onto that no longer serves me? Is it realistic for me to expect what has been, to always be? Am I resisting the change that time inevitably brings?

September 26

Batman Never Needed a Degree

What you do outweighs where you're from

英雄不问出处

yīng xióng bù wèn chū chǔ

Translation: "Heroes are not asked about their origins."
— Traditional Chinese proverb

Have you noticed how no one asks where Batman went to school? No one cares if he had a 4.0 GPA...they only care that he gets the job done.

This proverb reminds us that talent or capability is measured not by background, pedigree, or lineage, but by one's actions, character, and contributions. It recognises that the world continues to be shaped by privilege and inherited advantage. But it offers a sharp counterpoint: what you do ***can matter*** more than where you come from, if you are in an environment that recognises and rewards merit.

It is a call to build systems and cultures that prioritise merit, competence, productive effort, and meaningful results.

What it teaches us

- **Champion meritocracy**: Create environments where ability and effort are rewarded over privilege. Equal access to opportunity should be foundational, not aspirational.
- **Beware systemic inefficiency**: Without merit-based selection, cracks will show in the long run. Poor decisions by underqualified actors compound over time, leading to structural dysfunction and wasted resources.
- **Rise above the limitations:** Refuse the ceilings others set; talent, drive, and resilience can rewrite any part of your story.

> ***"We are a meritocracy. We select the best. If we do not find the best among the Singaporeans, we go abroad to find them."***
> — **Lee Kuan Yew**

The Dao Whispers: Do I have the best talents solving the problems at hand? Am I rewarding performance? Are the rules of my environment built on merit or something else?

September 27

On Effort and Being Proactive

Pies don't just fall from the sky

天上不会掉馅饼

tiān shàng bú huì diào xiàn bǐng

Translation: "Pies don't fall from the sky."
— Traditional Chinese proverb

If sitting around and hoping worked, we'd all be rich, fit, fluent in five languages and married to our celebrity crush. Sadly, life does not deliver results like online shopping. Though to be fair, you can now order pies online, at least no one's asking you to knead the dough.

This old Chinese saying is a not-so-subtle reminder that success does not just drop into your lap. You have to get up, roll up your sleeves, and do the work. It is not about hustle for hustle's sake. It is about not mistaking daydreaming for doing.

What it teaches us

- **Take initiative:** Progress usually needs proactive effort. Waiting rarely brings results.
- **Show up consistently:** Luck is lovely, but consistency and effort often build real results.
- **Be strategic:** While hope is great, it's not a plan. Pair effort with preparation and thoughtful execution, and you may just increase the odds that luck finds you.

> ***"All things excellent are as difficult as they are rare."***
> — **Baruch Spinoza**

The Dao Whispers

- Am I hoping things will magically improve, or actually doing something about it?
- Is this breather strategic, or just me procrastinating again?
- Hoping is human. But waiting for pies to fall from the sky? Rain, maybe... but pastry and cupcakes, unlikely.

September 28

Wait for the Right Wave

Those with the strongest moves tend to show them last

君子藏器于身，待时而动

jūn zǐ cáng qì yú shēn, dài shí ér dòng

Translation: "The wise conceal their abilities and act only when the time is right."
— Traditional Chinese proverb

You ever watch someone make a big move, and think, I should be doing something too? But maybe this isn't quite your time yet. Maybe this is the bit where you get ready, slowly, and at your pace. Possibly with a tub of chocolate ice-cream, or a nice glass of peaty whisky, and Netflix.

This old proverb reminds us that it's okay not to rush, and that we can grow without needing to show it too soon. You don't have to prove anything right now. Just use this time to get your act together.

What it teaches us

- **Get your tools in order**: Take time to upskill, make real connections, or learn the lay of the land.
- **Don't rush it:** Jump too early, and you risk falling flat. Wait too long, and the last train's gone.
- **Timing matters**: Knowing *when* to act can be just as important as knowing *what* to do.

> ***"Opportunity is missed by most people because it is dressed in overalls and looks like work."***
> — **Thomas Edison**

> ***"He who is prudent and lies in wait for an enemy who is not, will be victorious."***
> — **Sun Tzu** (The Art of War)

The Dao Whispers: Is my silence strategic or did it come from a place of fear and doubt? Am I investing to prepare for my next inflection point? When the right moment comes, will I be ready? And more importantly, will I recognise it?

September 29

Get the Definition Right

If you start with the wrong problem definition, you'll never get the solution right

名不正，则言不顺

míng bù zhèng, zé yán bù shùn

Translation: "If we get the name wrong, everything that follows becomes unclear."
— Confucius (孔子), Analects (论语)

You know those moments when something sounds fine on the surface, but deep down, something feels off? That's what Confucius was pointing to. When we use the wrong words, when we soften things, sugarcoat them, or spin the truth, it distorts how we think, how we speak, and how we act.

Misnaming a thing, a situation, a person...isn't just a language issue, it becomes a judgement problem, a leadership problem, a life problem. Because if you can't call something what it is, how can you deal with it properly?

Misnaming allows dysfunction to continue to hide in plain sight. Consider:

- A "friend" who drains you dry.
- A "teammate" who does absolutely nothing.
- A "leader" who's allergic to responsibility.
- A "caring boss" who throws you under the bus, then backs up and runs you over again.
- An "institution with values" that can't seem to find them when it counts.
- A "source of truth" that sounds suspiciously like TikTok on a spreadsheet.

> ***"Political language is designed to make lies sound truthful, and murder respectable, and to give an appearance of solidity to pure wind."***
> — **George Orwell** (Politics and the English Language)

The Dao Whispers: Am I seeing things as they are, or as I wish them to be?

September 30

The Many Faces of Wealth

Wealth can empower one to lift others up, or tempt one to be less compassionate

为富不仁

wéi fù bù rén

Translation: "One can be rich and yet lacking compassion (or generosity, benevolence)."
— Traditional Chinese proverb

In Confucianism, 仁 (rén) represents compassion, conscience, and humaneness, the core of ethical character. This proverb offers a sober reminder: when wealth becomes disconnected from compassion, it risks becoming a force for harm.

This is not a condemnation of wealth built through innovation, creativity, or service. Resources guided by values can heal, empower, and transform lives. But when gain loses touch with ethics, and empathy is eclipsed by ambition, wealth can degrade rather than dignify.

It speaks to those who profit through exploitation. Who treat people as disposable. Who protect their privilege while others labour without safety, voice, or dignity.

> ***"The neoliberal fantasy that markets are always efficient and self-correcting, and that government is always the problem, not the solution, has been repeatedly exposed by reality. Yet it persists, and with it, policies that benefit the powerful at the expense of the many. 'Freedom for the wolves has often meant death to the sheep'*** *(Isaiah Berlin).* ***In an unregulated market, the strong do what they will, and the weak suffer what they must."***
> **— Joseph Stiglitz**

The Dao Whispers: Wealth can be used to extract or to uplift. What would I choose, if that power were mine?

OCTOBER

勇

yǒng

勇 (yǒng) encompasses:

- Courage in action
- The strength to face fear or uncertainty
- Moral bravery, standing for what's right
- Persistence in hardship
- Daring to choose a harder path when it counts

The word 勇 (yǒng) means courage or bravery. It is not the absence of fear, but the choice to move forward despite it. In Chinese thought, courage is not recklessness; it must be paired with discernment and wisdom (智, zhì), so that boldness serves the right purpose at the right time. 勇 (yǒng) is the inner strength that allows one to endure, stand tall, and act when action is needed.

Mastering 勇 (yǒng) helps us:

- **Face discomfort:** Growth can sometimes feel uncomfortable, especially when we step into situations that scare us.
- **Stand for your values**: Real courage is holding to your principles even when it's unpopular.
- **Choose action over avoidance**: Courage is choosing to move forward instead of staying safe.
- **Balance boldness with wisdom:** Courage is most powerful when guided by sound judgement, not impulse.
- **Inspire others:** One brave act can give others permission to find their own strength.

October 1

The Ego Check We All Need

There's always someone faster, smarter, or stronger

人外有人，天外有天

rén wài yǒu rén, tiān wài yǒu tiān

Translation: "Beyond every person, there is one who is greater; beyond the sky, another sky (heaven)."
— Traditional Chinese proverb

You feel like you've done well. You've worked hard, achieved a few things, maybe even impressed your friends. Then along comes someone who's just like you, except they also play the cello, run ultramarathons, and rescue stray cats in their spare time.

This proverb is a gentle reminder that no matter how capable we are, there is always someone out there who might know more, do more, or see things we don't. Acknowledging this shouldn't diminish us, but rather, free us from the burden of comparison.

What it teaches us

- **Stay open to growth:** When we accept that others may know more, do more, or see more, we become open to mentorship, learning, and transformation.
- **Let go of the crown:** You don't need to be the best to live a meaningful, excellent life. You also don't need to stop participating or competing; compete to stretch, to grow, and to evolve. That alone is a win.
- **Expand your sky:** "Skies beyond skies" reminds us that current 'sky' is not the limit, stay curious.

> ***"It is impossible for a man to learn what he thinks he already knows."***
> — **Epictetus**

The Dao Whispers: When I meet someone better, do I learn from them or feel threatened? Am I open to skies beyond my own?

October 2

Don't Argue with Frogs in Well

Not everyone can imagine oceans they've never seen

井蛙不可以语于海，夏虫不可以语于冰

jǐng wā bù kě yǐ yǔ yú hǎi, xià chóng bù kě yǐ yǔ yú bīng

Translation: "You can't discuss the ocean with the frog that lives in the well, nor ice with an insect that lives only through summer."
— Zhuangzi (庄子)

The parable invites reflection, not ridicule. It reminds us that every person's understanding is bounded by the limits of their experience. A frog confined to a well cannot fathom the sea, just as an insect that lives through summer only may not be able to imagine the snow in winter.

Rather than judge those with narrower views or grow prideful of our own, it invites us to be humble, patient, and respectful.

What it teaches us

- **Practise empathy:** When someone speaks from their "well," listen, and resist the urge to dismiss them. You don't need to climb into the well with them, but you can at least peek over the edge. Understanding their patch of sky helps you see your own more clearly.
- **Respect others' knowledge gaps:** Avoid putting others on the spot for what they do not yet know, and celebrate what they bring, while filling in the blanks tactfully.
- **Seek wider horizons:** Your perspective has a ceiling, and your job is to keep raising it. Travel, read, talk to people who disagree with you. Stop confusing your well with the whole world.

"We see things not as they are, but as we are."
— Often attributed to **Immanuel Kant**

The Dao Whispers: Do I mock the limits of others, or remember I, too, once saw only a small patch of sky above the well? Am I open to seeing beyond my own well or mistaking its walls for the world?

October 3

The Last Piece Sometimes Takes the Longest

You've built the ship. Now you just need the wind

万事俱备，只欠东风

wàn shì jù bèi, zhǐ qiàn dōng fēng

Translation: "Everything is in order and ready, the only thing that is missing is the eastern wind."
— Traditional Chinese proverb

You've studied, built, worked, planned, refined, and yet, some outcomes still depend on final forces beyond your control.

This proverb speaks to the delicate dance between preparation and timing. The "east wind" represents timing, momentum, or fate. While it cannot be summoned, you can master your craft so fully that when the wind does arrive, you are ready to sail.

What it teaches us

- **Career strategy:** Preparation builds skill, but opportunities sometimes hinge on timing, luck, or the right connection. Stay ready so you can rise when the moment comes.
- **Entrepreneurial realities:** You can write the perfect plan, but markets, sentiment, or global forces like macroeconomics or geopolitics can rewrite the rules. Stay agile.
- **Resilience:** Some forces are beyond your control. Control what you can and use the time in waiting to refine your tools and strengthen your sails.

> ***"Luck is what happens when preparation meets opportunity."***
> — **Seneca**

The Dao Whispers: When the wind comes, will I be ready to sail or still patching holes in the ship?

October 4

Choose Your Company Wisely

Some people shine around you only when the spotlight is on them

君子之交淡如水，小人之交甘若醴

jūn zǐ zhī jiāo dàn rú shuǐ, xiǎo rén zhī jiāo gān ruò lǐ

Translation: "The friendship of a good person can be as plain as water; while one with the petty is as sweet as honeyed wine."
— Zhuangzi (庄子)

Zhuangzi offers a stark reminder by drawing a distinction between two kinds of relationships. The company of a noble person is like water, calm, reliable, and life-giving. In contrast, some friendships start like dessert wine, sweet, flattering, and intoxicating, but leave you with a headache later. Underneath the façade of sweetness may lie ego, envy, or self-interest.

What it teaches us

- **Real friends stick around when life gets tough:** Not everyone who claps when you win will stand by you when you fall. Look for those who show up when there's nothing in it for them.
- **Consistent care matters more than big gestures:** Sincere connections are often built through small acts of presence, including regular check-ins, honesty, time, and mutual respect.
- **Watch out for flattery:** If someone constantly praises you but avoids real talk or boundaries, ask why. Real friends don't flatter to gain favour; they tell the truth to protect you.

> ***"I had rather be alone than in the company of those who do not value truth."***
> — **Bernard of Clairvaux**

The Dao Whispers: A real friend celebrates your success without envy. 'Frenemies' on the other hand congratulate you with vibes that are off and dim your light to make theirs feel brighter. Be careful of who you share your pain with, but even more careful of who you share your joy with.

October 5

I Doubt, Therefore I Think

The smartest people ask questions

疑者，觉悟之机也

yí zhě, jué wù zhī jī yě

Translation: "Doubt is the beginning of awakening."
— Zen Buddhist saying

Very often, we find ourselves nodding along in agreement when everyone else is doing the same... and suddenly, we're thinking: ***"Wait... does this even make sense?"***

That flicker of doubt? It's a gift.

It pulls us out of autopilot and invites us to question what we've been taught, what we assume, and what we've inherited.

The proverb reminds us not to view doubt as indecision, or cognitive inferiority, but as inquiry. It's how our mind says, ***"I want to understand this for myself."***

What it teaches us

- **Growth starts with asking questions:** Don't fear them. Asking difficult questions helps us spot what we're missing in work, love, and life. Many turning points in life begin with, ***"Wait a minute, what if..."***
- **Don't trust everything you hear:** Just because everyone says it's true doesn't mean it is. Everyone's got biases, even the 'experts.'
- **Doubt makes you sharper:** Doubt is not the absence of belief. It's how you pressure-test your ideas until only the strongest ones survive.

> ***"Dubito, ergo cogito, ergo sum."***
> ***"I doubt, therefore I think, therefore I am."***
> — **René Descartes**

The Dao Whispers: What "facts" have I accepted that feel unsettling? Am I brave enough to ask the awkward questions no one else will? Am I doing my own thinking or outsourcing it to someone else?

October 6

What Goes Up Will Come Down

Hold steady when life hands you the highs and the humbling

宠辱不惊，闲看庭前花开花落

chǒng rǔ bù jīng, xián kàn tíng qián huā kāi huā luò

Translation: "Unfazed by favour or disgrace, he calmly observes the flowers bloom and wither in the courtyard."
— Zen Buddhist saying

This saying reflects a state of equanimity – calmness and composure whether you're being praised or criticised, lifted up or let down. It's about not getting too caught up in the highs and lows of life, but instead, watching everything come and go with peaceful awareness.

As the flowers bloom and fall, so do seasons of fortune and challenge. Instead of clinging to the highs or resisting the lows, this proverb reminds us to stay centred with balance, perspective, and trust in the bigger picture.

What it teaches us

- **Stay emotionally balanced:** Don't let success make you smug or failure make you spiral. Both are fleeting.
- **Accept life's impermanence:** Flowers fall. So do plans, people, and perfect LinkedIn updates. Accept the cycles.
- **Let go of the need for external validation:** ***If you need everyone's thumbs-up to feel good, you'll always be waiting.*** When you no longer need constant approval or permission, you'll feel more at ease in your own skin, with the freedom to simply be yourself.

> ***"The less you struggle to live, the less you live."***
> — Unknown

The Dao Whispers: Can I let go and let life unfold without holding on to the highs or bracing against the lows… and just be?

October 7

Don't Go It Alone

A single chopstick breaks easily, but a bundle of ten is as strong as iron

一根筷子易折断，十根筷子硬如铁

yì gēn kuài zi yì zhé duàn, shí gēn kuài zi yìng rú tiě

Translation: "A chopstick can be snapped easily, while a bundle of ten chopsticks can be as strong as iron."
— Traditional Chinese proverb

The Story

This proverb comes from a classic Chinese fable. A dying father, weary of his sons constantly fighting, calls them together. He hands each of them a single chopstick to break, and they break them easily. Then he bundles ten chopsticks and asks them to try again. None of them can break it.

The lesson is simple yet profound: alone, we are fragile. Together, we are unbreakable.

What it teaches us

- **Question the "lone-wolf" myth:** While independence has its place, glorifying total self-reliance can be misleading. Even wolves survive and thrive in packs. The lone wolf doesn't last long in the cold.
- **Invest in alliances:** In career, community, or personal life, lasting strength often comes from trusted relationships and a solid support system.
- **Lean on your support network:** In life's toughest seasons, we all need others to help us stand. Let the people who care about you help hold you up, and make sure you're there for them too. **Asking for help is an act of strength** – the courage to trust, and the confidence to know you don't have to carry it all alone.

The Dao Whispers

- Have I mistaken isolation for strength?
- Do the people I count on also know they can count on me?
- When I stood alone the longest... was I also most vulnerable to being pressured or misled?

October 8

The Power of Simplicity and Stillness

Slow down to see further

非淡泊无以明志，非宁静无以致远

fēi dàn bó wú yǐ míng zhì, fēi níng jìng wú yǐ zhì yuǎn

Translation: "Only in detachment does purpose become clear; Only in stillness (inner peace, a quiet mind) can the distant be reached."
— Zhuge Liang

Zhuge Liang, the legendary strategist of the Three Kingdoms era, wasn't the type to panic-scroll his scribe's messages at 2am. He knew that in chaos, even the sharpest minds get foggy. His advice? Simplify. Slow down. Be still.

It's easy to confuse motion with meaning. We fill our calendars, chase shiny goals, fight alligators all day and call it progress. But sometimes the real breakthroughs come not when we're doing more, but when we finally stop. When we clear out the clatter, the inbox, the social media feed, the pressure to be everywhere and do everything, something remarkable happens. Our own voice finally has space to speak.

What it teaches us

- **Simplify your priorities:** Clear away distractions such as unnecessary tasks, mindless scrolling, and external pressures to make space for what truly matters.
- **Reflect to define your purpose:** Quiet reflection, journaling, or even walking alone can bring unexpected clarity.
- **Stay focused on your long-term goals:** Long-term goals require focus. A calm mind can better weather storms without losing direction.

> ***"It is not that we have a short time to live, but that we waste a lot of it."***
> — **Seneca**

The Dao Whispers: Am I mistaking being busy, for progress? Have I taken time to simplify my life and realign with what's important to me?

October 9

The Power of Being: I Am Who I Am

The Dao follows the path that is natural

道法自然

dào fǎ zì rán

Translation: "The Dao follows what is natural."
— Laozi (老子), Dao De Jing (道德经)

In the Daoist worldview, the highest virtue is not effort, imitation, or striving. It is **zì rán** (自然): being natural, unforced, and true to your essence.

The mountain doesn't need to prove it is towering.
The river doesn't apologise for its winding course.
And the sage? She doesn't twist herself to earn approval. She just **is.**

When you say, ***"I am who I am,"*** you are echoing the Dao. You are returning... returning to a self that existed before all the titles, roles, trauma, expectations... The version of you that knew how to breathe before it had to perform, before you were cast in a role, handed a script, and told how to act. And in that return, you find your way back to yourself.

> ***"The greatest thing in the world is to know how to belong to oneself."***
> **— Michel de Montaigne**

The Dao Whispers

Today, give yourself one hour of joy.
No outcome. No productivity. No audience.
Just you, doing something that feels like you.

That's zì rán (自然), natural, unforced, going with the flow. That is the Dao.

October 10

Walk Your Path, Even If No One Follows

The real project isn't other people – it's you

人贵有自知之明

rén guì yǒu zì zhī zhī míng

Translation: "It is a rare virtue to truly know oneself."
— Ancient Chinese proverb

Here's what Confucius and Laozi both knew: the most powerful wisdom isn't about fixing others, it's about working on yourself.

What it teaches us

- **Being true to yourself:** It's cool to follow trends, helpful to be able to read a room... but the real game-changer? Knowing yourself – what matters to you, what drains you, and why you're here. That's how you live authentically, without having to fake it.
- **Remain centred when titles fall away**: Jobs end. Relationships change. When you step away from the 'safe' path, others might panic. But here's the secret: You're not your title. Strip all that away, and you're still very much there, solid, capable, ***enough.***
- **Where confidence really comes from:** You'll waste years waiting for others to 'get' you. Real freedom starts the day you realise that you no longer need others to write the report card on your life.

> ***"The privilege of a lifetime is to become who you truly are."***
> **— Carl Jung**

The Dao Whispers: If you've outgrown the room, do you shrink to try and fit in, or would you be willing to walk out and find a bigger one?

October 11

Do Not Interrupt Your Enemies

Steer clear when the tigers fight

坐山观虎斗

zuò shān guān hǔ dòu

Translation: "Sit on the mountain and watch the tigers fight."
— Ancient Chinese proverb

In ancient Chinese courts, when rival factions clashed for influence, the wisest ministers often said the least.
They were not indecisive.
They were not disengaged.
They were simply waiting.

They knew that power often shifts not in shouting matches or dramatic takedowns, but in the quiet aftermath, when the dust settles and opportunists reveal themselves.

This proverb reflects strategic patience in play, the decision to act by not acting. Let others wear themselves out, and the ministers watching from the sidelines will be the ones left standing, unscathed, and intact.

What it teaches us

- **Play the long game:** Skip the drama and draining conflicts. Let your opponents weaken each other while you conserve energy, resources, and optionality.
- **Stay safe in the chaos**: When things get messy or heated, sometimes the smartest move is to step back. Why get caught in the crossfire?
- **Check your motives**: This strategy can seem shrewd or opportunistic. The key is discernment... Sure, this sounds clever, but ask yourself, "Am I avoiding pointless fights, or just dodging when I should take a stand?"

> ***"Never interrupt your enemy when he is making a mistake."***
> — **Napoleon Bonaparte**

The Dao Whispers: Who benefits from the struggle I am caught in? Am I fighting a battle that was never mine to begin with?

October 12

Unstained in the Mud

The lotus can rise from the mud but stays untainted

出淤泥而不染

chū yū ní ér bù rǎn

Translation: "Rising from the mud yet unsoiled."
— Traditional Chinese proverb

There's something oddly admirable about people who can sit through a long, messy meeting, surrounded by egos and agendas, and somehow don't get flustered or pulled into the drama. Not smug, not fake, not worked up... just grounded, as if no mud can stick to them.

This proverb alludes to that. The lotus blossoms beautifully, untouched by mud on its buds or petals, despite growing in murky waters. It is used to symbolise those who stay untainted in messy environments – toxic work culture, family drama, or a conformist environment that rewards compromise over character.

The proverb means to say that if a lotus can rise from sludge and still glow, maybe we can, too.

What it teaches us

- **Be resilient:** Develop strength to resist external pressures and maintain personal agency in challenging environments.
- **Stand firm:** Uphold your principles, even when doing so makes you stand alone. Your values do not need anyone else's approval but your own.
- **Rise above toxic environments**: Some places bring out the worst in people. This proverb is a wake-up call to stay true to yourself, even when everything around you isn't.

> ***"The individual has always had to struggle to keep from being overwhelmed by the tribe. If you try it, you will be lonely often, and sometimes frightened. But no price is too high to pay for the privilege of owning yourself."***
> — **Friedrich Nietzsche**

The Dao Whispers: Am I absorbing any negativity that is not mine to carry? What have I compromised, knowingly or unknowingly, to get ahead in this secular world?

October 13

The Danger of Standing Out Too Soon

When tall poppies bloom too early, they get cut first

枪打出头鸟

qiāng dǎ chū tóu niǎo

Translation: "The bird that sticks its head out first gets shot."
— Ancient Chinese proverb

The nail that sticks out usually gets hammered down. In workplaces, social circles, and even families, standing out can make you a target. People get nervous about what they don't understand, and those who challenge the status quo often face pushback, envy, or quiet sabotage.

So here's the real question: Should you dumb yourself down or dull your shine just to survive? Or is there a smarter way to stay visible without getting knocked down?

What it teaches us

- **First, secure your sponsors:** Bold or impactful solutions, even when well-intentioned, may be met with resistance or sabotage in conservative, mediocre, or hierarchical cultures. Perhaps socialise your ideas with bosses and sponsors before going public. Make sure they have your back before you stick your neck out.
- **Visibility has a cost. Know it, and plan for it:** People who deviate from group norms in opinion, appearance, or behaviour often face criticism or exclusion. This isn't a call to conform but a reminder to understand the political and emotional dynamics before making bold moves.
- **Leadership carries risk**: Taking initiative or leading a complex project can expose you to blame if things go wrong, or envy if they go right. Visibility isn't always rewarded, so assess the risks before stepping into the spotlight.

"They'll either want to kill you, kiss you, or be you."
— Suzanne Collins

The Dao Whispers: Am I in an environment that celebrates excellence, or clings to mediocrity? Have I built enough strength and loyal allies to withstand visibility?

October 14

The Inevitability of Enemies

The tree that is taller than the forest is the first to meet the wind

木秀于林，风必摧之；堆出于岸，流必湍之

mù xiù yú lín, fēng bì cuī zhī; duī chū yú àn, liú bì tuān zhī

Translation: "A tree taller than the forest will be broken by the wind; a mound higher than the bank will be lashed by the current."
— Ban Gu (班固), Han dynasty historian

Excellence draws attention, and attention invites attack. Ban Gu's text offers a sober reminder that prominence, whether earned or accidental, rarely goes unchallenged.

Please pause here, find a quiet space, and turn up the volume – look up on YouTube for: ***"Margaret Thatcher recites 'No Enemies' by Charles Mackay to Queen Elizabeth – in the Crown, season four."*** In that powerful scene with Queen Elizabeth, Mackay's words are delivered with steely composure and fire, a reminder that standing tall always comes at a cost.

> ***"You have no enemies, you say?***
> ***Alas! my friend, the boast is poor;***
> ***He who has mingled in the fray***
> ***Of duty, that the brave endure,***
> ***Must have made foes! If you have none,***
> ***Small is the work that you have done.***
> ***You've hit no traitor on the hip,***
> ***You've dashed no cup from perjured lip,***
> ***You've never turned the wrong to right,***
> ***You've been a coward in the fight."***
> — **Charles MacKay**

The Dao Whispers: When you pursue something meaningful, excellent, or unconventional, **antagonism is inevitable.** That said, it is a sign that you are making an impact. Do not blame yourself or others for the foes you earn along the way. Perhaps, see them as proof that you're doing something that counts... Even friends may turn, and betrayal is part of life's education.

October 15

Shame: Humanity's Inner Compass

If you can't feel shame, you've lost your brakes

知耻近乎勇

zhī chǐ jìn hū yǒng

Translation: "Recognising shame is similar to (or close to, likened to) being courageous."
— The Doctrine of the Mean (中庸), Confucian classic

You know that little cringe you feel when you've acted out of line with your own standards? That's your moral GPS, loudly rerouting. Confucius called it, "Knowing shame is the first step to courage."

Of course, losing face or public humiliation is part of the consequence when you act out of line. But more importantly, it's that private, slightly uncomfortable nudge that says, ***"You're better than this."*** The ability to feel that nudge and act on it is what's needed for self-reflection, and moral improvement.

The real danger is in feeling nothing at all – no shame, just pride, fear, or greed. That's how people lose themselves.

What it teaches us

- **It's your inbuilt GPS:** Shame gets a bad reputation, but in the larger scheme of things, it's actually your gut saying, "Hey, we're off track." It's probably best to listen to it.
- **Fix it, not hide it:** Good leaders aren't perfect, they're the ones who know teams can mess up. They have the rare courage to admit it and course-correct by owning mistakes and fixing them.
- **There's dignity in accountability:** Owning a mistake dignifies both the self and others, especially when you have the power to shift blame downward, but don't.

> ***"The only tyrant I accept in this world is the still, small voice within."***
> **— Mahatma Gandhi**

The Dao Whispers: Shame isn't a "boo boo" feeling. It's proof you still care about what's right. The real question is, do your daily choices align with your sense of self-respect and personal agency – your ability to choose and act for yourself?

October 16

Don't Sleepwalk Through Your Days

Be here for your life, or you'll miss it as it happens

心不在焉，视而不见，
听而不闻，食而不知其味

xīn bù zài yān, shì ér bù jiàn, tīng ér bù wén, shí ér bù zhī qí wèi

Translation: "When the mind is absent, we look but do not see, listen but do not hear, eat but do not taste."
— Confucius (孔子), Analects (论语)

You go for a walk to "clear your head," and by the time you are back, you've been so lost in thought that you couldn't say which route you took, nor recall the interesting shops along the way. You lived the present through the past, deep in your head, or in multiple imagined versions of the future. You lived everywhere else except here, now.

What it teaches us

- **Practise mindfulness daily:** Put your phone away, slow down, and actually taste your food.
- **Engage fully in relationships:** When someone's talking, do you catch yourself mentally drafting your grocery list or tomorrow's priorities? They'll notice... gently reel it back in.
- **Appreciate life's details**: Next time you're out walking, try this... tune into the little things – the birds chirping, sunlight playing on the leaves, how clouds drift like they've got all the time in the world. Catch your mind drifting to yesterday's drama or tomorrow's to-do list? Gently bring it back to the here, and the now. Life's putting on a pretty amazing show, we just have to pause long enough to notice.

> ***"The greatest thing in the world is to know how to belong to oneself."***
> **— Michel de Montaigne**

Only when we truly belong to ourselves can we live in the present, instead of losing it to the past, the future, or someone else's problems.

The Dao Whispers: Do I take life's joys for granted, half-listen to others, or miss what's around me because I'm lost in thought?

October 17

I Jumped at a Shadow That Was Mine

Your brain is a brilliant storyteller, but it doesn't always tell the truth

杯弓蛇影

bēi gōng shé yǐng

Translation: "Mistaking the reflection of a bow in a cup for a snake."
— Chinese idiom

The Story

During the Western Jin dynasty, a man named Yue Guang was invited to a banquet. As he lifted his wine cup, he spotted what looked like a small snake wriggling in his drink.

Not wanting to offend his host, he forced himself to drink it. But once home, he couldn't shake the thought: "Did I just swallow a snake?" Consumed by paranoia, he fell ill.

A friend later invited him back to the same room. This time, Yue Guang noticed a bow hanging on the wall and its curved shadow falling into the wine cup. The "snake" had been nothing more than a reflection. The moment he realised that, his fear disappeared, so did his illness.

What it teaches us

- **Irrational fear:** In uncertainty or fear, our brains tend to fill in the blanks with the worst-case scenarios. Don't trust every thought. Unchecked narratives can distort your judgement and drive poor decisions.
- **Most worries never happen:** We lose sleep and spend so much energy rehearsing tragedies in our heads, and the stress ends up doing more damage than the events ever could.
- **Don't assume the worst:** Assuming "they meant to hurt me" often starts fights that never needed to happen. There's no need to always assume the worst in people.

> **"We suffer more in imagination than in reality."**
> **— Seneca**

The Dao Whispers: Am I running a horror movie in my head when there's nothing to fear?

October 18

Fix the Fence Before More Sheep Escape

It's not too late... until it is

亡羊补牢

wáng yáng bǔ láo

Translation: "Mending the pen after losing the sheep."
— Chinese idiom

The Story

The saying comes from a story about a shepherd who lost a sheep because there was a hole in the fence. He didn't bother fixing it right away. The next day, more sheep ran away. Finally, his neighbour yelled: *"Fix the fence!"* So he did and saved the rest of his flock.

The point? Feeling bad about a mistake is only useful if it pushes you to actually fix it. But sometimes, "next time" can be too late.

What it teaches us

- **Learn from mistakes**: Every mistake is tuition for life's lessons, but only if you learn and apply it. It's better late than never to start asking, "Okay, now how do I make this right?" It's even better early than late, if you can help it.
- **Stop crying over spilled milk:** Instead, start looking for a paper towel to clean up the mess. Wasting time ruminating on the "I should've..." and "Why me" just makes the problem bigger. Focus on the fix: apologise, adjust, reinforce – concentrate on what you can do now.

> ***"For what it's worth: it's never too late...to be whoever you want to be. I hope you live a life you're proud of, And if you find that you're not, I hope you have the strength to start over."***
> — **Eric Roth** (The Curious Case of Benjamin Button)

The Dao Whispers: Do I fix problems when they first appear, or only after I've paid a bigger price?

October 19

Embrace Lifelong Learning

As long as we are alive, we're enrolled in life's classroom

活到老，学到老

huó dào lǎo, xué dào lǎo

Translation: "As I live till an old age, so will I learn till then."
— Traditional Chinese proverb

This proverb says it simply: if you're alive, you're still a student. The moment we stop learning, we stop growing. Wisdom isn't a trophy you win once – it evolves with time, new experiences, and humility to admit you don't know everything yet.
Those who think they've "learnt enough" tend to get stuck, and risk becoming rigid, outdated, left behind. The ones who keep their curiosity alive stay sharp, adaptable, and full of new life... it doesn't matter if they are 18 or 88.

What it teaches us

- **Stay curious:** A lively mind keeps us young and ready for whatever curveballs life throws. Lifelong learning helps keep our mind sharp, adaptable, and resilient.
- **Relevance is earned:** The world keeps changing. It's never too late to learn about AI, new tech, or that one thing you've been avoiding.
- **Learning keeps you alive and intellectually engaged:** Engaging with new knowledge, tools, and ways of seeing the world enriches our perspectives and life's later years.

> ***"The illiterate of the 21st century will not be those who cannot read or write, but those who cannot learn, unlearn, and relearn."***
> **— Alvin Toffler**

The Dao Whispers: What's something I've been "too old" or "too late" to learn? What could change in my life if I started today?

October 20

The Illusion of Perfection

Perfection leaves no room for life

水至清则无鱼，人至察则无徒

shuǐ zhì qīng zé wú yú, rén zhì chá zé wú tú

Translation: "Waters that are too clear breed no fish; and a person too discerning finds no companions."
— Ancient Chinese proverb

If you've ever met someone who can't help pointing out every flaw, you'll know how exhausting it feels to be around them. This proverb reminds us that life and people aren't meant to be crystal clear or perfect. In nature, water that's *too* clear usually lacks the nutrients needed for life. In human relationships, someone who's ***too critical***, or unforgiving will eventually find themselves standing alone.

This contrarian wisdom reminds us that excessive perfectionism, hyper-clarity, or rigidity in one's worldview can become counterproductive. It's not a call to abandon standards... it simply hints that warmth, tolerance, and a bit of wiggle room can make life richer, for you and for those around you.

What it teaches us

- **Moderate your judgement:** Demand the best, but not perfection. People shut down if constantly measured against an impossible bar, feeling judged and inadequate.
- **Lead with balance:** The best leaders know when to bend. Flexibility and empathy build more loyalty than being too strict or uncompromising.
- **Embrace imperfection as fuel for growth:** Flaws aren't flaws if they make life fuller. In nature and in people, it's often the quirks, the mess, and the unpredictability that keep things alive.

> ***"The essence of being human is that one does not seek perfection."***
> — **George Orwell**

The Dao Whispers: Where in your life are you clinging to an impossible standard?

October 21

The Frog in the Well

The danger of mistaking your little view of the world for the whole picture

井底之蛙

jǐng dǐ zhī wā

Translation: "The frog at the bottom of a well."
— Traditional Chinese proverb, Warring States period

A long time ago, a Singaporean classmate, JJ, said to me, ***"You're such a sua ku..."***

I blinked, and asked, **"*What's a sua ku?*"**

He grinned, **"It's *Hokkien*** (a Chinese dialect) ***for 山龟 (shān guī) – mountain tortoise. A tortoise that's stayed on one mountain all its life and has never seen the world outside!"***

Apparently, I was the tortoise that day. I've since travelled widely… and hopefully, less of a suaku by now.

The idiom carries a similar sting. It paints a picture of a frog at the bottom of a well, believing the tiny circle of sky above is the entire universe. It warns us against narrow perspectives, untested beliefs, and the comfort of staying in a "small well" forever.

What it teaches us

- **Question your field of vision:** When things feel certain, ask, "Is this the full picture, or just the view from my well?"
- **Seek broader exposure:** Growth starts the moment we leave our little well, through travel, new ideas, or tough conversations.
- **Watch for blind spots:** Our worldview is only as wide as the world we allow ourselves to see. A limiting environment often leads to blind spots, biases, and flawed assumptions.

> ***"Your assumptions are your windows on the world. Scrub them off every once in a while, or the light won't come in."***
> — **Isaac Asimov**

The Dao Whispers: Am I seeing the full picture, or just the view from where I stand? How often do I climb out of my well to have a glimpse at the bigger sky?

October 22

Rumour with Teeth: Inventing Tigers

When repetition gives imagination the weight of truth

三人成虎

sān rén chéng hǔ

Translation: "Three people can make a tiger."
— Chinese idiom

The Story

In the Warring States period, a minister warned the king:

> "If one person claims a tiger is roaming the marketplace, you'll doubt it. If two people say it, you might still hesitate. But if three people insist, you'll believe it – even if no tiger exists."

He was right. When three citizens claimed they saw a tiger, the king panicked and ordered a citywide hunt. No tiger was ever found. But the rumour had already done its job: it changed what the king believed, and it shaped his actions.

The point? Repeat a lie often enough, and it stops feeling like a lie. Popular belief doesn't make something real, it just makes it powerfully convincing, rightly, or wrongly.

What it teaches us

- **Question popular consensus**: The louder and more often something is said, the more it needs fact-checking – not less.
- **Watch for echo chambers:** In politics, media, and even friendships, repetition can drown out reason.
- **Guard your mind:** Ideas spread like viruses. Be careful which "tigers" others ask you to fear or chase.

> ***"A lie doesn't become truth, wrong doesn't become right, and evil doesn't become good just because it's accepted by a majority."***
> **— Booker T. Washington**

The Dao Whispers: If a lie is repeated often enough, even you might believe it. What stories, repeated by many, have you accepted without ever checking if they were true?

October 23

The Art of the Workaround

You can yell at the mountain... or walk around it

山不转路转，路不转人转

shān bù zhuǎn lù zhuǎn, lù bù zhuǎn rén zhuǎn

Translation: "If the mountain doesn't move, the road can turn; if the road doesn't turn, the person can."
— Traditional Chinese proverb

"Hey, mountain... you're in my way. Mind moving?"

Sometimes life throws you a mountain – a stubborn boss, a broken system, or a situation that refuses to budge no matter how hard you push. You can keep shoving (and give yourself a headache)… or you can get smart and find another way through.

In the proverb, the mountain is a metaphor for life's obstacles. If the road can curve around it, great, take it. If there's no road, you adjust yourself: change your approach, your mindset, or your plan. Flexibility is knowing when to stop wrestling the immovable and start dancing around it.

What it teaches us

- **Pivot when you must:** Immovable barriers aren't always there to be smashed. Sometimes the win is in the workaround.
- **Be flexible when you plan:** Rigid plans can trap you, leaving you stranded. Flow around the obstacles, there's no need to keep pushing against a dead end. Alternatively, try another approach.
- **Change your angle:** If nothing outside changes, adjust what's inside – your expectations, your perspectives, your story, your route, or the weight you give the barrier.

> ***"Try not to resist the changes that come your way. Instead, let life live through you."***
> — **Rumi**

The Dao Whispers: What mountain in your life are you trying to push, when you could simply walk around it? Are you mistaking resistance for grit, when your real strength might lie in graceful redirection?

October 24

The Power of Saying Less

Executive presence: when less is more

言多必失

yán duō bì shī

Translation: "Too many words lead to mistakes."
— Traditional Chinese proverb

You sent a text and immediately thought, "I should've stopped three sentences ago..." And sometimes you sat in a meeting and realised the more someone talks, the less anyone is listening. That's the spirit of this proverb.

In classical Chinese wisdom, having some restraint in speech is a sign of intelligence, maturity, and self-mastery. Talking too much, especially without thinking, can land you in trouble, strain relationships, or even dilute your core message. The best communicators know that a few well-chosen words can hit harder than a torrent of meaningless talk. And sometimes, the most powerful thing you can do is to say nothing and let silence speak for you.

What it teaches us

- **Speak with purpose:** In work and life, clear, concise words build credibility. Rambling can bury your message and make you forgettable.
- **Stay cool in conflict**: In tense moments, the more you talk, the more likely you'll say something you regret. Restraint buys you time and keeps you out of trouble.
- **Lead like you mean it:** Great leaders use words sparingly but strategically. Over-talking can drain authority or make you look unsure.

> ***"Better to remain silent and be thought a fool than to speak out and remove all doubt."***
> **— Mark Twain**

The Dao Whispers: Do I add value when I speak? How can I be concise and land my message with impact without drowning it in a stream of words that dilute its power?

October 25

No One Ever Caught a Fish by Staring at It

Trade "I wish" for "I'll catch it"

临渊羡鱼，不如退而结网

lín yuān xiàn yú, bù rú tuì ér jié wǎng

Translation: "Rather than staring into the deep admiring the fish, why not take a step back and start weaving the net."
— Traditional Chinese proverb

The Story

There was once a young man who spent his days kneeling by the village well, wishing for riches. "If only I had gold like the merchant, or strong like the blacksmith." The well was rumoured to be magical, but his wishes never came true. One evening, an old farmer drew up water and asked, "What are you waiting for, boy?" Hearing his answer, the farmer laughed, "This is just a hole in the ground. The magic's in your hands, not the water."

The next morning, the young man apprenticed under the blacksmith, blistered his hands learning the trade, and bartered his skills for grain. Years later, looking at his calloused palms, he realised: he'd drawn up his own fortune.

What it teaches us

- **Be a strategist, not a spectator:** Instead of admiring what others have or what seems out of reach, focus on developing your strategy, building your skills, and mapping out your plans to turn vision into reality.
- **Turn green eyes into grit:** Instead of burning over someone's success, learn, or even, reverse-engineer it. How'd they do it? Study the playbook, then write your own.
- **Don't pray for the storm to pass, learn to sail in it:** Don't wait for permissions or dwell on what's missing... waiting for circumstances to change. Sail with the storm, problem solve proactively for what you want or need.

"The best way to predict the future is to create it."
— **Peter Drucker**

The Dao Whispers: Am I actually doing something about my problems, or just complaining? When I notice someone ahead of me, can I treat it as a roadmap instead of a rivalry?

October 26

Love Yourself, and the World Follows

Those who love themselves will be loved

自爱者，人恒爱之；自助者，天助之

zì ài zhě, rén héng ài zhī; zì zhù zhě, tiān zhù zhī

Translation: "Those who love themselves will always be loved by others; those who help themselves will be helped by heaven."
— Traditional Chinese proverb

This proverb is really about two sides of the same coin: self-love and self-help.

- **Self-love** (自爱, zì ài) is not just bubble baths and treats. It's carrying yourself with respect, keeping healthy boundaries, and taking care of your mind and body. When you treat yourself like you matter, other people tend to treat you the same way.
- **Self-help** (自助, zì zhù) means taking action instead of waiting for a rescue mission. It doesn't mean you go alone forever and never ask for help, but rather, show you're willing to meet the universe halfway. Funny thing is, when you do that, help often shows up when you least expect it.

What it teaches us

- **Set the standard:** The way you treat yourself teaches others how to treat you. Those who value themselves naturally attract mutual respect, in both friendships and love.
- **Build your backbone:** Self-care builds resilience, so you're steadier in life's storms.
- **Move first:** Take the first step toward what you want, the rest often falls into place.

> ***"Self-love is the only antidote to the chaos of existence. And if you don't love and care for yourself and your own needs, you will cause unnecessary suffering both for yourself and others."***
> — **Jordan Peterson**

The Dao Whispers: Choose yourself first. Treat yourself like someone worth protecting. And remember... heaven tends to help those already on the move.

October 27

Ask the Traveller Who Made It Back Alive

They know where the dragons and the shortcuts are

欲知前路，当问过来人

yù zhī qián lù, dāng wèn guò lái rén

Translation: "To know the road ahead, ask those who have travelled those roads."
— Traditional Chinese proverb

You can read all the maps, scan every "Top 10 Tips" list, and binge-watch YouTube tutorials… but some things you only learn from people who've actually done it, and survived to tell the tale.

This is a profound piece of advice that suggests that those who have already navigated a particular path possess invaluable insights. Their wisdom is not theoretical, it's forged through trial, error, and lived reality.

What it teaches us

- **Learn beyond theory:** Wisdom from the experienced folks is not theoretical, it's forged through trial, error, and lived experience. Listening to such voices helps us see around corners and dodge avoidable mistakes.
- **Fast-track your learning:** The quickest way to avoid rookie mistakes? Learn from someone else's.
- **Pick your mentors wisely:** Advice is only as useful as the insight, judgement, and self-awareness of the one giving it. Even well-intentioned advisors who aren't a good fit can end up giving poor guidance and leading you somewhere you never meant to go.

> ***"A wise man learns by experience of others; a fool, by his own."***
> — **Benjamin Franklin**

The Dao Whispers: Who has already done what I'm trying to do? Do I respect them enough to really listen to what they have to say? And can I take their wisdom without losing my own voice in the process?

October 28

It Gets Cold at the Top

Why reaching new heights can feel a little lonely

高处不胜寒

gāo chù bú shèng hán

Translation: "The higher one stands, the colder it gets."
— Traditional Chinese proverb

The higher you climb, the lonelier it gets... or so they say.

Smart people, visionaries, and those with real integrity often end up standing apart, not because they want to, but because seeing more can often mean feeling more. And let's be honest, most people don't get it. Greatness, brilliance, or deep wisdom can create distance from the crowd, making solitude an inevitable companion.

So, if you're someone who thinks deeply, cares fiercely, or refuses to follow the crowd? The price, sometimes, is loneliness.

The view from the summit is clear, but the air is thin.

What it teaches us

- **Embrace your altitude:** Solitude can be a mark of depth, not isolation. Intelligence offers elevation, but that height can come with a chill, and that's okay.
- **Find your tribe:** Seek the rare few who are on your wavelength, even if they are scattered across the world.
- **Protect your heart:** Just as mountain climbers dress for the cold, prepare yourself emotionally for the solitude that can accompany clarity, intellectual or spiritual elevation, and conviction.

> ***"Loneliness is the poverty of self; solitude is the richness of self."***
> — **May Sarton**

The Dao Whispers: Not everyone will 'get' you, and that's okay. Some won't even understand what you're asking, much less your answers. So, appreciate the few who ***do*** see you, even if they're not right beside you. And listen: Never dull yourself just to fit in. Instead, feed your own fire, the kind that keeps you lit from the inside, no matter how cold it gets outside.

October 29

When Pleasing Everyone Pleases No One

You can't season life to suit every taste

众口难调

zhòng kǒu nán tiáo

Translation: "It's impossible to please every palate."
— Chinese idiom

Try cooking for a big group... one wants more salt, another swears they can't have gluten, and someone else thinks coriander tastes like soap. At the end of it all, you have a big pot of beige mush on your kitchen hob that nobody likes. That's what happens when we try to please everyone in life. People carry different needs, values, and baggage. The more you try to accommodate everyone, the more you risk watering down your decisions and yourself.

The idiom reminds us that trying to please everyone often leads to diluted decisions, emotional exhaustion, or even resentment. Instead of chasing universal approval, learn to **discern, decide, and stand firm;** guided by your own compass, not the crowd's haphazard (mis-) directions.

What it teaches us

- **Personal boundaries:** People-pleasing is a fast track to losing your sense of self.
- **Leadership reality:** You can listen to every voice, but you can't cook every recipe at once. Leaders must balance competing voices – employees, customers, investors – and ultimately make hard calls grounded in values.
- **Decision-making in groups:** Consensus is useful, but not always possible. Sometimes, you just have to serve the dish and let people take it or leave it.

> ***"To avoid criticism, say nothing, do nothing, be nothing."***
> — **Aristotle**

The Dao Whispers: The surest way to fail is by trying to find a solution that pleases everyone. Sometimes, the bravest thing you can do is follow what feels right in your heart, you'll be criticised either way. And in the end… if you can live with your own choices, does it really matter who else likes it?

October 30

Don't Let Style Obscure Your Message

A message is only powerful if people understand it

不以文害辞，不以辞害志

bù yǐ wén hài cí, bù yǐ cí hài zhì

Translation: "Do not let literary style obscure expression, and do not let expression obscure intent."
— Emperor Qianlong, Qing Dynasty

You know, that speech you sat through that sounded impressive... until you realised you had no idea what the person actually said? It was just one impressive-sounding piece of rhetoric after another, strung together without a real message behind it.

Emperor Qianlong's point was simple: style is the garnish, not the main dish. Sure, a bit of polish can help the message land, but when you get lost in clever metaphors, corporate jargon, or endless word-spinning, you risk losing the point entirely.

The most powerful communication often sounds simple, but it's anything but easy. It's the difference between someone saying, "In the fullness of time, strategic synergies will be realised" and simply saying, "We'll work better together."

What it teaches us

- **Clarity in power:** A message is only powerful if people actually understand it.
- **Real talk = trust:** Some people can smell fake and insincerity from a mile away. Be it leading a team or texting a friend, honesty builds trust, no need for theatrics.
- **It's not just what you say, it's why you say it:** Sometimes, it serves you better to focus less on perfect delivery and more on your real message. When people feel your good intentions, they'll cut through the miscommunications.

> ***"Speak, so that I may see you."***
> — **Socrates**

The Dao Whispers: Before you speak or write, ask yourself: Am I dressing this up to clarify… or to cover up? Will the listener walk away remembering my point or just what I wore?

October 31

First, Understand the Core Principle

Clarity brings peace, balance, and better decisions

读书以明理为先，理明则心平气和

dú shū yǐ míng lǐ wéi xiān, lǐ míng zé xīn píng qì hé

Translation: "In learning, seek first to understand the first principles and have clarity of the subject matter. Once you have a good grasp of the principle, you'll better be able to find peace."
— Emperor Kangxi, Qing Dynasty

You've signed up for a brilliant course or cracked open a big-name book… and halfway through, thought, ***"Wait, what am I actually learning here?"*** We've all been there: plenty of buzzwords, but what do they actually mean and how is it relevant to what I want to accomplish?

Emperor Kangxi's reminder is simple: don't just collect knowledge for the sake of collecting. Go for the good stuff, in this case, the **理 (lǐ),** the underlying principles of how things actually work. Once you get that, you untangle mental knots, dodge nonsense, and think with clear purpose. According to Emperor Kangxi, that clarity brings not just peace, but equanimity – the ability to stay steady and balanced no matter what life throws at you.

What it teaches us

- **Make smarter choices:** Understand the why, not just the what, and solve problems at their root.
- **Know what you're solving for:** If you can define the problem you're solving for, that's half the battle.
- **Build a long-term vision based on reality:** See things as they are, not how you wish they were, so that your actions and plans are grounded on reality, not wishful thinking.

"The first principle is that you must not fool yourself – and you are the easiest person to fool."
— **Richard Feynman**

The Dao Whispers: When I read, do I first attempt to understand the principles? Do I question what I've been taught?

NOVEMBER

静

jìng

静 (jìng) encompasses:

- Inner calm and mental clarity
- Serenity amidst chaos
- Mindful presence in the moment
- Restraint in speech and action
- Harmony with self and surroundings

静 (jìng) literally means "quiet", but it isn't just about being quiet. It's got to do with the deep, intentional calm which brings clarity, peace, and inner strength. It's the art of finding tranquillity inside yourself, listening beyond words, and moving through life with your eyes wide open. This peace and stillness become the foundation of clarity and unwavering strength, and in turn, the practice of equanimity.

Mastering 静 (jìng) helps us:

- **Clear your head:** Slowing down sharpens your thinking so you can spot opportunities you might otherwise miss.
- **Stay grounded**: In turbulent times, composure keeps you anchored while others may spiral under pressure... sometimes in ways they never come back from.
- **Listen better:** Stop just waiting for your turn to speak. Listen proactively and observe, to better understand others and connect more deeply.
- **Conserve energy**: Protect your time, avoid distractions that drain.
- **Act with purpose**: Choose when and how to act without rushing, so you judge more clearly and make a greater impact.

November 1

Storms Don't Last Forever

If you can't beat it, outlast it

天下未有过不去之事，忍耐一时便觉无事

tiān xià wèi yǒu guò bù qù zhī shì, rěn nài yī shí biàn jué wú shì

Translation: "There is no challenge in the world that cannot be overcome or is insurmountable; if you simply hold steady for a while, you'll find that its weight will start to lift."
— Emperor Kangxi (康熙帝)

We've all faced problems that felt like the end of the world… only to look back later and wonder why we stressed so much.

Whatever you're dealing with right now, an impossible deadline, a boss who thinks 'urgent' means 3 a.m., a life curveball you didn't see coming, or maybe a haircut that went really wrong... these too shall pass.

That's the spirit of Emperor Kangxi's advice. The proverb reminds us that all difficulties, no matter how daunting, are temporary. Life's tough moments, no matter how big, don't last forever. If we keep our cool and ride them out, time will usually soften their edges. You don't have to fix everything today. Sleep on it. What feels unbearable now often feels lighter tomorrow.

What it teaches us

- **This chapter isn't your whole story:** Heartbroken? Lost a job? Knowing storms don't last forever keeps you from blowing the problems out of proportion.
- **Stay calm under pressure:** Staying composed under stress – in a high-stakes meeting or a family crisis – keeps your mind clear and your actions focused and logical.
- **Grow stronger:** Every trial you endure without losing your cool becomes training for the next one.

"This too shall pass."

— Attributed to Persian poets

The Dao Whispers: Trust that you will weather this storm, just as you have many times before, and come out a lot wiser and stronger for it.

November 2

Sailing Through Life's Weather

Equanimity in both storms and sunshine

风无常顺，兵无常胜

fēng wú cháng shùn, bīng wú cháng shèng

Translation: "The wind doesn't always blow in a favourable direction. Similarly, armies don't always win."
— Traditional Chinese proverb

Some days, life seems to be in your corner, clearing the path and giving you a helpful tailwind. Other days, it feels like it's playing a practical joke and you're the punchline. You start to wonder if you're a character in someone's comic book, written by an author with an odd sense of humour… one you're quite definitely not laughing at.

The proverb conveys the idea that life is inherently unpredictable. Outcomes may shift, fortunes may turn, and even the strongest encounter setbacks. Rather than trying to control the wind, perhaps you can trim your sails, adjust your course, and remember that storms and calm waters both come in cycles.

What it teaches us

- **Stay adaptable:** It's often the surprise changes, not the outcomes themselves, that throw us off. The more flexible you are, the quicker you find your footing, and the more likely you are to find new paths.
- **Stay humble in success:** Success may be lasting for some, fleeting for others. Be grateful and know that things can always change.
- **Stay balanced:** Don't let good luck make you reckless or bad luck break you. **Maintain equanimity** through life's highs and lows across relationships, work, and fortune.

> ***"Success is not final, failure is not fatal: it is the courage to continue that counts."***
> — **Winston Churchill**

The Dao Whispers: Can I let go of how I want things to be, and stay equanimous instead of being tossed around by life's ups and downs?

November 3

Half A Map Won't Get You Far

You need more than one voice to see the full picture

兼听则明，偏信则暗

jiān tīng zé míng, piān xìn zé àn

Translation: "Listening to all sides leads to clarity; believing only one side leaves you in the dark."
— Traditional Chinese proverb

You wouldn't judge a book by reading just one page, so why make up your mind after hearing only one version of a story? The truth has a way of hiding in the gaps, contradictions, and sometimes in the parts no one wants to tell you.

In ancient China, wise rulers gathered counsel from every side before deciding, aware that even their most loyal advisors had blind spots and biases. If you only listen to one side of the story, you're only getting half the picture. It's like trying to navigate with half a map.

What it teaches us

- **Resolving conflicts:** Listen to everyone involved before drawing conclusions. This way, you can avoid unfair judgments and uncover the full story.
- **Improving yourself:** If you want to improve at work, hobbies, or just life, ask different people for advice, including the tough critics. They might spot things you miss. The feedback you'd rather not hear is often the most useful.
- **Spotting misinformation:** Don't believe everything you read or hear. Compare a few sources before you decide what's true. One story might be biased but looking at a few may help you get closer to the real picture.

> ***"Leaders who don't listen will eventually be surrounded by people who have nothing to say."***
> — **Andy Stanley**

The Dao Whispers: Do I make the effort to listen to all sides, or do I have a tendency to settle for the story I like best?

November 4

There's No Need to Show All Your Cards

Leave some pages of your story untold

逢人且说三分话，未可全抛一片心

féng rén qiě shuō sān fēn huà, wèi kě quán pāo yī piàn xīn

Translation: "When meeting someone, speak only a third of what you think, never reveal your whole heart."
— Traditional Chinese proverb

Ever shared something personal, only to regret it the moment you saw the other person's face or worse, when it came back to you through someone else? This old saying is basically the ancient world's way of saying: ***test the waters before diving in.***

It doesn't mean being fake or closed off. It means revealing yourself in measured steps, once you understand the other person's intentions and integrity. In a world where oversharing can go viral in seconds, a little mystery and self-protection can go a long way.

What it teaches us

- **Build trust gradually:** In new friendships or work relationships, share a little at a time and watch how they handle it. Trust is earned in layers, not in a single conversation.
- **Preserve your leverage:** In workplace negotiations or team discussions, holding back part of your plan keeps you in control until the timing is right.
- **Protect yourself:** Venting to the wrong person can turn into gossip, misunderstanding, or a reputation you didn't intend to earn. What you share today can also be twisted and used against you tomorrow.

> ***"Never tell all you know – not even to the person you know best."***
> **— Baltasar Gracián**

The Dao Whispers: Am I speaking too freely to those who haven't earned my trust? What part of myself is better guarded in silence?

November 5

Lean into the Headwinds

How to turn life's resistance into your momentum

逆风扬帆

nì fēng yáng fān

Translation: "Raise the sail against the wind."
— Traditional Chinese proverb

You know those days when it feels like the universe has it in for you? The meeting gets cancelled, the client bails, the coffee spills... all before lunch. Most of us would drop anchor and wait for calmer seas, but the seasoned sailors? They adjust their sails and push right into the headwind.

This proverb says that headwinds can slow you down, sure, but they can also give you leverage, forcing you to focus and push harder. Sometimes, the very thing you think is holding you back can be what moves you forward.

What it teaches us

- **Overcoming obstacles:** Rejections, failed projects, and unexpected detours can each be a pivot point if you choose to learn, recalibrate, and try again.
- **Career resilience:** Navigating politics, shifting priorities, or impossible deadlines with adaptability turns you into the person people trust in a crisis.
- **Pursuing goals against resistance:** When family, society, or circumstance push back, use it as fuel to keep moving and to prove to yourself that you can chart your own course.

> ***"We must embrace pain and burn it as fuel for our journey."***
> — **Kenji Miyazawa**

The Dao Whispers: Am I waiting for calm seas… or will I raise my sail and face the headwind today?

November 6

The Risk of Shining Too Bright

Great achievements overshadow the master

功高震主

gōng gāo zhèn zhǔ

Translation: "Great achievements overshadow the master."
— Traditional Chinese proverb

Ever outshine your boss and thought, "They'll be thrilled"? And then… things got weird? You suddenly find yourself left out of key meetings, your projects mysteriously reassigned, or credit for your work is redirected elsewhere.

This proverb reveals a paradox: excellence, while admirable, can be dangerous. When your accomplishments outshine those in power, especially in the case of insecure or mediocre leaders who often see it as a threat rather than a win for the team. What should be a triumph ends up triggering envy, resistance, or sabotage. Secure managers, by contrast, make space for you to step up and will empower you to shine.

It's not a call to shrink or dumb down, but to direct it wisely. Influence is not built on talent alone, but on timing, discretion, and awareness of power and human nature.

What it teaches us

- **Workplace dynamics:** Outshining your boss too early or visibly may invite subtle backlash, unless your boss is highly secure and competent.
- **Leadership awareness:** Great leaders elevate rising stars. Weak ones resent them. Learn to tell the difference.
- **Power strategy:** Share credit, signal loyalty, and be deliberate in how much visibility you take.

"Never outshine the master."
— **Robert Greene**

The Dao Whispers: Is my success inspiring trust or is it painting a target on my back?

November 7

The Pedestal Conundrum

When putting someone too high sets the rest too low

捧上神坛

pěng shàng shén tán

Translation: "(To) Lift someone onto the altar of the gods."
— Traditional Chinese idiom

This idiom is about putting someone on a pedestal, treating them as flawless and almost godlike, when in reality no one is. This can happen in meetings where a boss' idea is treated as infallible, or when a team member becomes the "golden child" despite modest results. While the intention may stem from loyalty or admiration, it can end up undermining meritocracy and lead to overall lukewarm performance in the team.

What it teaches us

- **The distortion of merit:** When recognition is concentrated on just one person, it distorts the playing field. Effort and merit take a back seat, talented contributors slip under the radar, and decisions start favouring the "star" rather than what will move the whole team forward.
- **No space to share different ideas:** Once someone's crowned the office favourite, disagreeing can feel like poking a beehive. Great ideas stay hidden, real issues get glossed over, and the safest move is to nod along, even when the course is clearly wrong.
- **Toxic work culture**: When flattery runs the show, the same "chosen few" get the spotlight, cliques tighten, and the rest quietly disengage. It's not just bad for morale, it's bad for business.

> ***"Excessive praise is a form of deception, hiding weaknesses under flattery."***
> — Often attributed to **Sun Tzu**

The Dao Whispers: When I look at my team, do I recognise my team for their actual contributions, or just the glow of my favourites?

November 8

The Business of Keeping Fires Burning

Why some people can't let a crisis die

养寇自重

yǎng kòu zì zhòng

Translation: "Keep enemies or problems alive to stay relevant."
— Traditional Chinese idiom

Some people always seem to live in crisis, conveniently in charge of fixing it. The catch? The fix never quite arrives.

This idiom describes a manipulative tactic where a threat or dysfunction is kept alive in order to stay relevant, control the narrative, or secure more resources. It shows up in politics, corporate hierarchies, and even social groups... the rival still painted as dangerous years later, or the project that is "almost fixed" for the fifth quarter in a row. In the short term it can make the orchestrator look indispensable. In the long term it leads to the waste of resources, loss of trust, and leaves the whole system weaker.

What it teaches us

- **Perpetuation of dysfunction:** Perpetuating the problem allows someone's influence to survive at the expense of organisational performance. Over time, the dysfunction entrenches itself and spreads across the system.
- **Risk of exposure:** If colleagues, superiors, or clients discover the tactic, credibility disappears very quickly.
- **Resource misallocation:** Pouring time and money into manufactured crises starves actual priorities of resources, creating systemic inefficiencies in the long run.

> ***"Leaders who create problems to solve them soon find their problems outgrow their solutions."***
> **— John Maxwell**

The Dao Whispers: Is this crisis as real as it looks, or is someone milking it to look like the hero?

November 9

Push Hard Enough, They'll Push Back

Why even the nicest people have a breaking point

逼上梁山

bī shàng liáng shān

Translation: "Forced to go up Mount Liang."
— Water Margin (水浒传 shuǐ hǔ zhuàn)

Even the nicest person will snap if you back them into a corner. That's what this ancient Chinese saying is about.

The Story

Mount Liang was the remote stronghold of 108 legendary outlaws who resisted the corrupt Song Dynasty. Many hadn't started as criminals; they were honest officials, merchants, or farmers, a bit like Robin Hood or other unlikely heroes who resisted injustice. But injustice, betrayal, or abuse left them with no choice but to take up arms and join the rebels.

This proverb is for those times when you're not seeking a fight, but the fight finds you. When every peaceful path is blocked, even the most patient person may feel forced to push back.

What it teaches us

- **Don't corner people:** Push someone far enough and you may provoke a reaction you didn't expect. Even the nicest people can flip when you cross the line.
- **Pressure can change you:** Great pressure can reveal a clearer, bolder side of you that you didn't know was there.
- **Pushback comes with a price:** Taking a stand can alienate you from the status quo, so weigh your options carefully.

> ***"Those who make peaceful revolution impossible will make violent revolution inevitable."***
> — **John F. Kennedy**

The Dao Whispers: Have I left someone else with no safe option? Is my pushback driven by pride, or by principle?

November 10

How the Universe Balances Every Account

Ancient wisdom for when you think you're alone

举头三尺有神明

jǔ tóu sān chǐ yǒu shén míng

Translation: "Three feet above our head, there are gods."
— Traditional Chinese proverb

You know that feeling when you're alone and tempted to cut corners? This 2,000-year-old Chinese proverb puts it simply:

> ***"Three feet above your head, the universe is taking notes."***

It reminds us that nothing truly escapes accountability. In Eastern philosophy, divine forces, cosmic laws, or higher powers are always watching, not to punish, but to ensure moral balance in the universe.

What it teaches us

- **Your private actions define you:** The person you are when no one is watching is the ***real*** you.
- **Forget *"getting away with it"*:** Wrongdoing may go unnoticed for now, but no action is without consequence. The universe always settles its accounts.
- **Doing right for your own sake:** Do right not because someone is watching, but because you're answerable to yourself... your conscience.

> ***"Conscience is the inner voice that warns us somebody may be looking."***
> — **H.L. Mencken**

The Dao Whispers: Who you are in private is who you really are. Would you still choose the right path, even if no one was watching?

November 11

Do Your Best, Then Let Go

Give your best shot, then leave the rest to fate

尽人事，听天命

jìn rén shì, tīng tiān mìng

Translation: "Do all that is humanly possible, and then leave the rest to fate."
— Traditional Chinese proverb

You know that moment right before something big – that exam, the job interview, the wedding speech – where you've already done all the training, rehearsals, pep talks, and late-night Googling you can possibly do? At that point, no amount of frantic pacing or "just one more check" is going to make it better. That's when this proverb taps you on the shoulder and says: ***Relax. You've done your bit. The rest is out of your hands. It's bedtime, let's just go to sleep.***

It's the sweet spot between hustle and surrender. Push hard where you have control, then stop micromanaging the universe.

What it teaches us

- **Be disciplined, control what you can and let go of the rest:** Obsessing over results? Stop. Nail what you can (effort, attitude, preparation) and then trust that life will sort out the rest. Let the chips fall where they may.
- **Worrying ≠ working:** Stress won't change the weather, clear the traffic, or make the oven preheat faster. At some point, you've got to stop stirring the soup and let it cook.

> ***"God grant me the serenity to accept things that I cannot change, the courage to change the things I can, and the wisdom to know the difference."***
> — **Reinhold Niebuhr,** The Serenity Prayer

> ***"A wizard is never late, Frodo Baggins. Nor is he early. He arrives precisely when he means to."***
> — **Gandalf,** in Lord of the Rings

The Dao Whispers: Have I given my best effort? If yes, can I now let go of what I think the outcome should be?

November 12

When Doing Nothing is Doing Something

Let others reveal their hand before you play yours

以静制动

yǐ jìng zhì dòng

Translation: "Use stillness to control movement."
—Thirty-Six Stratagems (三十六计)

At a flea market, the seller names a price and stares at you, waiting for the counter-offer. You can simply smile and say nothing. A few seconds later, they may drop the price themselves, just to break the silence. You have not said a word, yet the game has already shifted in your favour.

It works outside the market too: in meetings, a well-timed pause after someone's proposal can make them elaborate, backtrack, or offer a better deal without you having to lift a finger.

That's the heart of this idiom. Holding still is not the same as doing nothing; it is control. The impatient reveal themselves first, often too much and too soon. Patience lets you see the whole picture before you commit.

What it teaches us

- **Notice more by saying less:** Holding back gives you space to catch small shifts such as tone changes, hesitations, or power plays. Others miss them when they are busy reacting. These details can often reveal intentions, weaknesses, or hidden opportunities.
- **Let silence do the heavy lifting:** In negotiations, conflicts, or moments of uncertainty, silence often compels others to fill the gap, revealing their hand, their priorities, or even their vulnerabilities before you make your move.

> ***"Tactics is knowing what to do when there is something to do. Strategy is knowing what to do when there is nothing to do."***
> — **Savielly Tartakower**

The Dao Whispers: Does my need to respond quickly give away more than I realise? Can I take a step back and let others show their hands first?

November 13

The Spotlight Test

Power exposes character faster than anything else

小人得志，便猖狂

xiǎo rén dé zhì, biàn chāng kuáng

Translation: "When a person who is of poor character (or petty, narrow-minded) gains power, they become reckless and arrogant."
— Traditional Chinese proverb

Some climb the ladder of success only to use it as a platform to look down on everyone else. A promotion, a little fame, or even just 5,000 extra Instagram followers, and suddenly they are talking down to waiters, name-dropping at every opportunity, or giving unsolicited TED Talks at dinner. The proverb tells us of exactly that sort of individual – the 小人 (*xiǎo rén*: petty, narrow-minded, of poor character), who, once they taste success, inflates like a hot-air balloon. Lacking humility or a moral compass, power often makes them more obnoxious, not more admirable.

What it teaches us

- **Power can be a slippery slope:** Money, fame, or authority amplifies who someone already is. Without a moral compass, it is likely a slow crash waiting to happen.
- **The spotlight doesn't change you, it exposes you:** Struggle reveals grit, while success reveals character. The real test isn't climbing the ladder; it's how you act once you're at the top.
- **Insecurity speaks loudly:** The louder someone shouts ***"Look at me, I'm the man!"*** the more they reveal their insecurities. Real confidence tends to be understated. Think of the difference between the nouveau riche, eager to prove they have arrived, and old wealth, secure enough to let actions, values, and presence speak for themselves.

> ***"Power tends to corrupt, and absolute power corrupts absolutely."***
> **— Lord Acton**

The Dao Whispers: When I succeed, do I stay grounded or start to believe I'm above others?

November 14

The Truth Can Sometimes Sound Ugly

What sounds pleasant may not always be true

信言不美，美言不信

xìn yán bù měi, měi yán bù xìn

Translation: "The truth may sound ugly, while beautiful sounding words are not truthful."
— Laozi (老子), Dao De Jing (道德经)

The proverb conveys the idea that truthful, sincere words are often plain or even uncomfortable, while eloquent, polished words may lack sincerity or truth. It highlights the value of authenticity over superficial charm in communication, warning us not to be seduced by charm or eloquence, and calls us to seek substance over style. Not all that sounds good is good.

What it teaches us

Not all words carry the same weight. Some flatter, some deceive, some cut through with honesty. The trick is knowing which is which.

- **Sense check the smooth talk:** If something feels too good to be true, or makes you feel unusually flattered, be wary. Flattery is often a tactic to win favour, while honest words may sting or sound unrefined, though they carry the greater weight.
- **Honesty rarely comes polished:** Overly slick language, especially in critical situations, often glosses over the truth. Rough words spoken with sincerity deserve more trust than elegant lies.
- **Train your gut feel**: Learn to separate genuine help from hidden agendas, especially when they come dressed in a shiny bow.

> ***"People don't want to hear the truth because they don't want their illusions destroyed."***
> — **Friedrich Nietzsche**

The Dao Whispers: Truth can be uncomfortable, even ugly, but it clears the fog. Who in my life tells me what I don't want to hear? Do I mistake politeness for trustworthiness?

November 15

Action Breaks Paralysis

Stop staring at the problem. The longer you glare at it, the bigger the monster gets

为之，则难者亦易矣；不为，则易者亦难矣

wéi zhī, zé nán zhě yì yì yǐ; bù wéi, zé yì zhě yì nán yǐ

Translation: "Tackle the task, and difficulties ease; dodge it, and the manageable becomes daunting."
— Traditional Chinese proverb

We often avoid tasks that feel difficult, and the longer we delay, the more overwhelming they seem. What once was manageable can now feel insurmountable.

The proverb speaks to the transformative power of action, ***action breaks paralysis.*** By facing tasks head-on with effort and grit, even the toughest problems become manageable.

What it teaches us

- **Procrastination magnifies the task:** The longer you put it off, the scarier it feels. Procrastination often distorts our perception of the challenge and magnifies both the problem and the stress.
- **Don't let your mind spiral, take action instead:** Our mindset can shape and transform how we perceive challenges. We can either spiral into anxiety, or take action to break the paralysis.
- **Start small, keep moving:** Break a problem into bite-sized steps and start solving them... even if the first answers aren't perfect. You'll notice the weight lifting almost immediately.

> ***"It is not because things are difficult that we do not dare; it is because we do not dare that they are difficult."***
> — **Seneca**

The Dao Whispers: What's the one thing I've been avoiding because even thinking about it makes me anxious? What small step could I take today to prove I can begin, even if I don't feel ready?

November 16

On Loyalty to Our Leaders

The unseen force that holds teams together

忠君如忠天

zhōng jūn rú zhōng tiān

Translation: "Loyalty to the ruler is like loyalty to heaven."
— Traditional Chinese proverb

If you were the boss, wouldn't you want a team you can trust, people who won't undermine you, who'll rally to help you succeed? Your boss feels the same.

In traditional Chinese thought, loyalty to a leader was seen as sacred, even heaven-ordained. It rested on the belief that a good leader governed with righteousness and thus deserved support.

This isn't about being a yes-man or following a bad leader off a cliff. It simply affirms that there are merits in standing by a good and fair leader. Loyalty, coupled with good judgement, can be the glue that holds institutions, teams, and societies together.

What it teaches us

- **Committed teams get things done:** Ever been on a team where everyone's committed? That's how ordinary groups pull off extraordinary things.
- **Mutual loyalty builds strength:** Loyalty is a two-way street. The more leaders invest in their people, the more their people stand with them.
- **Loyalty as a shield:** Teams with deep trust and loyalty are harder to fracture, even when outsiders try to sow division.

> ***"Obedience is the virtue of the servant.***
> ***Loyalty is the virtue of the sovereign soul."***
> — Anonymous (frequently misattributed)

The Dao Whispers: Do I have a leader, mentor, or peer who has my best interests at heart? What does loyalty to them look like in practice? And am I building a circle of people who bring not only skill, but loyalty and shared purpose?

November 17

Love, Obsession... and the Trouble In-Between

How too much of a good thing changes everything

从痴有爱，则我病生

cóng chī yǒu ài, zé wǒ bìng shēng

Translation: "From obsession comes love, and from love, my illness is born."
— Traditional Chinese proverb

A poetic and philosophical expression, the line describes how excessive attachment or obsession can lead to emotional suffering.

Love can lift you to the clouds or drag you into the swamp. This proverb captures the slippery slope: deep affection tipping into fixation, and the joy of love slowly turning into a source of pain. It speaks to recognising how our own intensity can change it... when passion turns possessive, or when we hold on so tightly that the love becomes more about control, fear, or fantasy than connection.

What it teaches us

- **Moderation in emotions:** Too much attachment, even to something beautiful, can spiral into suffering. It is important to balance needs and desires in relationships.
- **Awareness of obsession:** The line between deep affection and fixation is thin. Recognising when love turns into emotional captivity can save years of heartache – especially if you're stuck in unrequited love – and even stop the bad late-night texting.
- **Healthy relationships:** True love makes space for freedom and respect; it doesn't trap, smother, or demand that you lose yourself.

> ***"We are never so defenceless against suffering as when we love."***
> **— Sigmund Freud**

The Dao Whispers: Am I in love with the person or with how they make me feel? Do I love them or the idea of them? Is it love or fear of being without it?

November 18

Turning on Our Own

Why must we hurt the ones we were meant to protect?

本是同根生，相煎何太急

běn shì tóng gēn shēng, xiāng jiān hé tài jí

Translation: "We are born of the same root, so why are we so eager to harm each other?"
— Cao Zhi (曹植), poet of the Three Kingdoms period

The Story

This verse comes from Cao Zhi's poem ***The Quatrain of Seven Steps** (七步诗)*, a poem which legend says was composed under threat of execution by his brother, Emperor Cao Pi (曹丕). Suspected of treason, Cao Zhi was ordered to compose a poem within seven steps or die. He responded with a verse that has since echoed through centuries:

> ***"They burn the beanstalks to boil the beans, and the beans in the pot cry out, 'We are of the same root, why would you choose to harm us?'"***

What it teaches us

- **Family feuds cut the deepest:** The people closest to us can hurt us most. Before striking out, remember you share the same blood.
- **Take a step back before you attack:** The harsh word you're about to say to family, friends, or allies? Once spoken, it can't be taken back, and you'll likely regret it most with those who matter.
- **Global solidarity:** Humanity shares the same roots. Borders, politics, and differences aside, we are all human. What unites us runs deeper than what divides us.

> ***"We must learn to live together as brothers or perish together as fools."***
> **— Martin Luther King Jr.**

The Dao Whispers: What happens to us, as a family, a people, or a planet, if we burn what we were meant to protect together?

November 19

The Long Road to Your Table

Each bite is a chapter in a farmer's story

锄禾日当午，汗滴禾下土。
谁知盘中餐，粒粒皆辛苦？

chú hé rì dāng wǔ, hàn dī hé xià tǔ

shuí zhī pán zhōng cān, lì lì jiē xīn kǔ?

Translation: "Hoeing millet under the sun at noon, his sweat drips onto the soil beneath the crops; do we know that each grain on our plate came from the toil of these farmers?"
— Li Shen (李绅) poet from the Tang Dynasty

This line has been recited to Chinese children for centuries, usually recited when children stared at a plate of food they didn't want to finish. It's basically the ancient Chinese version of the ***"There are starving children in the world!"*** reminder, only more poetic, and with vivid imagery. It reminds the children that the food on their plate didn't appear by magic. Someone planted it, grew it, harvested it, transported it, cooked it. Countless hands worked for the food to reach the table, so we shouldn't waste it.

What it teaches us

- **See the invisible work behind everything:** That morning coffee? Someone grew those beans under the sun for months. Your warm jacket? Countless hands stitched it together. The clean streets? People woke before dawn to make them that way. Waste isn't just about money... it's disrespect to the human labour behind every item.
- **Responsibility to avoid waste:** Forget the ESG press releases. As individuals, we can just buy what we need, eat what we buy, not waste food, honour the circle of life, and the people who make it possible.

> ***"Gratitude is not only the greatest of virtues, but the parent of all others."***
> **— Cicero**

The Dao Whispers: How much of what I waste was once someone else's hard work, and do I even notice?

November 20

Predator, Prey... or Protector?

In the food chain of life, are you eating or being eaten?

大鱼吃小鱼，小鱼吃虾米

dà yú chī xiǎo yú, xiǎo yú chī xiā mǐ

Translation: "The big fish eats the small fish, while the small fish eats the shrimp."
— Traditional Chinese proverb

It's not just the ocean. Offices, politics, and markets often work the same way. The big fish swallow the small fish. The small fish eat the shrimp. And the shrimp? Well, they just get eaten.

This proverb isn't concerned with seafood (I know that you know that...). It's a metaphor for systems of power. Power tends to flow upward, pressure flows downward, and the smallest often have no defence. The danger is that even when we're not at the top, we might pass that pressure along without even realising it. We have to realise that sometimes, this isn't always personal. It's often structural and baked into the system. The real question is, are we unconsciously passing that pressure downward?

What it teaches us

- **Recognise the food chain:** Hierarchies often favour the top at the expense of the vulnerable. Think of small businesses, junior staff, or the elderly. Awareness is the first step to protecting the "small fish" and "shrimp."
- **Break the chain:** Even if we're not the apex predator, we can choose not to push pressure downward.
- **Uplift the smallest:** If you have power, use it to support those most at risk. Education, resources, and advocacy can disrupt the predatory cycle.

> ***"The true measure of any society can be found in how it treats its most vulnerable members."***
> — Often attributed to **Mahatma Gandhi**

The Dao Whispers: Do I pass down pressure, or hold it to shield others? When power comes my way, do I uplift or simply take more from others?

November 21

Why Aim for One, When You Can Hit Two

Efficiency is the art of solving twice with a single stroke

一箭双雕

yī jiàn shuāng diāo

Translation: "One arrow, two hawks."
— Traditional Chinese proverb

The Story

In ancient times, a master archer stood under the open sky and drew his bow. He studied the wind, locked onto his target, and released with a single, flawless shot.

Two hawks fell mid-flight.

It wasn't luck. It was clarity, precision, timing, and strategy. The archer hit both targets by doing the **right thing**, at the **right time**, in the **right way.** That single shot didn't just hit the mark. It solved two problems at once.

What it looks like in practice

- **Tactical trade:** A well-timed concession can build trust *and* shift the balance of power.
- **Leadership by example:** A single act of humility can earn respect internally and strengthen credibility externally.
- **Smart design and human capital:** Solve for a redesign or investment in people that lifts efficiency, morale, and impact all at once.

> ***"It's been said that the cleverest way to solve a hard problem is to give it to someone lazy. They'll find the most efficient shortcut."***
> — Popular saying, origin uncertain

The Dao Whispers: The smartest plays solve more than one problem. It's not about doing more. It's about ***doing the right thing, at the right time, in the right way.***

November 22

Same Pages, But A Different You

Every re-read reflects the person you've become

旧书不厌百回读，熟读深思子自知

jiù shū bù yàn bǎi huí dú, shú dú shēn sī zǐ zì zhī

Translation: "An old book never grows dull, no matter how many times it is read, with each careful reading, new insights appear."
— Traditional Chinese proverb

You can read the same book a hundred times and somehow discover a hundred different lessons. The pages stay the same, but you don't. Each pass reflects who you are at that moment, what you've lived through, what you now understand, and what you're finally ready to see. The text is constant, but you aren't, and that's where the magic lies. It grows with you.

What it teaches us

- **Timeless learning:** A great book is not an item to check off a list. It's more like a familiar path through the woods, you walk it again and again, and each time, you notice a different detail: a new mushroom after the rain, the way the light filters through the branches at a certain hour. The book hasn't changed, but you have. The timeless learning is like a conversation with the author that continues across a lifetime.
- **Reflection can transform us:** The second, third, or tenth read often turns "information" into understanding.
- **Unpick layers with revisits:** Choose a few great works (books, poems, teachings) and revisit them often. With each encounter, read more slowly, and think just a little more deeply. Let the layers of meaning show themselves over time.

> ***"The only constant in life is change... you cannot step into the same river twice."***
> — **Heraclitus**

The Dao Whispers: A book changes as I change. So too does my life. What am I finally getting now that I didn't get before?

November 23

No One is Infallible

Even the smartest people make mistakes

智者千虑，必有一失；愚者千虑，必有一得

zhì zhě qiān lǜ, bì yǒu yī shī; yú zhě qiān lǜ, bì yǒu yī dé

Translation: "The wise may have a thousand thoughts, one of which may be wrong; the foolish may have a thousand thoughts, one of which may be right."
— Traditional Chinese idiom

Most of us like to think we're pretty smart, maybe not Einstein-level, but at least the one who spots typos in PowerPoints and Instagram Reels. And yes, we usually get it right most of the time. But even the sharpest minds drop the ball sometimes. And the people we usually roll our eyes at will, every so often, come out with something that lands perfectly. It's a reminder to keep the ego on a leash and stay open to surprise – even a broken clock is right twice a day..

What it teaches us

- **Check your blind spots:** Being smart can sometimes make us overconfident. No one has all the answers, so it's worth scrubbing our own assumptions. Say if you are the leader and the room goes awkwardly silent when you think you're saying something brilliant, maybe, you aren't.
- **Don't brush people off:** Even someone with less experience might see something we've missed. The best insights can come from unexpected places.
- **Stay humble, stay open:** The smartest leaders know they're not perfect. That's why they surround themselves with people who challenge them and keep them grounded.

> ***"The greatest of faults, I should say, is to be conscious of none."***
> **— Thomas Carlyle**

The Dao Whispers: Do I assume I'm always right, and others are not? When was the last time I learned from someone I underestimated? Am I too quick to dismiss what challenges my logic?

November 24

Don't Play Mozart to a Cow

Save your best for those ready to value it

对牛弹琴

duì niú tán qín

Translation: "Playing the lute (qin) to a cow."
— Traditional Chinese proverb

Imagine pouring your heart into a beautiful melody, but your audience is a cow. It keeps chewing grass, unmoved. The music isn't the problem; the cow was never going to hear it.
Good judgement isn't just about knowing what to say, but about choosing who, when, and where to say it so it actually lands.

What it teaches us

- **Choose your audience wisely:** Share your ideas with those who can appreciate or act on them, otherwise you're wasting time and energy.
- **Some minds won't open, no matter how hard you knock:** No matter how clearly you explain, some people simply aren't ready or willing to hear you.
- **Read the room**: If your message doesn't seem to land, step back and redirect your effort to a more receptive space.

> ***"Never argue with a fool, onlookers may not be able to tell the difference."***
> — **Mark Twain**

The Dao Whispers: Not everyone is ready to hear what you have to say, and that's okay. Good communication is knowing when to speak, when to wait, and when to walk away. Offer your thoughts where you'll be valued.

November 25

When the Game is Brutal

Better I betray the world than let it betray me

宁教我负天下人，休教天下人负我

nìng jiào wǒ fù tiān xià rén, xiū jiào tiān xià rén fù wǒ

Translation: "I would rather betray the world than let the world betray me."
— Cao Cao (曹操), warlord, strategist, and poet of the Three Kingdoms

This famous line from Cao Cao is one of the most ruthless statements in Chinese history. **It's the mindset of the hostile takeover, the political pre-emptive strike, or the boardroom move that freezes out a rival before they make their first play.** It is not a moral ideal, but a survivalist creed: ***self-preservation at any cost, even at the expense of others.***

It reflects realpolitik in its rawest form, where trust is fragile, betrayal is common, and the naïve often become prey. Yet, while it can serve as a defensive shield in cut-throat arenas, taken literally it corrodes trust, isolates allies, and can turn the survivor into the very thing they once feared.

What it teaches us:

- **Balance self-preservation and trust:** This mindset can protect you in dangerous environments, but carried too far, it leaves you isolated at the top. It's easier to topple someone who's alone than one backed by loyal allies.
- **Learn from betrayal, not fear:** Betrayal should sharpen your judgement and guide you toward building smarter alliances, not close your heart.
- **Winning dirty isn't really winning:** Power won at the cost of your soul is probably not worth having.

"Only the paranoid survives."
— **Andy Grove**

The Dao Whispers: Do I guard my interests without becoming someone I no longer recognise? Have I grown too cynical to believe in loyalty, or too trusting to protect myself? The hard part is knowing where to draw that line and having the courage to keep it.

November 26

Larger Than Life Leadership

Lead with ambition, strategy, and relentless will

夫英雄者，胸怀大志，腹有良谋，
有包藏宇宙之机，吞吐天地之志者也

fū yīng xióng zhě, xiōng huái dà zhì, fù yǒu liáng móu,

yǒu bāo cáng yǔ zhòu zhī jī, tūn tǔ tiān dì zhī zhì zhě yě

Translation: "A hero harbours grand ambitions, holds wise strategies, can hold the workings of the universe; and carries the will to conquer heaven and earth."
— Cao Cao (曹操), warlord, strategist, and poet of the Three Kingdoms

Some people dream so big they rattle even themselves. They keep you up at night and pull you out of bed in the morning. This was the ambition Cao Cao spoke of in Romance of the Three Kingdoms. A leader who doesn't just run a team or win a battle, but carries a vision vast enough to bend the course of history. Think Alexander the Great, or a modern CEO aiming for Mars, not just market share.

What it teaches us

- **Set visionary goals:** Game-changing leaders don't just tweak things, they reimagine the systems and themselves. Big Hairy Audacious Goals need pragmatic and street-smart plans, and these leaders know it.
- **Think strategically:** Vision requires sharp foresight. The best leaders combine bold aspirations with practical, adaptable plans. They spot trends early, pivot fast and always have a Plan B... and Plan C.
- **Expand perspective:** A global, open-minded outlook can help us better seize opportunities. The best opportunities sometimes hide in places you've never looked.

> ***"The greatest danger for most of us is not that our aim is too high and we miss it, but that it is too low, and we reach it."***
> — **Michelangelo**

The Dao Whispers: Am I limiting my leadership by aiming too small for myself, my team, or my cause?

November 27

The Dark Side of Human Nature

The case for discipline, culture, and conscious moral scaffolding

人之性恶，其善者伪也

rén zhī xìng è, qí shàn zhě wěi yě

Translation: "Human nature is inherently evil, what is good has to be cultivated."
— Xunzi (荀子)

Here's a blunt take: according to Xunzi, we're all born selfish, messy, and a bit chaotic. If we want to be decent human beings, we have to work at it. No free pass, no "born good" fairy dust. It's the exact opposite of Mencius' rose-tinted view of humanity.

In modern terms? Think of goodness like a gym bod: you don't wake up with one, you train for it. Parents, teachers, mentors, and good leaders are basically the personal trainers of our moral muscles. Left alone, our natural instincts lean toward cutting corners, chasing comfort, and taking the easiest path when no one's watching.

What it teaches us

- **We're not born saints, we become them:** Since goodness isn't innate, building character takes deliberate effort through education, practice, and the company we keep.
- **Trust doesn't just happen, it has to be earned:** People look out for themselves, that's human nature. Which is why trust has to be built with clear rules: do what you say, show up, and stay honest.
- **Role-model the values you want in your teams:** Leaders must actively model fairness, empathy, and discipline, and not assume these traits arise organically within a team or society.

> ***"Everyone is a moon, and has a dark side which he never shows to anybody."***
> **— Mark Twain**

The Dao Whispers: Do I assume my team will "be good," or do I build systems that make it easier for them to shine?

November 28

Pay Peanuts, Get Monkeys

And other truths about building a high-performing team

无能不官，无功不赏

wú néng bù guān, wú gōng bù shǎng

Translation: "Without ability, there shall be no office; without merit, there shall be no reward."
— Xunzi (荀子)

If you want great results, hire great people, reward performance, and put the capable in roles where they can accelerate success.

Xunzi's point echoes that: give responsibility to the capable, reward the ones who deliver. Anything else – nepotism, cronyism, "just because" promotions – kills morale, culture, and performance. In essence, the proverb is a warning to leaders against the temptation of favouritism and a timeless prescription for building a respected, effective, and successful organization.

What it teaches us

- **Hire A-Players:** Don't hire cheap and hope for the best. Hire skill, hire potential – or pay the price. To build a world-class organisation, you need world-class talents. Pay peanuts and you risk losing your business.
- **Sustain a culture of excellence:** When merit is rewarded, excellence becomes the norm. When it's ignored, you may have to watch your best people leave and have mediocrity grow.
- **Protect standards:** Lowering the bar for comfort or convenience invites mediocrity in… and it rarely leaves.

"Pay peanuts and you get monkeys."
— David Ogilvy

The Dao Whispers: Do I have the courage to choose talents better than myself, not just the safest or the cheapest? Am I in a place that rewards excellence, or protects mediocrity?

November 29

To Know and Not Do, is To Not Know

Move from knowing better to doing better

知而不行，只是未知

zhī ér bù xíng, zhǐ shì wèi zhī

Translation: "To know but not act, is simply, to not know."
— Traditional Chinese proverb

We all have that thing we ***know*** we should be doing and yet, somehow, it keeps getting pushed to "tomorrow."

According to this proverb, if you're not acting on what you know, you may as well not know it at all.

That's true, isn't it? Ideas that are not acted upon are no different from ignorance. Intellectual insight only becomes wisdom when it impacts how we live, work, and treat others. Knowledge that stays in the mind remains a theory. Admirable, but with very little to show for it.

What it teaches us

- **Growth is a verb, not a thought:** Reading about push-ups won't get you fit. Knowing you should call your mom isn't the same as calling her. Knowing green tea is a great antioxidant or ginger tea can help a sore back is different from actually taking the pack off the kitchen cabinet and making the drink.
- ***"Someday I'll do it"* is not good enough:** "Someday, I'll start exercising, prepare healthy meals, fix my sleep hygiene, network with mentors, track my expenses, pay off debt, end toxic relationships, set boundaries, declutter, forgive…" Inaction leaves you with the same reality as not knowing – you end up with no change.

> ***"Knowing is not enough; we must apply.***
> ***Willing is not enough; we must do."***
> **— Johann Wolfgang von Goethe**

The Dao Whispers: What's one thing I know I should do, yet keep postponing?

November 30

The Clock Doesn't Stop

Making the most of the time you have left

对酒当歌，人生几何？譬如朝露，去日苦多

duì jiǔ dāng gē, rén shēng jǐ hé? pì rú zhāo lù, qù rì kǔ duō

Translation: "We sing with a glass of wine in front of us – how long is our life, really? Just like the morning dew, the days that have passed far outnumber those that are to come."
— Cao Cao (曹操)

Cao Cao wasn't exactly the kind of guy you'd invite for a light chat about weekend plans. The warlord, strategist and poet hardened by relentless battles and the impermanence of life was also, in his own way, a philosopher. His conclusion? **Life is short**, time is moving, and it's not waiting for you.

While this isn't a call to indulgence (though a little karaoke and dessert never hurt), it is a call to **live deliberately,** to stay conscious of time's passing, and choose meaning over mindless delay. Every time we overthink or hesitate, we lose the one thing we'll never get back: **now**.

What it teaches us

- **Seize the moment:** Don't postpone the trip, the call, or the "I love you." What matters most rarely waits.
- **Live with intention:** Make your choices on purpose, not by default. If you don't choose how to spend your days, someone else will.
- **Don't dwell on lost time:** Yes, you could have started earlier. But you are here. Start now.

> ***"Live as if you were living already for the second time and as if you had acted the first time as wrongly as you are about to act now."***
> **— Viktor Frankl**

The Dao Whispers: Lost time is lost. We can grieve it, but we can't get it back. The only choice is to begin again and make the best of what remains. Am I living deliberately, or letting hours drift by? And am I giving my time to people and causes that are worthy of my energy and life? (Yes, your time ***is*** your life.)

DECEMBER

志

zhì

Meaning of 志 (zhì):

- Will
- Ambition
- Aspiration
- Determination
- Quiet strength

志 (zhì) acts as an internal compass. It points us toward what's important in life and drives how we act. It is not the sort that rushes. Instead, it is sustained through deliberate intention and steady perseverance.

Mastering 志 (zhì) allows you to:

- **Aspire – know what you actually want:** You stop chasing other people's goals. You start aiming for things that genuinely light you up and feel right for ***you.***
- **Endure – not quit when it gets hard:** You understand that some days you'll take giant leaps, and other days you'll barely take a step. The point is you're still facing the right direction, and you stand firm through hardship, setbacks, or slow progress.
- **Focus on what's important:** You stop wasting time on things that don't matter. You can say "no" to distractions.
- **Decide for yourself:** Instead of asking "What does everyone else think?" you start asking "What aligns with my purpose?" You stop following the crowd.
- **Grow with intention:** You grow your ambitions with patience, foresight, and thoughtful strategy.

December 1

The Cobra Principle

Stay low until it's time to strike

静如处子，动如脱兔

jìng rú chǔ zǐ, dòng rú tuō tù

Translation: "Stay composed as a lady; then move as swiftly as a startled hare."
— Sun Tzu, The Art of War

This famed line from the Art of War teaches a powerful duality: calm composure while in wait, and speed without hesitation in action. It is often used in military strategy to advocate for quiet preparation and hidden strength until it's time to strike. In strategy, life, and leadership, this principle calls for emotional control, precision timing, and the wisdom to know **when to hold back and when to make a move.**

What it teaches us

- **Preparation matters:** The best opportunities don't just fall into your lap, they're the late-night research, the rejected drafts and the practice runs that no one sees. Study, plan, and drill when no one's watching, so you're ready when the window opens.
- **Strategic restraint;** Not every move is worth making. Hold your ground, then act when the conditions tilt in your favour. For example, market entry, making key hires, launching products, closing deals, or buying your house at the right place at the right time.
- **Energy mastery**: Being fully off, then fully on, is more sustainable than staying in 'half-effort, always-on' mode.

> ***"I may lose a battle, but I shall never lose a minute."***
> — **Napoleon Bonaparte**

The Dao Whispers: Let the strike be swift, the win clean, and the battle short. Like a cobra, it can be still for hours, yet deadly when it decides to strike.

December 2

It's Never Too Late to Dream

Do what you want, go where you like, be who you are

老骥伏枥，志在千里。烈士暮年，壮心不已

lǎo jì fú lì, zhì zài qiān lǐ; liè shì mù nián, zhuàng xīn bù yǐ

Translation: "Just as the old steed in the stable still aspires to run a thousand miles; so too does a warrior with great resolve, even in his later years, continue to harbour bold ambitions."
— Cao Cao (曹操)

Cao Cao's words are a reminder that age isn't the real barrier, mindset is. You can be 25 and feel "too old" to start over, or 70 and still be chasing new horizons. Dreams don't have an expiry date unless you give them one.

What really stops you isn't the passing of time; it's ***you*** convincing yourself that it's too late. Spoiler: It's not.

What it teaches us

- **New adventures aren't just for the young:** Starting a business at 50? Learning guitar at 60? Backpacking at 70? Adventures and pivots need not be youth's privilege; they are open to all.
- **Age is just a number – self-doubt is the real enemy:** Let go of age-related fear, allow yourself to dream up bold choices, from solo travel to playing a new sport, fall in love, or learning to dance.
- **Defy stereotypes:** Society often underestimates older individuals, yet their experience is not just relevant, it's essential. While others are still figuring it out, you've got the skills, the patience, and the grit to make moves. Why not use it?

> ***"Do not grow old, no matter how long you live. Never cease to stand like curious children before the Great Mystery."***
> **— Albert Einstein**

The Dao Whispers: Time is irrelevant to purpose. What dreams have I buried, believing my time has passed? Do I let societal expectations shrink my dreams?

December 3

See the Forest, Not Every Leaf

You can't steer a ship if you're counting barnacles

不聋不瞎，不配当家

bù lóng bù xiā, bù pèi dāng jiā

Translation: "If you cannot play deaf or blind at times, then you are unfit to lead."

— Emperor Qianlong of Qing (乾隆帝)

The emperor used humour in this proverb to suggest that leadership is not about catching every fault but knowing which to overlook. A wise leader must sometimes choose silence over scrutiny when small mistakes serve no meaningful consequence. Endless correction paralyses teams, creates unnecessary stress, and distracts from what's important. Good judgement and deliberate discretion, not perfectionism, make the difference.

What it teaches us

- **Focus on the big picture:** Not every typo, hiccup, or opinion needs your attention. Micromanaging and obsessing over details can derail your team and pull you off course.
- **Your time is finite, spend it wisely:** Trivial tasks are black holes for energy. By not getting bogged down by trivial details and minor imperfections, you can free up your energy for things that actually ***move the needle***.
- **Achieve more by delegating:** If you try doing everything yourself, you risk being the bottleneck. Trust your team – delegation doesn't mean you lose power; it's how you can grow your teams, scale your organisation, and amplify your leadership impact.

> ***"The art of leadership is not saying 'yes' to everything but knowing when to say 'no' – or nothing at all."***
>
> — Adapted from multiple thinkers

The Dao Whispers: Do I get stuck in the weeds, or can I be 80/20? If the details don't change the answer, why waste time on them? Am I willing to empower others to lead in their own way?

December 4

The Wheel of Life Will Keep Spinning

The eternal dance of union, division, and renewal

天下大势，分久必合，合久必分

tiān xià dà shì, fēn jiǔ bì hé, hé jiǔ bì fēn

Translation: "The great trend of the world is that long division must unite, and long union must divide."
— Romance of the Three Kingdoms

The ***Romance of the Three Kingdoms*** captures one of life's greatest patterns: kingdoms that split apart will later reunite, allies that fall out, later reconcile... The wheel keeps spinning and each turn reshapes what comes next. In simple terms:

- Division cannot last forever: fragmented states, systems or relationships eventually move toward integration.
- Unity cannot last forever: even the strongest alliances or empires will one day fracture.
- Change is the only constant: no relationship, political order, or emotional state remains static forever.

What it teaches us

- **Impermanence is normal:** Jobs change. Relationships evolve. You'll outgrow old versions of yourself. Nothing lasts forever and this is part of life's design.
- **Don't hold on too tightly:** When something has run its course, whether a role, a system, or an idea, holding on only makes the break more painful.
- **Know that the wheel will spin:** If you're in a rough patch and everything seems to be falling apart, trust that the tide will turn. Be ready to move when it does.

"Civilizations are born, mature, decay, and die. This cycle is the fundamental reality of history."
— Oswald Spengler

The Dao Whispers: Am I holding on to something that is already slipping away? When the wheel turns, will I be ready for it? How can I prepare myself for the change that's coming?

December 5

The Habit of Becoming

Great lives are built in small days. We are what we do daily

苟日新，日日新，又日新

gǒu rì xīn, rì rì xīn, yòu rì xīn

Translation: "Every day we renew ourselves; renew daily, and then, renew again when tomorrow begins."
— Text from 'The Great Learning' (大学)

Confucius repeats the word xīn (新, new) three times here to make a point. Growth is not a one-time event. It is something you choose to do every single day. Think of it like taking a shower. You do not do it once because you were dirty once. You do it to stay fresh. Renewal works the same way whether it is for your mind, your spirit, or your habits.

What it teaches us

- **Progress is incremental:** Small daily improvements compound into meaningful transformation over time.
- **Growth requires daily rituals:** A few minutes of reading, practising a skill, or reflecting each day adds up and keeps you from regressing.
- **Be the change:** You do not just prepare for change. You become the change. Small improvements in mindset, habits, and skills help you stay relevant and agile.

> ***"We are what we repeatedly do.***
> ***Excellence, then, is not an act, but a habit."***
> — **Aristotle**

The Dao Whispers: What two or three micro habits could I adopt to become just one percent better than yesterday? Am I letting past mistakes or past wins stop me from starting fresh today? How can I make renewal a natural part of my daily life?

December 6

Love at Home is the Best Armour Outside

A warm heart makes the world less cold

家和万事兴

jiā hé wàn shì xīng

Translation: "When the family is harmonious, all other undertakings prosper."
— Traditional Chinese Wisdom (民间俗语)

Let's face it, nothing throws off your day like an argument that begins at breakfast and ends three hours later with a slammed door. This old proverb reminds us that a peaceful, supportive home isn't just "*nice to have,*" it's rocket fuel for everything else we do.

When there's love, laughter, and understanding under your roof, you show up in the world calmer, stronger, and less likely to bite someone's head off in a meeting. But when home is a battlefield, even the smallest outside challenges feel twice as heavy.

What it teaches us

- **Work through family tensions with empathy**: A bit of understanding, plenty of respect, and the occasional "I'm sorry" can keep things from spiralling.
- **Make home your safe haven:** When your space feels warm and supportive, you've got the mental breathing room to chase your goals without extra drama weighing you down.
- **Count on your family's love:** In the middle of illness, heartbreak, or job loss, knowing your people have your back makes you twice as tough.

> ***"Family is not an important thing. It's everything."***
> **— Michael J. Fox**

The Dao Whispers: Does my home help my family feel loved, secure, and ready to face the world?

December 7

Strategic Warfare: Win Before You Fight

The best generals don't just win – they make the fight irrelevant

上兵伐谋，其次伐交
其次伐兵，其下攻城

shàng bīng fá móu, qí cì fá jiāo,
qí cì fá bīng, qí xià gōng chéng

Translation:
"The highest form of warfare is to subdue the enemy's strategy.
Next best is to disrupt their alliances.
Next, to attack their armies.
The worst is to besiege walled cities."

— Sun Tzu (孙子), The Art of War (孙子兵法, sūn zǐ bīng fǎ)

Sun Tzu's timeless wisdom teaches that victory is achieved not through destruction but through foresight and strategy. His hierarchy prioritises outsmarting opponents over fighting them:

- **Outmanoeuvre their game plan:** Spot their playbook early, then rewrite the rules. Strike smart deals, misdirect their focus, or broker peace that keeps everyone off the battlefield.
- **Disrupt alliances**: Shift loyalties or defuse tensions through diplomacy.
- **Attack armies:** Only when other tactics fail.
- **Storm cities**: Taking over cities should be a last resort as it is costly, inefficient, and destructive to all. It's equivalent to smashing your phone because an app froze... it works, but now you've probably got bigger problems.

His hierarchy of warfare applies beyond warfare as it focuses on the following strategic principles:

- Resolve tension at the root.
- Dismantle destructive forces before they grow.
- Prevent escalation before it begins.
- Fighting only when all other better paths have failed.

Win Before the Battle: Diplomacy

Strategic mastery is often about making fights unnecessary, not diving in just to win them outright. It takes discipline to de-escalate, and intelligence to create outcomes where no one has to lose. It's the harder path, yes; but usually the smarter, more sustainable one.

Confrontation can feel very satisfying, but it often destroys more than it solves. Sun Tzu ranks full-on battles as the least desirable path not because wars cannot be won, but because even "victory" can leave a trail of ruin behind it.

What it teaches us

- **Lead with foresight:** Step back before engaging. The best moves come from seeing the whole board, not just the next square. Aim for a non-confrontation, a win-win if possible, and an intelligent resolution.
- **Exhaust smarter plays first:** Try every smart workaround (deals, misdirection, alliances) as your first line of offence. Save the punches for when all else fails.
- **Leave the field standing:** Perhaps the best win is in solving the problem without burning everything down, and everyone can walk away intact.

> ***"Diplomacy is the art of letting someone else have your way."***
> — **Daniel Vare**

The Dao Whispers: Can I resolve this tension without burning all the bridges to the ground?

When all you have is a hammer, everything starts to look like a nail. Am I charging in with a hammer when a small nudge could have done the trick?

December 8

Blind Spots and the Bigger Picture

When four blind men touch the elephant, the one who grabs the leg swears it's a pillar

盲人摸象

máng rén mō xiàng

Translation: "When the blind men touch the elephant."
— Traditional Chinese idiom

The Story

Four blind men touch an elephant for the first time:

- The one who grabs the leg says, *"It's a pillar!"*
- The one who touches the tail says, *"It's a rope!"*
- The one who feels the belly says, *"It's a wall!"*
- The one who holds the trunk says, *"It's a snake!"*

This parable mirrors life. In complex systems, organisations, or relationships, we're often fumbling in the dark, each holding just one fragment of a bigger reality. Realising this shifts everything. We stop being so certain we're right, we listen instead of waiting for our turn to talk, and we recognise that others may be carrying the missing pieces we need.

What it teaches us

- **Don't be too sure:** Many big mistakes, from market crashes to relationship breakdowns, start with people convinced they know it all when they've only got half the story.
- **Seek broader perspective:** Surround yourself with others who see different parts of the "elephant," especially in strategy, governance, or conflict resolution.
- **They may not be wrong:** Just because someone only sees part of the picture doesn't mean they're wrong. They're working with what they've got, just as you are. Their piece of truth might be small, but it's still real.

> ***"We are blind to our blindness. We have very little idea of how little we know."***
> **— Daniel Kahneman**

The Dao Whispers: Can I accept that I may never see the whole truth alone?

December 9

Self-Sabotage in Disguise

My spear pierces all things, and my shield blocks everything

自相矛盾

zì xiāng máo dùn

Translation: "I own a spear that pierces all things, and a shield that blocks everything."
— Traditional Chinese idiom

The Story

A merchant sells a spear claiming, "It can pierce through anything!"

Moments later, he holds up a shield and shouts, "This shield blocks everything!"

A customer asks: "What happens if you use the spear against the shield?"

The merchant then freezes on the spot.

This idiom describes when someone's words, actions, or beliefs contradict each other.

What it teaches us

- **Keep your stories straight:** In strategy, leadership, or communication, inconsistency tends to damage credibility and trust. Stay logically consistent.
- **Own your contradictions:** Defending bad logic just digs the hole deeper. Instead, take a step back and ask: ***"Where did I miss the plot?"***
- **Spot your self-sabotage:** When your goals and actions clash, like wanting health but skipping sleep or aiming for promotion while avoiding responsibility, you're working against yourself.

> ***"You can't talk your way out of something you behaved your way into."***
> — **Stephen Covey**

The Dao Whispers: Am I fighting for my future… or against it?

December 10

The Man Who Moved the Mountain

When willpower is stronger than stone

愚公移山

yú gōng yí shān

Translation: "The foolish old man who decides to move the mountains."
— Traditional Chinese idiom

The Story

Once upon a time, an old man named Yugong lived in a village hemmed in by two towering mountains — Taihang and Wangwu. These peaks made travel difficult, isolating his family from the world beyond. One day, Yugong decided to remove the mountains. With only a shovel and the help of his family, he began digging.

His so-called "wise" neighbour mocked him, and said, *"You're old, you'll never finish."* Yugong simply replied, "True, but when I die, my children will continue. Then their children. One day, the mountains will be gone."

His unwavering spirit moved even the heavens. In some versions, celestial beings, touched by his perseverance, descended to carry the mountains away.

Yugong's story isn't just about being stubborn. It's about trusting the long game, rallying others to a shared goal, and chipping away at something a little each day, even if you won't get to see the finish line yourself.

> ***"You may never know what results come from your actions. But if you do nothing, there will be no results."***
> **— Mahatma Gandhi**

The Dao Whispers: What is the "mountain" in my life that I have been avoiding because it feels too big to change? If I started today and kept going, where could I be in a year?

December 11

When You're the Only One Giving

When relationships are 90/10, how long can they last?

剃头挑子一头热

tì tóu tiāo zi yì tóu rè

Translation: "The barber's pole is hot, but on one end only."
— Traditional Chinese proverb

The Story

During the Qing Dynasty, street barbers carried their tools on a shoulder pole (挑子) with two baskets:

- One end held a coal-fired hot water pot for shaving.
- The other end carried cold tools and supplies.

Once set down, only one end of the pole gave off warmth.

This proverb has since come to symbolise one-sided effort in relationships where one person is emotionally invested while the other remains distant in love, friendship, or work.

What it teaches us

- **Stop being the only one trying:** Relationships should be a two-way street. If you are always giving at work, in love or with friends, you'll run dry fast. Ask yourself, "Is this worth my energy?"
- **Life is too short to keep heating cold spaces:** Don't chase people who won't meet you halfway. It's better to invest that passion where it's appreciated.
- **If you *are* the one carrying the 10 in a 90/10**: If the relationship truly matters to you, honest conversations, clearer boundaries, or shifting expectations can turn it back into a two-way exchange.

> ***"Don't set yourself on fire to keep others warm."***
> — Unknown

> ***"Invest in people who invest in you.***
> — Unknown

The Dao Whispers: Where am I the only one putting in all the work? Is this relationship a keeper, one to rebalance, or to release?

December 12

Not Everything That Glitters Is Gold

A reminder to judge what's underneath

金玉其外，败絮其中

jīn yù qí wài, bài xù qí zhōng

Translation: "Gold and jade on the outside, but rotten rags within."
— Traditional Chinese proverb
Note: The original sharp tone in the proverb and the quote by Machiavelli has been preserved to reflect the spirit of what was written. Readers are invited to interpret it with personal agency and judgement.

Some people just seem to be perfect – impeccably dressed, smooth with words, carrying themselves like they've got life figured out. And then, a little later, you realise their follow-through is… let's say, less couture. This proverb speaks to exactly that, the beautiful packaging that hides a disappointing product.

The saying also applies to jobs that sound glamorous but leave you drained, investments that have a slick pitch deck but sink in reality, or friendships that are high on charm but low on trust. The shine can be blinding. Which is why this saying is a jolt to take a step back, look closer and ask: ***"What's really underneath?"***

What it teaches us

- **Yes, the world judges by appearances:** Whether we like it or not, people form impressions based on how we present ourselves. So, it helps to be mindful of the signals we send.
- **Pretty wrapping doesn't mean a good gift:** The very fact that appearances are so persuasive makes it easier to disguise flaws. This proverb reminds us not to judge a book by its cover, not everything polished is good.
- **Looks can't carry you forever:** Superficial charm, good looks and smooth talk run out of power in the long run. Eventually, you'll need to prove you have some substance.

> ***"The vulgar crowd always is taken by appearances, and the world consists chiefly of the vulgar."***
> — **Niccolò Machiavelli** (The Prince)

The Dao Whispers: What in my life is all polish, but no real depth?

December 13

Self-Care or Self-Centred?

The fine line between responsibility and indifference

各人自扫门前雪

gè rén zì sǎo mén qián xuě

Translation: "Everyone only sweeps the snow from their own doorstep."
— Traditional Chinese proverb

Picture a street after a heavy snowfall. The air is sharp, your breath rising in little clouds. Each neighbour steps outside, broom or shovel in hand, clearing only the space in front of their door. Some work quickly, keeping their little patch spotless. Others stop to chat, leaning on their shovels. The snow between houses remains untouched; slippery, uneven, and therefore everyone's problem.

The proverb carries a dual meaning:

1. Human nature: People tend to look out for #1 (i.e., themselves), especially when selfishness gets rewarded. In broken systems, this undermines shared responsibility.
2. Down-to-earth lesson: Clean your own doorstep before judging your neighbour's. It's hard to complain about someone else's mess when yours is untouched.

What it teaches us

- **Personal responsibility:** Our choices, actions, and results are ours to own. Accountability starts with us.
- **Help is only help when it's wanted:** Jumping in to 'fix' someone else's problems without being asked usually backfires. You can't help those who don't want help.
- **Fix the system, not the symptom:** Misaligned incentives create silos and dysfunction. If your teams are not working together, check the incentives and operating model.

> ***"If everyone swept in front of their own door, the whole world would be clean."***
> — **Johann Wolfgang von Goethe**

The Dao Whispers: When is it wise to step in, and when should I step back?

December 14

The Old Stallion Knows the Way

Experience remembers paths that maps have forgotten

老马识途

lǎo mǎ shí tú

Translation: "An old horse knows the way."
— From Han Feizi (韩非子)

The Story

Long ago, Duke Huan of Qi (齐桓公) led his army deep into unfamiliar territory. On their journey home, the troops lost their way in a vast, desolate wilderness. The paths were confusing, the terrain disorienting, and anxiety began to spread through the ranks.

One of the duke's trusted ministers, Guan Zhong (管仲), stepped forward with a calm suggestion.

"Old horses know the way. Let the old horses lead, and they will guide us home."

So, the soldiers released the older horses to the front, allowing them to walk freely.

Step by step, without command or hesitation, the horses followed an invisible memory of the path. And before long, they led the army out of the wilderness safely home.

"The years teach much which the days never know."
— **Ralph Waldo Emerson**

The Dao Whispers

- Experience is an invisible compass. Don't underestimate those who've weathered storms.
- In times of uncertainty, lean on those who've walked the path before. Real wisdom often hides in quiet people with scarred hands and steady hearts.
- Do we see that calm older person in the storm? They're not naïve. They've simply been through enough to not panic.

December 15

Surf the Storm with Emotional Intelligence

Emotions are like water, ride the wave but don't drown

情绪如水，智者观其流

qíng xù rú shuǐ, zhì zhě guān qí liú

Translation: "As emotions are like water, the wise would simply observe their flow."
— Traditional Chinese proverb

Emotions move like water, sometimes calm, sometimes raging, sometimes deceptively deep. Fighting the current rarely works. The better choice is to watch, understand, and act only when the time is right.

The proverb doesn't ask you to suppress your feelings. It's about knowing when to ride the wave, when to linger in the frothy whirlpool of emotions, and when to let them pass.

What it teaches us

- **Name it to tame it:** When you're able to label the emotion ("I'm feeling defensive," "This is anxiety," "I'm feeling stressed," "I am angry at..."), it takes the edge off. That's emotional intelligence at work; the better you understand your feelings, the less they control you, and the smarter your decisions become.
- **Detach to gain perspective:** By observing your emotions like a bystander, you can avoid being consumed by them. "Interesting... why does this annoy me?"
- **Learn self-control:** Resist the impulse to react. Delaying your response makes space for logic and discernment to lead instead of raw emotions.

> ***"You can't stop the waves, but you can learn to surf."***
> **— Jon Kabat-Zinn**

The Dao Whispers: How can I observe the flow of my emotions today without letting them drown me, or derail me?

December 16

How You Carry Yourself Speaks for You

We judge books by their covers, and people by how they present themselves

不学礼，无以立

bù xué lǐ, wú yǐ lì

Translation: "If one does not study propriety (礼), one cannot establish oneself."
— Confucius (孔子), Analects (论语)

Ambition and talent can open the door, but the way you conduct yourself decides whether you are invited to stay.

According to Confucius, our personal strength doesn't start with ambition or power, but with lǐ (礼) – propriety – a principle often overlooked today. More than rituals or manners, lǐ is the practice of respectful conduct, social grace, and ethical awareness. It polishes the self, fostering dignity, discernment, and empathy. Far from being superficial, propriety complements authenticity. It allows you to be a polished version of yourself.

What it teaches us

- **Refinement is a daily practice:** Built through self-awareness, values, and etiquette.
- **Your presence shapes trust:** How you speak, behave, and carry yourself determines how others remember you.
- **How you show up matters:** The way you carry yourself can affect how you are trusted, followed, and remembered. Grace and composure under pressure can be as influential as assertiveness and decisiveness.

> ***"Excellence is an art won by training and habituation. We do not act rightly because we have virtue or excellence, but rather we have those because we have acted rightly."***
>
> — **Aristotle,** *Nicomachean Ethics* (paraphrased)

The Dao Whispers: Am I open to feedback on how I speak, behave, and carry myself? Do I treat etiquette as a surface act, or a path to self-mastery?

December 17

Mentors Open Doors You Can't Find Alone

Guidance for the paths you don't yet know exist

无师，吾安知礼之为是也

wú shī, wú ān zhī lǐ zhī wéi shì yě?

Translation: "Without a teacher, how would I know what is proper in the matters of propriety (the right way)?"
— Traditional Chinese proverb

There are doors in life you will never even notice, let alone open without the right guide. A good mentor doesn't just give you answers, they show you where to look, what to ask, and how to read the room in ways you never imagined. They guide us in navigating the world, from unspoken rules to unseen dynamics, and help us walk paths we cannot travel alone.

Connection to previous sayings

- **Know thyself,** 知己 (zhī jǐ): They hold up an honest mirror, helping us see what we cannot.
- **Learn and think,** 学而不思则罔 (xué ér bù sī zé wǎng): The best mentors do more than instruct; they provoke reflection.
- **Leverage strengths,** 用人如器 (yòng rén rú qì): They help us recognise our strengths and develop our unique value.
- **Daily renewal,** 苟日新 (gǒu rì xīn): They challenge us to keep learning, adapting, and becoming better than we were yesterday.
- **Lure the snake out** 引蛇出洞 (yǐn shé chū dòng): Wise mentors guide us through subtle strategies to navigate complexity and focus on solving the right problem.
- **Reap what you sow,** 种瓜得瓜 (zhòng guā dé guā): They steer us toward planting the seeds worth our effort.
- **Enduring ambition,** 老骥伏枥 (lǎo jì fú lì): They help us stay grounded while pursuing our long-term aspirations.

The Dao Whispers: When I feel lost, do I seek guidance or pretend I know the way, trust mentors for their judgement, not their status, and pay forward the wisdom they gave me?

December 18

Move Beyond Penny-Pinching

To advance, we must discard a scarcity mindset

欲成大事者，不惜小费

yù chéng dà shì zhě, bù xī xiǎo fèi

Translation: "Those who seek great achievements must not begrudge small costs."
— Empress Wu Zetian (武则天)
Empress Wu Zetian remains a controversial figure. Revered for her leadership, condemned for her ruthlessness. Some argue that history judged her more harshly for being a woman in power than for her actions.

Empress Wu Zetian, feared by some and revered by others, understood that ambition demands investment. A scarcity mindset, left unchecked, can sabotage long-term growth. Some doors don't stay shut because we lack talent, they stay shut because we wouldn't spend $20 on the book, the course, or the coffee that could have moved us forward. Big goals don't grow out of scraps. If you're going after meaningful goals, you have to invest your time, energy and yes, the occasional few dollars.

What it teaches us

- **Invest in multipliers**: Choose tools, training, or resources that turn small spends into big returns. The right $20 book, software, or AI tool could earn you $5,000 not because of luck, but because it multiplies what you can do.
- **Invest in your relationships:** Behind every role, title, or logo is a human being. Nurture those relationships with genuine care and contribution, they are your real network.
- **Be proactive and build brick-by-brick:** Show up, learn, connect, contribute. Every course you take, event you attend, or person you help plants seeds that can open doors that you may not yet know exist.

> ***"The man who does more than he is paid for will soon be paid for more than he does."***
> — **Napoleon Hill**

The Dao Whispers: What future did I trade away for the comfort of saving a few pennies?

December 19

The Measure of a Man's Character

A person with nothing to hide walks with ease, while some others are always looking over their shoulder

君子坦荡荡，小人长戚戚

jūn zǐ tǎn dàng dàng, xiǎo rén cháng qī qī

Translation: "Those of good character are calm and composed; those of poor character are often anxious."
— Confucius (孔子), Analects (论语)

Confucius didn't bother with polite euphemisms – he drew a sharp line between the steady and the restless. Through this proverb, he explains that solid characters feel steady, while shady characters feel... sort of twitchy.

The ***junzi*** – a person of virtue or good character – is typically characterised by openness, sincerity, and inner tranquillity. Anchored by moral integrity and a clear conscience, they remain steady in both calm and storm. The ***xiaoren*** – petty, insecure, self-serving – tend to live on edge, second-guessing, scheming, and are often consumed by suspicion and defensiveness.

What it teaches us

- **Inner peace is earned:** When your actions match your values, you walk lighter, sleep better, and don't need a PR spin to feel okay.
- **Honesty builds trust:** Being open and honest in communication creates space for trust.
- **Grow through honest reflection:** Self-awareness isn't always fun, but it's how you spot the cracks before they turn into earthquakes. When we confront our thoughts, feelings, and behaviours with honesty and introspection, we begin to notice patterns and understand how we affect others and ourselves.

> ***"The measure of man's real character is what he would do if he knew he would never be found out."***
> **— Thomas Macaulay**

The Dao Whispers: What sort of person am I?

December 20

Pick Fights You Can Win Early

Early quick wins stack the odds for bigger battles ahead

故善战者，胜于易胜者也

gù shàn zhàn zhě, shèng yú yì shèng zhě yě

Translation: "The skilled warrior wins by defeating those who are easy to defeat."
— Sun Tzu (孙子), The Art of War

Some people always seem to win. They're not necessarily stronger or smarter, they just pick games they can't lose. The mate who only challenges you to pool after you've had three pints, or the colleague who volunteers for the project that's already 90% done.

Life isn't about charging at every fight just to prove you're tough. It's about racking up the wins that matter, the ones that build confidence and fuel bigger challenges ahead. You don't need to win every arm-wrestling match to prove your worth.

Sun Tzu understood this. Even the sharpest generals knew better than to waste time and troops on battles they couldn't win. The smart ones chose fights where the ground, the timing, and the odds were already in their favour; stacking up quick wins that built strength and position for what came next.

What it teaches us

- **Stack quick wins early**: Pick fights you can actually win and projects that play to your strengths. A few quick wins build confidence and momentum.
- **Stop hiking uphill just to prove you can**: Life's tough enough, stop taking the "hard way" as a badge of honour. Double down on your intrinsics and play to your strengths.
- **Conserve your ammo:** Ego loves a "glorious struggle," but the smartest wins come from focusing time and resources where the return is highest.

"You don't have to swing at every pitch.
The trick is to wait for the fat pitch."
— **Warren Buffett**

The Dao Whispers: Am I going after battles stacked against me, or focusing on the low-hanging fruit that changes the game?

December 21

Stay the Course: One Goal, One Finish Line

Grit is in sticking to your goals, even when they become boring, hard, or inconvenient

无志者常立志，有志者立常志

wú zhì zhě cháng lì zhì, yǒu zhì zhě lì cháng zhì

Translation: "The unmotivated are always setting goals; the truly motivated set one and keep it."

— Traditional Chinese Wisdom (民间俗语 mín jiān sú yǔ)

Some people have a new "big goal" every other Monday. Lose weight. Start a business. Run a marathon. Learn French. Knit a sweater. Learn piano. Three weeks later… a new list and the same unfinished plans.

This proverb calls it out. It says that those without true resolve are always starting anew... setting fresh goals, chasing distractions, and making empty declarations. Whereas driven people tend to choose one goal, sticking with it when it gets boring, hard, or inconvenient, and not quitting even when the novelty wears off.

What it teaches us

- **Purpose fuels persistence:** A clear "why" will keep you going long after motivation fades.
- **Avoid empty promises:** A track record of "I'll start Monday" makes people stop believing you… including you.
- **One finished beats fifty false starts:** Scatter your energy, scatter your results. Stay positive and don't let self-limiting beliefs creep into your thoughts, or stop you from finishing what you've started.

> ***"Perseverance is not a long race; it is many short races one after the other."***
>
> — **Walter Elliot**

The Dao Whispers: Which goals do I keep announcing but never finish? What would happen if I picked just one and didn't stop until it was done?

December 22

The Best Policies Fail Without the Right People

Laws alone do not guarantee order; you need the right people to enforce them

法者，治之端也；君子者，法之原也

fǎ zhě, zhì zhī duān yě; jūn zǐ zhě, fǎ zhī yuán yě

Translation: "Laws are useless without virtuous leaders enforcing them."
— Xunzi (荀子)

The best rules in the world mean nothing in the wrong hands. A nation can draft a flawless constitution, a company can publish a gleaming governance manual, or a school can set out the clearest code of conduct. But if those enforcing them lack integrity, courage, or competence, the system will fail.

Xunzi put it simply: "Laws are useless without virtuous leaders enforcing them." Words can create structure, but only people can create order.

What it teaches us

- **A leader walks the talk:** Rules only stick when leaders live them, such as showing up on time, taking responsibility, and calling out bad behaviour.
- **Execution needs ownership:** Big visions flop without someone clearly in charge. Transformations need clear governance, oversight, and people who own delivery and outcomes.
- **Practise what you preach:** As a parent, teacher, or mentor, saying one thing and doing another invites pushback. Others will be tempted to test your boundaries.

> ***"A nation is great not by its laws alone, but by the moral stature of those who uphold them."***
> — **Lee Kuan Yew**

The Dao Whispers: Do I focus too much on designing systems, and too little on the people entrusted to run them? Do my actions align with the principles I claim to value?

December 23

When Full Becomes Too Much

Strength is also in knowing when to stop

水满则溢，月满则亏

shuǐ mǎn zé yì, yuè mǎn zé kuī

Translation: "When the water is full, it overflows; when the moon is full, it wanes."
— Traditional Chinese proverb

Some victories are lost not in battle but by overstaying. A wine glass poured to the brim will spill with the slightest nudge. A moon at its fullest has already begun to fade. This proverb reminds us that knowing when to stop, before the point of overflow, is what keeps success intact.

It teaches that excess, even in good things, can turn into a bad thing. Success, energy, and resources all have a sweet spot, and pushing past it often causes more harm than gain. Knowing your limits is not weakness; it is the discipline that sustains momentum.

What it teaches us

- **Don't max out your calendar:** There's a fine line between being productive and burning out. Avoid overcommitting to projects, working excessive hours, or setting unrealistic deadlines. Leave breathing room so you can bring out the best of you.
- **Spend smart, not hard:** Financial wisdom is knowing when enough is enough. It means not splurging impulsively, or hoarding so excessively that you block off opportunities for growth.
- **Learn in sips, not gulps:** You don't have to read ***every*** book or take ***every*** course. Focus on a few and put them into practice instead of drowning in ideas you'll never use.

> ***"Excess generally causes reaction and produces a change in the opposite direction."***
> — **Plato**

The Dao Whispers: Am I pushing too hard in some areas of my life? Where do I need to slow down now so I don't lose what I've gained?

December 24

Beyond the Surface

Beneath still waters flow currents strong enough to shift the world

静水流深

jìng shuǐ liú shēn

Translation: "Still water runs deep."
— Traditional Chinese idiom

Not everyone likes the spotlight. Some people who are comfortable in their own skin prefer to observe. Underneath that unassuming exterior, we often find profound depth, strength, or complexity in character. The proverb suggests that quiet or reserved individuals may possess deep insight, resilience, or influence that may not be immediately visible. Silence may sometimes be plain yellow, but at other times it is golden.

What it teaches us

- **Spot the silent observers:** In meetings dominated by vocal personalities, the best ideas often come from those who listen more than they speak. A simple ***"What's your take on this?"*** can unlock game-changing insights.
- **Make space for reflection:** Busy lives leave little room for deep thinking. Try journaling for just 10 minutes a day. You might be surprised how much clearer your thinking becomes when you slow down.
- **Value genuine connections:** Some of the most loyal and wise friends or family members are modest and reserved. Be grateful for their profound loyalty rather than judging them by their lack of charisma.

> ***"Live the questions now, and perhaps without knowing it, you will live along someday into the answers."***
> — **Rainer Maria Rilke**

The Dao Whispers: Some of the most powerful currents run beneath the surface. Who around me holds insights I've overlooked that they may not be sharing, rightly or wrongly?

December 25

Roots Before Branches

Before all else, be grateful to those who gave us life

百善孝为先

bǎi shàn xiào wéi xiān

Translation: "Among all virtues, filial piety (honouring your parents) comes first."
— Confucian Principle

Rooted in Confucian thought, this proverb teaches that respect, care, and gratitude for our parents is the foundation of a good life and the starting point for cultivating other traits like kindness, loyalty, and integrity. While it doesn't demand blind obedience, it does encourage us to consider the conscious act of returning the kindness, patience, and sacrifice we were given, a debt we can never fully repay.

What it teaches us

- **Stronger as a family**: While independence is prized, many underestimate the resilience that comes from a strong family bond. Little acts of love like checking in, helping out, or sending a text give us strength when life gets messy.
- **Seeing our parents differently**: As we grow older, we begin to see something powerful. Our parents are not only "Mum" and "Dad;" they are people, imperfect, loving, doing their best, and often sacrificing in silence. That realisation changes everything.
- **The invisible gifts**: There are countless small, unseen ways our families shape us. The meals cooked, the worries left unspoken, the traditions passed down; all of these have given us life and moulded us into who we are.

> ***"Parents are to be honoured above all others, for they gave us life and nurtured us when we were helpless."***
> — **Aristotle**

The Dao Whispers: Today, let's honour our parents. A simple call, a visit, or a WhatsApp message, not out of obligation but out of love.

December 26

Embrace Good Fortune and Fate

Some days we drink from a full cup, other days, it's half full

得之我幸，不得我命，如此而已

dé zhī wǒ xìng, bù dé wǒ mìng, rú cǐ ér yǐ

Translation: "If I gain, it is good fortune; if I lose, it is fate. That's all there is to it."
— Traditional Chinese proverb

Detachment from outcome is the ultimate display of control.

We are told to hustle, grind, and force our way to success, but this proverb offers another view. Sometimes things are simply not up to us. Luck, timing, or plain old fate can change everything.

The message tells us to keep moving while releasing our need to control the outcomes or cling to fixed expectations. When we win, do it without arrogance; when we lose, don't fall into a spiral. This way, we can learn to navigate life with equanimity and emotional sovereignty.

What it teaches us

- **Give your all, then let go:** When you go after your goals, give your all but remember that not everything is in your control. If Plan A falls apart, adapt. Your worth is not tied to what didn't work out.
- **Let relationships evolve:** Text them, say sorry, put in the effort. But if your energy isn't matched, that's your cue to move forward. Not all relationships are meant to last, and that too is part of life.
- **Learning with patience:** Mastery takes time. It's messy, full of plateaus and tiny wins, but they all add up. Celebrate milestones and keep going.

> ***"Attachment is the leash by which others lead you."***
> — Unknown

The Dao Whispers: Can I fully embrace both the wins and the losses as part of my journey?

December 27

Do Your Desires Serve You, or Rule You?

We can't get rid of desires, but we can control them

欲虽不可尽，可以近尽也

yù suī bù kě jìn, kě yǐ jìn jìn yě

Translation: "Desires cannot be eliminated, but they can be regulated."
— Xunzi (荀子)

We all crave love, success, recognition, beauty, and influence. That's just part of being human.

The ancient philosopher Xunzi explains that being wise is not about pretending that we don't have these desires or suppressing them completely. It's how we manage them that makes the difference.

Self-control is not in saying no to everything. It's in knowing ***which desires we can follow, which we must control, and which we can simply leave unfulfilled***.

What it teaches us

- **Emotional discipline in relationships:** We crave closeness and affirmation, but real connections don't need constant validation. Space, patience, and emotional restraint are also acts of love.
- **Material balance:** Wanting comfort is natural, but excessive wants often lead to dissatisfaction. If we can learn to want less, we'll suddenly discover that we have more.
- **Ambition with awareness:** Striving is natural, but obsession with status or perfection can leave us unhappy and resentful. Not every life needs to be lived at breakneck pace; there's only one Elon Musk in eight billion.

> ***"He who is not contented with what he has, would not be contented with what he would like to have."***
> — **Socrates**

The Dao Whispers: Are my wants driving me? What if I simply choose "**enough**?"

December 28

Kindness Is Like Water

Kindness leaves a mark without leaving scars

上善若水，水善利万物而不争

shàng shàn ruò shuǐ, shuǐ shàn lì wàn wù ér bù zhēng

Translation: "The highest form of kindness is like water; it benefits all things without competing or fighting."
— Laozi (老子), Dao De Jing (道德经)

As we near the end of the year, let's soften up a little.

In this proverb, Laozi invites us to learn from water. It is soft yet unstoppable, humble yet powerful. Water slips into low places, takes the shape of whatever holds it, and nourishes everything it touches without asking for anything back. It does not shout, compete, or demand credit. It simply flows, and in doing so it shapes rivers, carves valleys, and sustains life. Kindness can work the same way, quiet, steady and without ego, changing the world not through force but through presence.

What we can learn from water

- **Lead like you care:** Servant leadership means lifting others up, listening deeply and empowering your team, putting their growth first and helping them succeed. This way, your team wins; and you win as a leader.
- **Discard the "my way or the highway" mentality:** Like water flowing around obstacles, we can adapt to the needs of others without insisting they follow our way.
- **Nurture without expecting reciprocity:** Give generously in the relationships that matter most, without expecting something in return.

> ***"Waste no more time arguing what a good man should be. Be one."***
> — **Marcus Aurelius**

The Dao Whispers: Am I giving out of real generosity, or do I do it for recognition or self-validation?

December 29

When Things Don't Work Out, Look Within First

We can't always control the outcome but we can examine our part in it

行有不得，反求诸己

xíng yǒu bù dé, fǎn qiú zhū jǐ

Translation: "When things do not go as planned, seek the cause from within yourself."
— Mengzi (孟子, Mencius)

When we hit a wall or suffer a setback, it's easy to look outward, blaming others, bad luck, or the world.

Mencius offers another way by urging us to look inward first. His proverb calls for self-reflection before shifting blame, encouraging personal responsibility, self-awareness, and growth through introspection.

This is not to say that we're always at fault, or that external injustice doesn't exist. But rather, it reminds us that growth requires self-awareness. And let's just say that we've been wronged, we ultimately still have the power to choose how we respond.

What it does *not* mean:

- Blame yourself for everything.
- Ignore external harm or injustice.
- Spiral into guilt.

What it *does* mean:

- Start with honest self-reflection before pointing fingers.
- Focus on what you ***can*** control, such as your mindset, effort, and choices.
- Refine your character without punishing yourself.

> ***"Until you make the unconscious conscious, it will direct your life and you will call it fate."***
> — **Carl Jung**

The Dao Whispers: When I hit a setback, do I look inward or shift the blame?

December 30

The Inevitability of Fate

I once believed I was the smartest under Heaven...but now I know, no one escapes fate

我常以为吾乃天下第一聪明人...
然今知无人能逃天命

wǒ cháng yǐ wéi wú nǎi tiān xià dì yī cōng míng rén...
rán jīn zhī wú rén néng táo tiān mìng

Translation: "I once thought I was the smartest person in the world...but now I know no one can escape fate."
— Empress Dowager Cixi (慈禧太后)

In her final days, Empress Cixi, once the most powerful woman in ancient China, is said to have spoken these words. She outwitted princes, foreign powers, and internal rivals, ruling behind the curtain for nearly half a century. But as the Qing dynasty fell and modernity loomed, she was confronted with the reality that no mind, power, or cunning can escape destiny. Her story reminds us of how even the best must know when to give way to the inevitability of fate, and that letting go is grace, not failure.

What it teaches us

- **Limits of intellect:** Intelligence alone does not guarantee peace, wisdom, or control.
- **Some things are bigger than you:** Forces greater than the human will – timing, nature, mortality – don't care about your plans. Sometimes, we must know when to let go.
- **Legacy beyond control:** You cannot control how you will be remembered. Live well and let go of the rest; as we care little for most who lived a century ago, so it shall be a century from now.

> ***"Whatever happens at all happens as it should; you will find this true, if you watch narrowly."***
> — **Marcus Aurelius**

The Dao Whispers: Have I mistaken power or intelligence for invincibility?

December 31

Life Is but a Dream

So live as if you're awake

人生如梦

rén shēng rú mèng

Translation: "Life is like a dream."
— Traditional Chinese proverb

At the end of the year, or perhaps at the end of anything, we're reminded of how strange and impermanent life can feel. It's like waking from a vivid dream... it feels so real, yet it fades quickly. The highs, the lows, the heartbreaks, the triumphs… all slip through our fingers like sand.

This proverb does not ask us to despair; it invites us to awaken. If life is indeed like a dream, then we are dreamers with some power to influence it, release our hold, or walk away with grace. It calls us to hold success and grief loosely, to live more consciously, and to stop confusing what is urgent with what is really important.

What it teaches us

- **Detach with grace:** When you realise that anger, ambition, and validation will all pass, you'll start to live with more freedom and less fear.
- **Live with presence:** Even if life is a dream, it is ***your*** dream. Show up for it fully, because only you hold the key to make it beautiful.
- **Choose what matters:** Don't waste the dream chasing shadows or letting others turn your dream into a nightmare. Spend it on people, purpose, and peace.

> ***"It is not death that a man should fear but never beginning to live."***
> — **Marcus Aurelius**

The Dao Whispers: When my story ends, will I know that I was truly awake, or was I sleepwalking through the dream all along?

A Final Word

For those who hold power and authority, may you use it with wisdom, and leave a legacy worthy of the trust humanity has placed in you.

For followers, may you rally behind your leaders, lending strength to the voices in power – so they may lift you higher too.

For leaders, may you lift your followers as you ascend, so that your rise carries all, not just yourself.

For those who can preserve or end livelihoods, may you choose the path that protects dignity – by honouring the labour of others, supporting talents, and creating paths for people to grow and to contribute.

For those blessed with privilege or good fortune, may you share a grain of generosity with those who have less – and the discernment to give in ways that truly uplift, rather than enable.

For those who are strong, may you use your strength to shield rather than to merely extract, to protect rather than to diminish.

For those with talents and abilities, may you not only keep them for yourself, but also apply them where they bring value – to your craft, your community, and our shared humanity.

For those who cross paths with the young, the vulnerable, or those in need, may you leave them stronger, safer, and in a better place than when you first found them.

For those still searching for your voice, may you find the courage to keep exploring, the people who believe in you along the way, and the moment of certainty when your voice finally feels like your own.

For those who have found your voice, may you have the courage to use it, the strength to own it, and the grace to uplift others with it.

For those who are wise, may you have the patience to guide those still growing – remembering that wisdom deepens when shared, and that others were once patient with you.

For all of us, may we carry wisdom with humility, power with compassion, and clarity with grace.

Acknowledgement

This book was never a solo act. It grew out of notes scribbled in a blue Moleskine, ideas shaped during a leadership course, late-night sparks that refused to wait until morning, and conversations that stretched my thinking and enriched my perspective.

Still, whatever clarity or perspective these pages offer is not mine alone. This book stands on the shoulders of giants. Not only the ancient sages of China and the philosophers of the West, but also the schools that taught me, the workplaces that stretched me and enriched my insights, the mentors and friends who guided me, and the experiences that sharpened my perspective. If these pages offer you any shade or insight, it is because of the giants who lifted me higher.

I am grateful to my family, who have always loved me enough to let me wander, write, and question. To my father, for working through the themes with me, and for the many conversations — from historical contexts to clarifying details — as well as pointing me to resources and nudging me toward sages and emperors I might never have thought to include. To my mother, for patiently teaching us Chinese proverbs over the years, your lessons echo through these pages more than you know. To my sister, who kept pushing me beyond "good enough" and challenged me to raise the bar, and to my brother, for teasing that my Chinese still needs work, you both made me sharper in your own ways.

To friends who walked with me during difficult seasons, your presence was a whisper of its own.

To teachers, mentors, and colleagues across London Business School, Columbia Business School, the National University of Singapore, the Hong Kong University Business School, Singapore Management University, and Stanford, thank you for shaping the questions I still carry. Professor Wong Poh Kam and Dr. Amy Bradley, and Mladen Tcherveniakov, I am especially grateful for your encouragement and for lending your words to these pages.

To those who offered thoughts on design and structure, and to my quiet co-editor in the digital realm, thank you for tolerating endless late-night tweaks and rewrites.

Finally, to the thinkers and sages of China and beyond, including Confucius, Laozi, Zhuangzi, Sun Tzu, the poets, and the emperors and empresses whose words have endured against time, this book is a small echo of the wisdom you entrusted to us.

And to you, reader, thank you for opening these pages.

Without your curiosity, there would be no Dao to whisper at all.

Printed in Great Britain
by Amazon

a99a9d6a-6bcb-49db-ad4b-029570622b5eR01